DATE DUE

DEC 15

Demco, Inc. 38-293

MACROECONOMICS

An Introduction to Advanced Methods

MACROECONOMICS

An Introduction to Advanced Methods

WILLIAM M. SCARTH

McMaster University

Harcourt Brace Jovanovich

Toronto • Orlando • San Diego • London • Sydney

Copyright © 1988 by Harcourt Brace Jovanovich Canada Inc.,
55 Horner Avenue, Toronto, Ontario   M8Z 4X6

Published in the United States by Harcourt Brace Jovanovich, Inc., Orlando, Florida 32887.

Requests for permission to make copies of any part of the work should be mailed to:
Permissions, College Division, Harcourt Brace Jovanovich, Canada, 55 Horner Avenue,
Toronto, Ontario   M8Z 4X6.

Edited by LENORE D'ANJOU
Drawings by JAMES LOATES
Cover and interior design by ROBERT GARBUTT PRODUCTIONS
Cover illustration by KVETA JELINEK

Canadian Cataloguing in Publication Data

Scarth, William M., 1946–
   Macroeconomics : an introduction to advanced methods

Bibliography: p.
Includes index.
ISBN 0-7747-3077-3

1. Macroeconomics.   I. Title.

HB172.5.S33 1987   339   C87-095227-7

Printed and bound in Canada
5 4 3 2 1 88 89 90 91 92

TO MY PARENTS

CONTENTS

PREFACE

In the late 1970s, Thomas Sargent and Robert Lucas argued that conventional macroeconomic methods were "fatally flawed": since then, macroeconomics has become a most exciting part of our discipline. After all, it is stimulating to be involved in the very initiation of a new research agenda. But while all this activity has been exciting for researchers in the field, it can be frustrating for students and their instructors. Journal articles by original researchers rarely represent the best pedagogic treatment of a subject, especially when the analysis involved becomes quite technical.

I have taught both graduate students and upper-level undergraduates throughout the last fifteen years, and have found that these developments in our subject have created an increasing demand, from year to year, for an organized set of lecture notes. This book is the result — an attempt to fill the gap between intermediate texts and the advanced analysis found in the journals. While it can be used on its own with upper-level undergraduates, at the MA level the book is intended to complement, rather than to replace, the journal readings.

The theme of the book is that a useful synthesis of Keynesian and New Classical ideas *can* be constructed, and is indeed now emerging. For example, the internal consistency that follows from well-specified micro foundations is an advantage of the New Classicals, but this methodology can be exploited by Keynesians if their analysis is based on well-defined reasons for market failure.

Some Keynesians do not regard the imperfect micro underpinnings of their models as an important limitation. They consider the methods used by rational-expectations theorists to solve nonuniqueness problems just as arbitrary as not basing macroeconomics on formal constrained maximization. Instead, these Keynesians focus on certain empirical-prediction problems in some of the New Classical models. New Classicals, on the other hand, downplay such empirical limitations on the grounds that it is no victory for Keynesian models to obtain better fits simply by allowing more of what they call free parameters.

Strengths and weaknesses such as these, on both sides of the debate, are explored throughout the text. Among the issues considered are: nonuniqueness problems with rational expectations, stabilization policy analysis (incorporating the Lucas critique), stock-flow dynamics, open-economy issues, micro models of sticky wages, and the effects of the rational expectations approach on empirical work. A brief chapter-by-chapter summary of the book's contents is provided on pages 4–5 of Chapter 1.

Using basic mathematics throughout, this text will introduce its readers to the actual research methods of macroeconomics. But in addition to explaining methods, the book presents the underlying logic at a common-sense level to help elucidate the essence of each controversy.

Before writing this book, I asked myself why, if a text like this one is so necessary, hasn't someone already written it? I think there are two parts to the answer. First, the literature was initially developing at such a pace that only a daring author would attempt to set down what the key conclusions might be that would have lasting significance in the years to come. But now that some of the issues are more settled, important elements of a synthesis have come to light. Thus, and only quite recently, has the extent of the gamble for the prospective textbook writer decreased significantly. The second consideration is that many macroeconomists are either in one camp or the other, and so are not particularly interested in expositing a synthesis.

It is obvious that my particular emphasis on the different issues will not coincide with that favored by all instructors. One reason for keeping the book a concise, reasonably priced paperback is to allow instructors to assign numerous ''favorite'' journal articles to be read along with the text. The book is meant to make those articles more accessible.

Comments and suggestions from users are most welcome, and may be sent to my attention, in care of the publisher.

I have many debts to acknowledge. The following economists have either made helpful comments on an earlier draft, or have been a general source of insight during numerous conversations on macro issues, or have helped in both capacities: Roy Bailey, John Burbidge, James Butkiewicz, Thomas Cargill, Peter Howitt, Peter Kennedy, David Laidler, Bennett McCallum, Tony Myatt, Thomas Moutos, Gord Myers, Michael Parkin, Craig Riddell, Brian Scarfe, John Smithin, and Junsen Zhang. I also wish to thank Tom Sargent for his encouragement to complete this project. It should, of course, be emphasized that none of these individuals can be held responsible for how I may have filtered their remarks.

As to the production of the book, many individuals at Harcourt Brace Jovanovich, Canada were most helpful. In particular, Keith Thompson, Darlene Zeleney, and Lenore d'Anjou were remarkably understanding and flexible, while making signficant contributions at every stage.

But my greatest debt is to my wife, Kathy, whose unfailing love and support have been invaluable.

MACROECONOMICS

An Introduction to Advanced Methods

CHAPTER 1

MICROECONOMIC FOUNDATIONS

1.1 INTRODUCTION

Fifty years have elapsed since the publication of Keynes's *The General Theory of Employment, Interest and Money*, yet the controversy between his followers and those macroeconomists who favor a more classical approach has never been more active. The purpose of this book is to examine this controversy and to draw attention to developments suggesting that progress toward a synthesis of important ideas from both traditions can be—and is being—accomplished.

To ensure a useful selection of macro models, the economist must use two broad criteria. First, models must be subjected to empirical tests, to see whether the predictions are consistent with actual experience. This criterion is fundamentally important. Unfortunately, however, it cannot be the only one for model selection, since empirical tests are often not definitive. Thus, while progress has been made in developing applied methods, and further work in this area is most important, macroeconomists have no choice but to put at least some weight on a second criterion for model evaluation.

Since the hypothesis of constrained maximization is at the core of our discipline, many argue that macro models should be evaluated as to their consistency with optimizing underpinnings. Without a microeconomic base, there is no well-defined basis for arguing that an ongoing stabilization policy improves welfare. Keynesians must acknowledge this point. They must also admit that it is utility and production functions that are independent of government policy; agents' decision rules do not necessarily remain invariant to shifts in policy. A specific microeconomic base is required to derive how private decision rules may react to major changes in policy. Another advantage is that a specific microeconomic rationale imposes more structure on macro models, so the corresponding empirical work involves fewer "free" parameters (parameters that are not constrained by theoretical considerations and can thus take on whatever value will maximize the fit of the model). It must be admitted that the empirical success of a model is compromised if the estimation involves many free parameters.

Despite these clear advantages of an explicit microeconomic base, those who typically stress these points—the New Classicals—must make some acknowledgments too. They must admit that thus far their models are inconsistent with several important empirical regularities (as we shall see in Chapter 11). Also, since the primary goal of this school of thought is to eliminate arbitrary assumptions, its followers cannot downplay the significance of aggregation issues or of the nonuniqueness problem that often plagues the solution of their models. (This latter problem is thoroughly discussed in Chapter 6.)

Where does all this leave today's student of macroeconomics? Controversy always provokes a variety of reactions: some people are excited by it, while others are confused. Some see the discipline as becoming fragmented into schools of thought that do not interact; others take the opportunity to combine the best features of the competing approaches so that real, lasting progress occurs. Happily, a growing number of macroeconomists have recently been having the latter reaction, with promising results. This group, sometimes referred to as the New Keynesians, acknowledges that stabilization policy must be justified by reference to a clear source of market failure—one that any well-trained microeconomist would recognize. This group is beginning to exploit the concepts and solution methods used with the rational expectations hypothesis, seeking to bring more rigor to Keynesian notions such as multiple equilibria. These economists are trying to combine the rigor of the New Classicals with the policy concern that stems from the Keynesians' belief in certain market failures. Given today's limits on tractability, this group of economists often disappoints strict New Classicals to some degree regarding the completeness of their model's underlying microeconomic rationale. New Keynesians respect this criticism, however, and are attempting to overcome it. We hope that by highlighting their work, this book will support the development of a constructive synthesis.

The Structure of Models

The purpose of any model is to provide answers to a series of if–then questions: if one assumes a specified change in the values of the exogenous variables (those determined outside of the model), what will happen to the set of endogenous variables (those determined within the model)? A high degree of simultaneity seems to exist among the main endogenous variables (for example, household behavior makes consumption depend on income, while the goods market-clearing condition makes income depend on consumption). To cope with this simultaneity, we define macro models in the form of systems of equations for which standard solution techniques can be employed. A model comprises a set of structural equations—definitions, equilibrium conditions, or behavioral reaction functions that are assumed on behalf of agents.

Mainstream macroeconomists have disciplined their selection of alternative behavioral rules by appealing to microeconomic models of households and firms. In other words, their basis for choosing structural equations is constrained maximization at the individual level, without much concern for problems of aggregation. To keep the analysis manageable, they often restrict attention to particular components of the macroeconomy one at a time, recording the resulting decision rules (the consumption function, the investment function, the money-demand function, and so on, which are the first-order conditions of the constrained maximizations) as a list of structural equations. This series of equations is then brought together for solving as a standard set of simultaneous equations in which the unknowns are the endogenous variables.

In other words, the procedure has two stages:

Stage 1: Derive the structural equations, which define the macro model, by presenting a set of unconnected constrained maximization exercises (that is, do a set of independent microeconomic problems).

Stage 2: Use the set of structural equations to derive the solution or reduced form equations (in which each endogenous variable is related explicitly to nothing but exogenous variables and parameters) and perform the counterfactual exercises (for example, derivation of the policy multipliers).

Until about 1970, macroeconomics developed in a fairly orderly way, following this two-stage approach. In recent decades, however, the discipline has seen some changes in basic approaches following from the fact that macroeconomists have tried to consider even more consistent and complicated theories of household and firm behavior. That is, the specification of the constrained maximizations in stage 1 of the analysis has been made more general by allowing for such things as dynamics and the fact that agents must make decisions on the basis of expectations of the future.

This expansion has led to some conceptual and methodological complications. Many analysts now regard it as unappealing to derive any one component structural equation without reference at stage 1 to the properties of the overall system. For example, if agents' behavior turns out to depend on expected inflation, it is tempting to model their forecast of inflation so that it is consistent with the actual inflation process, which is determined as one of the endogenous variables within the model. From a technical point of view, such an approach means that stages 1 and 2 must be considered *simultaneously*. It also means that the form of at least some of the structural equations and, therefore, the overall structure of the model itself depends on the assumed time paths of the exogenous variables. Thus, it may be a bad practice for economists to use an estimated model found suitable for one data period when they predict what would happen in another period under a different set of policy rules. We shall consider this problem, which is referred to as the Lucas critique, at various stages in later chapters; for the introductory material in this and the next three chapters, however, we shall restrict ourselves to models whose structures are assumed to be independent of the behavior of the exogenous variables.

The Plan for This Book

The overall plan of the book is as follows. The remainder of this chapter will present the basic microeconomic foundations for standard macroeconomics. Then, in Chapters 2 and 3, we shall review the standard aggregate demand and supply model to clarify the key distinctions between Keynesian and Classical positions and to explain the formal methods for deriving policy multipliers and stability (convergence) conditions. Expectations of inflation will be introduced in Chapter 4, as we focus on the question: is an increased degree of wage flexibility a good thing for macroeconomic stability?

The question of how to model expectations has been at the core of recent controversies in macroeconomics, so Chapters 5 and 6 will be devoted to examining how the hypothesis of rational expectations affects the debate on whether ongoing stabilization policies should be pursued. Once our assumptions concerning expectations are more explicit, we can distinguish the effects of unanticipated disturbances from the anticipated results of current and future policy measures. Important issues such as nonuniqueness and the credibility of policy rules will be examined here.

A macro model is necessarily dynamic if it includes accumulation identities that relate the stock and flow variables. Examples of such accumulation identities include: (1) in a closed economy, the increase in the stocks of money and government bonds must equal the government budget deficit; and (2) in an open economy, a balance of payments deficit (which reduces the central bank's holdings of foreign exchange reserves) must change the level of some other central bank asset or liability and, therefore, the stocks of money or government bonds outstanding. Chapters 7 to 9 will examine the implications of these sources of intrinsic dynamics, so that we can reach conclusions concerning the importance of budget deficits and the relative efficacy of fixed and floating exchange rates.

One important theme emerging from the macroeconomic analyses is that "sticky" wages are important for the Keynesian explanation of business cycles. Thus, in Chapter 10 we shall consider a series of microeconomic models that have been proposed to explain sticky wages. In Chapter 11, we shall discuss two empirical issues: (1) using the data as the criterion, how does the sticky-wage approach to explaining business cycles fare compared to Classical theories? and (2) how does the rational expectations approach change the way in which analysts undertake empirical work on particular structural relationships?

Also in Chapter 11, we shall return to a discussion of how policy can be used to affect the built-in stability characteristics of the economy. It is emphasized that the macroeconomic tools that have been pioneered by the New Classicals can be fruitfully applied to policy proposals that are typically advocated by Keynesians. This permits us to end our study by clarifying the payoff that follows from learning these methods, whatever the individual's policy priors may be.

Before we begin our progression through macroeconomic issues, we must determine whether the usual intertemporal theories of decision-making by households and firms can provide an adequate microeconomic rationale for macroeconomics. This issue will occupy us for the remainder of this chapter. (These sections, as well as the remaining chapters of the text, have been written so that the material on micro foundations can be read at any stage. Thus, if the reader wishes to postpone consideration of these issues, he or she can proceed directly to the analyses of macro models in Chapter 2.)

1.2 FIRMS IN THE STANDARD MACRO MODEL

In the standard macro model, we assume firms produce real output, Y, by combining labor, N, and capital, K, according to a production function:

$$Y = F(N, K).$$

The assumptions that both marginal products are positive but diminishing are incorporated by two restrictions: $F_N, F_K > 0$ and $F_{NN}, F_{KK} < 0$, where subscripts stand for partial derivatives. We also assume that the two factors are complements: $F_{NK} = F_{KN} > 0$.

Now consider a set of perfectly competitive firms that wish to maximize the present value of net revenues for their owners:

$$PV = \sum_{t=0}^{\infty} \left(\frac{1}{1+r}\right)^t \left[P \cdot F(N_t, K_t) - WN_t - P_I I_t - bP_I I_t^2\right],$$

subject to the accumulation identity,

$$I_t = (K_{t+1} - K_t) + \delta K_t,$$

where I stands for gross investment, P for product selling price, P_I for the purchase price of investment goods, W for the money wage, r for the real interest rate, and δ for the depreciation rate. The t subscripts indicate time periods.

At each point in time, net revenue equals sales, PY, minus the wage bill, WN, minus the purchase costs of investment goods, $P_I I$, minus the installation costs for capital, $bP_I I^2$. With $b > 0$, we have assumed that firms incur disruption costs when adjusting their capital stocks. The quadratic functional form is the simplest specification that has these adjustment costs increase more than in proportion to the amount of investment undertaken, as shown in Figure 1.1.

Figure 1.1 Installation Costs Incurred during Investment

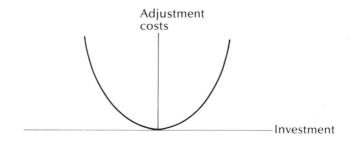

Notice that we are assuming adjustment costs for capital but not for labor. Given this assumption, it turns out that firms will always hire the desired quantity of labor but will only gradually close the gap between desired and actual capital stocks. But before we derive this result, it is important to point out that standard macroeconomics (including this book) treats investment inconsistently. The usual models ignore longer-run growth issues and so restrict the analysis to time periods during which the aggregate capital stock is fixed. Given adjustment costs, even individual holdings of capital are fixed at a point in time. The assumption is that the passage of time is insufficient for the newly purchased capital goods to be installed and used but that their purchase still has an effect on aggregate demand within the time periods we are studying (the "short run"). Hence, while the capital stock accumulation identity is used by firms at the individual level (our stage 1) to determine the optimal investment plan, it is not included as a structural equation at the aggregate level (our stage 2). To let the aggregate demand effects of investment matter in the short run while assuming away the aggregate supply effects of the larger capital stock in the same time frame is deemed a justifiable simplification if investment is a significant portion of national output but a small proportion of the accumulated capital stock (that is, if the I/Y ratio is large compared to the depreciation rate). In any event, we follow this standard simplification.

The Firm's Decision Rules

Since each firm is perfectly competitive, it takes P, P_I, W, and r as given by the market. It picks N_t and K_t to maximize PV; the optimal value for I_t follows residually from the accumulation identity (which simply states that gross investment is the sum of new additions to the capital stock, plus replacement investment). Replacement is required since the existing capital stock is assumed to wear out at rate δ per period. This simple framework requires no decision about the utilization rate of capital. Since no adjustment costs for labor are assumed, it is always rational for firms to utilize their existing stock of capital fully.

By not including a time subscript for P, W, P_I, r, or F, we are assuming that technology is constant and firms have static expectations. This approach presents a problem that we shall encounter over and over in this book. If the resulting decision rules of firms are embedded in a macro model in which wages, prices, and interest rates are not constant (as is virtually always the case), we are in the awkward situation of assuming that agents choose decision rules that involve their making systematically incorrect forecasts. Many economists find it unappealing to assume that agents are fooled in such a systematic or predictable way. Nevertheless, this approach is often standard practice.

Let us now proceed to derive the investment and labor demand functions that follow *if* static expectations are assumed. Profit-maximizing behavior can be derived by differentiating with respect to the firm's choice variables (all N_ts and K_ts) and setting these derivatives to zero. The first-order conditions are

$$\frac{\partial PV}{\partial N_t} = \left(\frac{1}{1+r}\right)^t (PF_N - W) = 0;$$

$$\frac{\partial PV}{\delta K_t} = \left(\frac{1}{1+r}\right)^t [PF_K + P_I(1-\delta) + 2bP_I(1-\delta)I_t]$$

$$+ \left(\frac{1}{1+r}\right)^{t-1} [-P_I - 2bP_I I_{t-1}] = 0.$$

The first condition is simply the familiar proposition that labor should be hired (at every instant) up to the point at which its marginal product is just matched by its rental cost, which is the real wage. (We shall use this condition later in the chapter when explaining the microeconomic rationale for the Phillips curve.)

To simplify the derivation that follows, it is useful to see what the labor demand condition implies when combined with the assumptions of static expectations and constant returns to scale. These assumptions are sufficient to make both marginal products, F_N and F_K, constant, no matter how the firm varies N_t and K_t. To appreciate this point, consider a particular constant-returns-to-scale production function, the Cobb/Douglas: $F(N, K) = K^\alpha N^{1-\alpha}$, where α is the technology coefficient and $0 < \alpha < 1$. For this function,

$$F_N = (1-\alpha)(N/K)^{-\alpha}$$

and

$$F_K = \alpha(N/K)^{1-\alpha},$$

so

$$F_K = \alpha[W/P(1-\alpha)]^{(\alpha-1)/\alpha},$$

using the first of the first-order conditions. Since W/P and α are constant, F_K is constant. This fact very much simplifies the derivation that follows from the second of the first-order conditions; it becomes the standard investment function.

We are now ready to simplify the second of the first-order conditions in several ways. First, assume that, installation costs aside, consumption and investment goods can be acquired or purchased at the same price ($P_I = P$). Second, multiply the equation through by $(1 + r)^t$. Third, substitute in a piece of summary notation: $B = [F_K - (r + \delta)]/2b$. The first-order condition then becomes

$$I_t - \left(\frac{1+r}{1-\delta}\right)I_{t-1} + \frac{B}{1-\delta} = 0.$$

Our job is to keep reexpressing this decision rule until it is in a form to which economic intuition can readily apply. Since we are abstracting from underlying growth, we define full equilibrium as obtaining when $K_t - K_{t-1} = 0$, and we denote full-equilibrium values by asterisks: $I^* = \delta K^*$. We obtain expressions for these full-equilibrium values by substituting $I_t = I_{t-1} = \ldots I^*$ into the last equation to get $I^* = \delta K^* = B/(r + \delta)$. We can then reexpress the last equation in terms of deviations from full equilibrium:

$$(I_t - I^*) = \left(\frac{1 + r}{1 - \delta}\right)(I_{t-1} - I^*).$$

It is important to note that both the interest rate and the depreciation rate are fractions: $0 < r$, $\delta < 1$. Thus, $(1 + r)/(1 - \delta)$ exceeds unity and, therefore, any initial deviation of investment from its full equilibrium value must get ever larger. That is, I_t has three time paths consistent with this decision rule; I_t can approach $+\infty$, approach $-\infty$, or always equal I^*. In full equilibrium, the firm must have $I^* = \delta K^* = B/(r + \delta)$, which is finite. The firm can simultaneously obey this long-run constraint and this first-order condition only by setting $I_t = I^*$ at all times.

Substituting $I^* = B/(r + \delta)$ and the definition of B into this rule gives:

$$I = \frac{1}{2b}\left(\frac{F_K}{r + \delta} - 1\right).$$

Another manipulation of this result follows from noting that $I = \delta K^*$ and $I = \dot{K} + \delta K$ (the continuous time version of the accumulation identity) together imply that

$$\dot{K} = \delta(K^* - K).$$

Hence, the decision rule that follows from this microeconomic analysis can be described verbally in several ways:

1. Invest whenever the marginal product of capital, F_K, exceeds its rental cost, $(r + \delta)$.
2. Set net investment equal to a fraction of the gap between desired and actual capital. (Note, however, that this partial adjustment coefficient cannot be treated as a free parameter; rather, it equals the depreciation rate.)
3. Set gross investment equal to what optimal replacement investment would be if the optimal capital stock had already been acquired.

The intuition behind the third way of wording the firm's optimal behavior runs as follows. If firms do not set investment equal to the same amount in every period, adjustment costs will be high in some periods and low in others. But since these costs are nonlinear, they can be reduced by cutting investment in the high investment periods and raising it in the low ones. These savings will not be exhausted until investment is the same in all periods.

There is a fourth interpretation of this theory of the firm that can be appreciated by realizing that in a well-functioning stock market, the market value of equities equals the present value of the income derived from owning capital. If capital is held into the indefinite future, its per-period earnings will be national output, $P \cdot F(N, K)$, minus the wage bill, WN. To obtain the present value of this flow, it is discounted by the sum of the real interest rate and the depreciation rate. (Not only must future income be discounted to calculate present value, but also the capital stock must be maintained.) Since $F = F_K K + F_N N$ (given constant returns to scale) and $F_N = W/P$, the market values of equities $= PF_K K/(r + \delta)$. We can define q as the ratio of the market's valuation of capital to its actual purchase cost, P_K. This means $q = F_K/(r + \delta)$. We see that q can be interpreted as either the ratio of the marginal product of capital to its rental cost or as the ratio of the market's valuation of capital to its replacement cost—in other words, the real value of an equity. Tobin (1969) prefers the second interpretation.

We have almost completed our review of the standard microeconomic rationale for the firm's factor demand functions. Several more points about the investment function are worth noting, however. Macroeconomic analyses often employ a less specific form of what we have just derived. We found that investment depends positively on capital's marginal product, F_K. But since F_K increases with the level of employment—that is, $F_{KN} > 0$—and since the production function, $Y = F(N, K)$, dictates a positive one-to-one relationship between output and the employment of labor (when the capital stock is held constant), investment must be higher at higher levels of output. This point can be clarified formally by taking the total differential of the production and investment functions, $Y = F(N, K)$ and $I = (1/2b)[(F_K/(r + \delta)) - 1]$. Setting $dK = 0$, we have

$$dY = F_N \, dN,$$

and

$$dI = \frac{F_{KN}}{2b(r + \delta)} \, dN - \frac{F_K}{2b(r + \delta)^2} \, dr.$$

After eliminating dN by substitution, the result is

$$dI = \left[\frac{F_{KN}}{2b(r + \delta)F_N} \right] dY - \left[\frac{F_K}{2b(r + \delta)^2} \right] dr.$$

Since both the coefficients within square brackets in this equation are positive, we are justified in interpreting the partial derivatives in the standard investment function, $I = I(Y, r)$, as:

$$I_Y = \frac{F_K}{2b(r + \delta)F_N} > 0,$$

and

$$I_r = \frac{-F_K}{2b(r + \delta)^2} < 0.$$

It is customary to use this less-structured version of the investment function.

Our review of the theory of the firm has assumed no inflation. If there is a constant rate of expected inflation, π, this analysis can be reworked to yield almost the same factor demand functions. The only difference is that it becomes explicit that it is the real interest rate, r, not the nominal rate, i, that is involved in the investment function. (The real and nominal interest rates differ by the expected inflation rate: $i = r + \pi$.)

It should be emphasized, however, that this derivation is appropriate only for firms within a model that involves constant wages, prices, and interest rates (or constant inflation *rates* in wages and prices). That this limitation is severe can be illustrated by the following example. Economists often use a given macro model to simulate the effects of such things as a wage–price control policy. To use the same investment function in the model both with and without the hypothesized controls scheme is inconsistent since doing so involves the assumption that firms will *always* make their investment decisions as if wage and price controls existed. Despite this limitation, we present this conventional derivation. The point of going through micro underpinnings of this sort is precisely to check on the standard model's likely range of applicability.

We can consider treating capital symmetrically with labor; that is, by assuming no adjustment costs for capital. In this case, $b = 0$, so $1/2b$ approaches infinity; therefore, firms always trade existing capital at each point in time, and interest rates and prices adjust so that they can always hold exactly the desired amount of capital stock (determined by marginal product equals rental cost: $F_K = r + \delta$).

Notice that in this case, investment is undefined. Neoclassical growth theory is specified in this way, and has no independent investment function. If the model includes no independent investment function, investment is residually determined by the goods market-clearing condition. In this case, fiscal policy involves complete crowding out of preexisting private investment expenditure. But in short-run macroeconomic analyses that focus on stabilization issues, both the Keynesian and the Classical approaches presume that investment does not passively adjust to savings. Thus, all branches of textbook macroeconomics involve the assumption that adjustment costs for capital exist—that is, $b > 0$.

1.3 HOUSEHOLDS IN THE STANDARD MACRO MODEL

To provide an economic rationale for the remaining structural equations of the standard macro model, we shall now consider households. Like firms, households must make an intertemporal decision—how to arrange their level of consumption through time. For pedagogic simplicity, we follow Gray (1984) and assume that households are risk-neutral. As explained in Chapter 10, this assumption implies that the household utility function is linear in consumption, so we can assume that individuals maximize the present value of consumption, C, rather than the present value of the utility of consumption. We write this assumption as

$$ \text{PV} = \sum_{t=0}^{\infty} \left(\frac{1}{1+\rho} \right)^t C_t, $$

where ρ is the rate of time preference. We further assume that individual house-holds do not make labor supply decisions; the implication is that income in each period is exogenous to the household's consumption/savings choice. (The characteristics of the labor market in this model are described in the next section of this chapter.)

Households maximize the present value of consumption subject to the following constraint:

$$C_t = Y^d - (A_{t+1} - A_t) - h(A_t/Y^d),$$

where A_t is the quantity of liquid assets owned by the household at a point in time.

The constraint says that household consumption is limited by—actually, is equal to—real disposable income, Y^d, minus the real value of any accumulation of liquid assets during the period and also minus the transactions costs incurred during the trading process. The expression $A_{t+1} - A_t$ is the accumulation of liquid assets. The $h(\cdot)$ function specifies the nature of the transactions technology. The first derivative of this function, h', is assumed to be negative, so that the higher the agent's liquid asset holdings compared to his income, the lower the transactions costs incurred. The second derivative, h'', is assumed to be positive, so that increases in liquid assets are progressively less helpful in avoiding transactions costs.

Since this transactions or trading costs term may be unfamiliar, some further discussion is warranted. When Friedman (1957) introduced the permanent income hypothesis, he argued that consumption should be proportional to broadly defined wealth. But, he said, the factor of proportionality should vary with the ratio of human wealth to total wealth because human wealth is relatively illiquid. Permanent income was defined as the yield on broadly defined wealth; if we assume that agents have static expectations, we can denote this expected yield on broadly defined wealth as a constant, Y^d. Thus, the A_t/Y^d term in the household's constraint is just a way of capturing Friedman's idea that consumption depends on the liquid-to-total-assets ratio, as well as on the (expected) yield on total wealth.

One of the long-standing questions in monetary economics is why agents hold money. At the microeconomic level, one can identify three main approaches to this issue. One is reflected in what are referred to as cash-in-advance models. They are based on Clower's (1965) notion that one-half of every transaction must involve money. Our $h(\cdot)$ function can be considered a less-structured way of giving all liquid assets some role in the trading process. A second approach to the micro foundations for money stresses its role as a store of value, instead of its role in the transactions process. This approach involves the overlapping-generations model, in which money and other paper assets are used to transfer spending to future periods and generations. The third approach involves less structure: the role of money is not explained, it simply enters the agent's utility function. These second and third approaches, which are not used in this book, are thoroughly explained in Sargent (1987). As Gray (1984) shows, our $h(\cdot)$

function in the household constraint serves the same function as would the supposition that liquid assets directly enter the utility function.

The Household's Decision Rules

Before deriving the first-order condition for the household's decision problem, we must clarify what liquid assets, A, are and how disposable income, Y^d, is defined. The two components of liquid assets are equities, V, which are issued by firms, and money, M, which is issued by the government. Since we have already seen that q represents the real value of an equity, we can define liquid assets as:

$$A_t = q_t V_t + M_t/P_t.$$

Households must make two decisions: the accumulation decision (how much to add to their stock of liquid assets during each period), and the allocation decision (the form in which to hold their liquid assets at each point in time). Like households, we can treat these two decisions separately so long as trading paper assets—equities and money—involves no adjustment costs.

Before examining the household's two decisions, it is useful to define disposable income. The economy has three sectors—households, firms, and government—and the flow financing constraints between each must be specified. In the standard model, firms retain no earnings, so to finance their new (net) investment each period, they must issue equities. Thus, the firm's financing constraint is

$$q_t(V_{t+1} - V_t) = K_{t+1} - K_t.$$

For simplicity at this stage, we assume that the government levies no conventional taxes and issues no bonds. (These simplifications are removed in Chapter 7.) Given this assumption, the government simply buys real goods and services, G, by issuing money. So the government financing constraint is

$$P_t G_t = M_{t+1} - M_t.$$

We are now in a position to clarify the definition of Y^d. Household disposable income must be the sum of consumption, saving, and capital gains:

$$Y_t^d = C_t + A_{t+1} - A_t.$$

From the definition of A_t, this relationship can be expanded to:

$$Y_t^d = C_t + q_t(V_{t+1} - V_t) + V_t(q_{t+1} - q_t) + \frac{1}{P_t}(M_{t+1} - M_t) - \frac{M_t}{P_t}\left(\frac{P_{t+1} - P_t}{P_t}\right).$$

Using the capital stock accumulation identity, $I_t = K_{t+1} - K_t + \delta K_t$, as well as firms' and the government's financing constraints, the disposal income definition becomes

$$Y_t^d = C_t + I_t - \delta K_t + V_t(q_{t+1} - q_t) + G_t - \frac{M_t}{P_t}\left(\frac{P_{t+1} - P_t}{P_t}\right).$$

Now, substituting in the goods market-clearing condition, $Y_t = C_t + I_t + G_t$, we have

$$Y_t^d = Y_t - \delta K_t + V_t(q_{t+1} - q_t) - \frac{M_t}{P_t}\left(\frac{P_{t+1} - P_t}{P_t}\right).$$

If agents have static expectations for income and equity price levels (as we have been assuming throughout this chapter) and if we limit attention to a constant expected inflation rate, π, for goods prices, expected disposable income becomes simply net national product minus the inflation tax on real money balances:

$$Y^d = Y - \delta K - (M/P)\pi.$$

Notice that we have dropped the time subscripts to emphasize our assumption of static expectations for all variables except the level of goods prices.

One purpose of this derivation of Y^d was so that we can justify separate treatment of the additions-to-A decision and the allocation-of-A decision. With static expectations for goods prices too, π is 0, and Y^d is independent of M/P. Therefore, households can treat both their portfolio allocation decision (which concerns choosing M/P at each point in time) and the level of Y^d as independent of their consumption/savings decision.

The decision rule for the consumption/savings choice is formally derived by substituting the household constraint into the definition of the present value of consumption so as to eliminate C_t and by differentiating with respect to A_t. The result is

$$\frac{\partial PV}{\partial A_t} = \left(\frac{1}{1+\rho}\right)^t\left[\frac{-h'(A_t/Y^d)}{Y^d} + 1\right] - \left(\frac{1}{1+\rho}\right)^{t-1} = 0.$$

We simplify this condition by multiplying through by $(1 + \rho)^t$, which yields

$$h'(A_t/Y^d) = \rho Y^d.$$

Since we have assumed that the rate of time preferences is constant, this first-order condition dictates that households will plan to maintain a constant level of liquid assets as long as they expect disposable income to stay constant. Once this $A_{t+1} = A_t$ rule is substituted into the constraint, the household consumption function follows immediately:

$$C = Y^d - h(A/Y^d).$$

By taking the total differential of this consumption function, we see that the marginal propensity to consume out of (permanent) income, $\partial C/\partial Y^d$, is $1 + h'(Y^d)^2$, which is a fraction. We also see that a Pigou effect—$\partial C/\partial A = -h'/Y^d > 0$—has been rationalized. Some analysts (for example, Hall 1978) ignore liquidity effects here, stressing that with static expectations, the permanent income hypothesis leads to the assumption that the marginal propensity to consume is unity. Other analysts ignore the Pigou effects (as we do in Chapter 2). Both these propositions follow from our analysis when liquidity effects are formally excluded, by setting $h' = 0$.

We must now consider the household's portfolio-choice problem: how to allocate A across the two available forms—money and equities. Denoting the desired quantities of each of these assets by D superscripts, the liquid-asset constraint dictates that

$$(M/P) + (qV) = (M/P)^D + (qV)^D = A,$$

so that

$$(M/P)^D - (M/P) = (qV) - (qV)^D,$$

which means that the excess demand for money must equal the excess supply of equities. This implication of the budget constraint on liquid assets is referred to as Walras's Law. From it, we know that if households have the money holdings they desire, the equity market must be clearing.

In considering the household's allocation choice, we assume that money is the more useful of the two liquid assets for reducing trading or transactions costs and that, therefore, the demand for money depends positively on the level of national product, Y. We also assume that the nominal yield paid on money is zero, so the real yield differential between the two assets is $(i - \pi) - (0 - \pi) = i$, which denotes the nominal yield on equities (in other words, the nominal interest rate in the system). The demand for money is assumed to depend inversely on this yield differential. If we define the money and equity demand functions as $L(Y, i, A)$ and $V(Y, i, A)$ respectively, we can summarize the assumptions made thus far as $L_Y > 0$ and $L_i < 0$. Since the liquid wealth constraint dictates that $L_Y + V_Y = 0$, that $L_i + V_i = 0$, and that $L_A + V_A = 1$, we have already implicitly assumed that $V_Y < 0$ and $V_i > 0$ as well.

In basic macroeconomic models, it is often assumed that agents want to hold all new additions to liquid assets as equities, so that $V_A = 1$ and $L_A = 0$). This simplification keeps the position of the *LM* curve independent of the quantity of bonds in the system. (Intermediate treatments usually refer to all nonmonetary paper assets—our "equities"—as "bonds.")

We conclude that this simple model of the household provides a microeconomic rationale for both the money demand function and the consumption function that are contained in the standard macro models, at least for the case of static expectations. But if the assumption that households have static expectations is unreasonable, we should rederive the consumption and the demand for money functions. The fact that this rederivation is not often done is the main reason the New Classicals regard standard macroeconomics as ad hoc.

1.4 THE LABOR MARKET

The interaction between households and firms on the labor market is the remaining area for explanation in our overview of standard macro models and their micro-economic bases. We have derived the firm's labor demand function, $F_N = W/P$, but not the nature of wage-setting. To provide some justification for conventional macroeconomics at this stage, we present a variation on Mussa's (1981) and McCallum's (1980) model of sticky prices. (Alternative theories of wage determination are considered more fully in Chapter 10.)

We assume that households supply labor inelastically in the sense that, on average, they want to work (and do work) a fixed amount, $\bar{N}$. Households recognize, however, that negotiations and other costs preclude the instantaneous adjustment of the money wage that would be required to keep firms forever satisfied with this level of employment. As a result of this understanding, households agree to a money-wage contract that saves some of these costs and gives firms the right to determine unilaterally the level of employment in the short run. Thus, strictly speaking, labor supply is perfectly elastic at an instant in time. Households allow short-run deviations from $\bar{N}$, since they can count on optimal adjustments of the money wage through time.

To see how optimal wage changes can be defined, consider that money wage-setting involves two sorts of costs. First, agents incur costs whenever the wage, W, differs from $\bar{W}$, the equilibrium wage, which is the wage that would make actual employment equal the long-run desired level ($N = \bar{N}$). Workers dislike working at levels that differ from their long-run desires, and firms incur costs when they employ labor at a level that does not correspond to the minimum point of their average cost curve. Second, households and firms incur adjustment costs whenever wages have to be renegotiated. These negotiation costs are assumed to depend positively on the gap between the actual rate of wage change and the percentage change in the equilibrium wage, $\bar{W}$. Whenever wages tend toward an increase that is more than that dictated by full equilibrium, firms resist; whenever wages tend toward an increase that is less than that dictated by full equilibrium, workers resist.

The optimal rate of wage change is the one that permits a minimization of these two kinds of costs—those incurred because agents are away from full equilibrium and those incurred because wages are changed at a rate other than the underlying equilibrium amount. (In the model we assume that individuals delegate this decision to representatives—labor negotiators—so this cost minimization is separate from households' individual choices regarding consumption/saving and asset holding and from firms' factor demand decisions.)

The simplest formal specification is to have wages adjust through time so as to minimize the following quadratic cost function:

$$\sum_{t=0}^{\infty} \left(\frac{1}{1+r} \right)^t \left\{ (w_t - \bar{w}_t)^2 + \beta[(w_t - \bar{w}_t) - (w_{t-1} - \bar{w}_{t-1})]^2 \right\}$$

in which the lower-case w stands for the natural logarithms of W (that is, $w = \log W$), and β is a parameter indicating the relative importance of the adjustment costs compared to the costs of being away from full equilibrium. If the discount rate and the $\bar{w}$ time path are taken as given to this decision problem, wage-setting behavior is defined by setting the derivative of this cost function with respect to w_t equal to zero. The result is

$$2\left(\frac{1}{1+r}\right)^t [(w_t - \bar{w}_t) + \beta(w_t - \bar{w}_t) - \beta(w_{t-1} - \bar{w}_{t-1})]$$

$$- 2\left(\frac{1}{1+r}\right)^{t+1} [\beta(w_{t+1} - \bar{w}_{t+1}) - \beta(w_t - \bar{w}_t)] = 0.$$

We simplify by multiplying through by $(1+r)^{t+1}/2\beta$ and by grouping terms:

$$(w_{t+1} - \bar{w}_{t+1}) - [2 + r + (1+r)/\beta](w_t - \bar{w}_t) + (1+r)(w_{t-1} - \bar{w}_{t-1}) = 0.$$

The characteristic equation of this second-order difference equation is

$$\gamma^2 - (2 + r + (1+r)/\beta)\gamma + (1+r) = 0,$$

and γ, the characteristic root, is

$$\gamma = \frac{2 + r + (1+r)/\beta \pm \sqrt{[2 + r + (1+r)/\beta]^2 - 4(1+r)}}{2}.$$

Simple inspection shows that one of the two values of γ must exceed one; and if that root were to operate, the deviation of w from $\bar{w}$ would become ever wider through time. Since this path cannot be the cost-minimizing wage-adjustment path, agents choose the value of γ that corresponds to the negative square root. Then, taking the fractional value for the characteristic root, the wage-setting rule is

$$w_{t+1} - \bar{w}_{t+1} = \gamma(w_t - \bar{w}_t),$$

where $0 < \gamma < 1$.

If w_t is subtracted from, and $\bar{w}_t$ added to, both sides, this decision rule can be reexpressed as

$$w_{t+1} - w_t = \bar{w}_{t+1} - \bar{w}_t + (1 - \gamma)(\bar{w}_t - w_t). \tag{1.1}$$

From this point on, we take γ as a constant. This presumption is not contentious as far as parameter β is concerned. Since β can be considered as either a taste or a technology parameter, it should be independent of the time paths of all macro variables. However, the real interest rate is not usually modeled as a constant in standard macroeconomics. γ should be expected to be constant only if agents' having static expectations is an appropriate assumption. Notice that this limitation is the same one that lies behind the interpretation of all the other structural equations we considered earlier in this chapter.

From Wage-Setting to Price-Setting

Our remaining task is to connect the wage-setting rule to the price change equation that is used in standard macroeconomic analysis. That common equation is the expectations-augmented Phillips curve:

$$\frac{\dot{P}}{P} = f \cdot \left(\frac{Y - \bar{Y}}{\bar{Y}} \right) + \pi,$$

where the dot above P stands for a time derivative and f is a parameter that stands for the steepness of the short-run Phillips curve. Using lower-case p and y to stand for logarithms of price and output, we can write this standard price-change equation as

$$\dot{p} = f \cdot (y - \bar{y}) + \pi. \tag{1.2}$$

To relate equations 1.1 and 1.2 we must, of course, have both relationships in either discrete or continuous time. Since the manipulations are slightly easier in a continuous time specification, we rewrite the wage-adjustment rule as

$$\dot{w} = \dot{\bar{w}} + a(\bar{w} - w), \tag{1.3}$$

where $a > 0$.

Two points concerning this new form of specification are worth noting. First, the essence of this sticky wage model is that w cannot jump instantaneously to make $n = \bar{n}$. For the wage rate to change, time must actually pass. This important assumption is unaffected by the switch to continuous time. Second, a continuous time formulation right from the beginning would have provided a slightly more concise treatment for all three of the intertemporal optimizations considered in this chapter. We avoided this approach, however, so that calculus of variations was not needed.

We now combine equation 1.3 with log-linear versions of the production function, $Y = K^{\alpha} N^{1-\alpha}$, and the labor demand function, $W/P = F_N = (1 - \alpha) Y/N$, which follow from the Cobb/Douglas functional form mentioned earlier:

$$y = \alpha lnK + (1 - \alpha)n;$$

$$w - p = ln(1 - \alpha) + y - n.$$

We also use a log-linear version of the aggregate demand for goods. This function combines standard *IS* and *LM* relationships to eliminate the real interest rate. The result is that aggregate demand depends positively on government spending, G, the real money supply, M/P, and the expected inflation rate, which for the moment we write as the actual inflation rate, $\dot{p}$. A log-linear approximation of this aggregate demand summary is

$$y = \phi g + \theta(m - p) + \psi \dot{p}.$$

As before, the lower case letters stand for the logarithms of the variables already defined in upper case; $\phi, \theta,$ and ψ are positive aggregate demand parameters.

The expression for the (log of the) wage level that makes employment be $\bar{n}$ follows directly from the labor demand function:

$$\bar{w} - \bar{p} = ln(1 - \alpha) + \bar{y} - \bar{n}.$$

This relationship and the labor demand function imply

$$(w - \bar{w}) = (p - \bar{p}) + (y - \bar{y}) - (n - \bar{n}),$$

and

$$\dot{\bar{w}} = \dot{\bar{p}}.$$

These expressions can be substituted into the wage-adjustment rule to yield

$$\dot{w} = \dot{\bar{p}} + a[(\bar{p} - p) + (\bar{y} - y) - (\bar{n} - n)].$$

We can simplify further by substituting expressions for the terms on the right-hand side of this wage-change relationship. For example, given the production function, $y - \bar{y}$ can be replaced by $(1 - \alpha)(n - \bar{n})$. To use the aggregate demand function, we assume a trial form for the price-change relationship:

$$\dot{p} = f \cdot (y - \bar{y}) + \dot{m}. \tag{1.4}$$

Simple economic inspection of the system suggests this format; the job of this derivation is discovering how the summary parameter f (which remains arbitrary for the moment) is related to the other coefficients—$\alpha, a, \phi, \theta, \psi$—that have underlying economic interpretation.

Using trial solutions is part of what mathematicians call the undetermined coefficients solution method. It is worth a brief aside because it may be more familiar to economics students than they realize. Consider the familiar example of compound interest. The basic relationship (the economic model) of compound interest is $x_t = (1 + r)x_{t-1}$, where r is the interest rate and x the accumulated value. We know that the solution equation for this dynamic process is $x_t = (1 + r)^t x_0$, where x_0 is the initial amount that is invested. To derive this solution equation, we simply posit a trial solution of the form $x_t = \lambda^t A$, where the arbitrary parameters, λ and A, are yet to be determined. Substituting the trial solution into the model, we have: $\lambda^t A = (1 + r)\lambda^{t-1}A$ or $\lambda = (1 + r)$. Similarly, substituting $t = 0$ into the trial solution, we have $A = x_0$. As a result, the initially arbitrary reduced-form coefficients, λ and A, are now determined as functions of the economically meaningful parameters, r and x_0.

Let us proceed by using equation 1.4 as a trial solution in the log-linear summary of the aggregate demand function:

$$y = \phi g + \theta(m - p) + \psi \dot{m} + \psi f(y - \bar{y}).$$

From this relationship we know that

$$\bar{y} = \phi g + \theta(m - \bar{p}) + \psi \dot{m},$$

so $(p - \bar{p}) = -(1 - \psi f)(y - \bar{y})/\theta$, and $\dot{p}$, the equilibrium inflation rate, equals

$\dot{m}$ (since $\ddot{y} = \dot{g} = \ddot{m} = 0$). Thus, the final version of the wage-change equation is

$$\dot{w} = a(\alpha + (1 - \alpha)(1 - \psi f)/\theta)(n - \bar{n}) + \dot{m},$$

which is a standard expectations-augmented Phillips curve.

Finally, we can use this analysis to defend a simple Phillips curve involving price changes instead of wage changes. The time derivative of the production function is $\dot{y} = (1 - \alpha)\dot{n}$; of the labor demand function, $\dot{w} = \dot{p} + \dot{y} - \dot{n}$; and of the aggregate demand function combined with the trial solution (equation 1.4) before time differentiation (to avoid a $\ddot{p}$ term), $\dot{y} = \theta(\dot{m} - \dot{p})/(1 - \psi f)$. These relationships can be used to eliminate $\dot{w}, \dot{y}$, and $\dot{n}$ in the Phillips curve for wages. After substitution, the result is

$$\dot{p} = \frac{a(1 - \psi f)}{\theta}(y - \bar{y}) + \dot{m}. \tag{1.5}$$

Since $\dot{\bar{p}} = \dot{m}$, we see that the Mussa/McCallum version of the expectations-augmented Phillips curve follows from the specification of the labor market that we have just discussed.

By comparing the trial solution (equation 1.4) with the result (equation 1.5), we can now define the previously arbitrary coefficient, f (which signifies the steepness of the short-run Phillips curve), by the following condition:

$$f = 1/(\psi + \theta/a). \tag{1.6}$$

Equation 1.6 can be used to examine the implications of alternative degrees of wage flexibility. Wages become more flexible as the costs of adjustment are lessened—that is, as a increases. Equation 1.6 makes it clear that $\partial f/\partial a > 0$. Thus, this theory verifies the common presumption that the short-run Phillips curve becomes steeper as wages become more flexible. We shall use this result extensively in Chapter 4.

We conclude that micro underpinnings have been provided for the Phillips curve $\dot{p} = f(y - \bar{y}) + \dot{\bar{p}} = f(y - \bar{y}) + \dot{m}$, but *not* for the Phillips curve $\dot{p} = f(y - \bar{y}) + \pi$, where π is the expectation of the current (not the equilibrium) inflation rate. We have also seen that the Phillips curve involving the expected equilibrium inflation rate can be justified on the basis of the same kind of intertemporal adjustment-cost theory as we used to defend the firm's investment function and the household consumption function. Thus, this microeconomic rationale involves the same limitation we noted earlier—principally, static expectations.

Finally, it is worth noting that the slope of the short-run Phillips curve depends on the slope of the aggregate demand curve, θ. Thus, any policy that alters the slopes of the *IS* and *LM* schedules can be expected to affect the slope of the short-run Phillips curve. This effect of aggregate demand policies is rarely modeled. New Classicals regard this sort of oversight as another illustration of the arbitrariness involved in macroeconomic analyses that pay little attention to microeconomic underpinnings.

To see how this dispute matters in an important policy issue, consider the following example, which follows from equation 1.6. We know that the more a central bank tries to peg the interest rate, the more the economy behaves as if its *LM* curve were horizontal—that is, the closer the economy is to having aggregate demand independent of the money supply. In our notation, the parameter θ moves closer to zero. When central banks were trying to fight inflation in the early 1980s, many moved from pegging interest rates to more monetarist positions. We can model this movement by considering the policy shift as causing an increase in θ. Such an increase has two implications: it makes the aggregate demand curve flatter (the conventional effect), and it reduces the steepness of the short-run Phillips curve (since $\partial f/\partial \theta < 0$ from equation 1.6). The second effect is not usually noted, so many people were surprised that the policy-induced recession of the early 1980s was as long and deep as it was. The outcome is less surprising when the microeconomic underpinnings for the Phillips curve are provided.

1.5 CONCLUSIONS

This chapter has had two purposes: first, to introduce the subject and preview the contents of the remaining chapters; and second, to review the standard theories of intertemporal optimization in order to clarify the limitations in the microeconomic rationale behind the mainstream macro model.

The main limitation, we discovered, is that the derivation of the model's structural equations (stage 1) assumes static expectations for several variables. Yet when these equations are combined to analyze the properties of the macroeconomy (stage 2), the same variables are shown to vary systematically between full equilibria. Many economists find it unappealing to examine agents who are assumed to make systematic forecast errors like this. This limitation is not fundamentally solved by assuming rational expectations (an approach explained in Chapters 5 and 6) while continuing to assume the same behavioral rules. Ideally, the structural equations have to be *rederived* with assumptions about expectations that are consistent with the properties of the overall macro model. Tractability problems have severely limited developments in this direction, as macroeconomists try to meet the Lucas critique.

Another consideration has kept many macroeconomists from working toward a more elaborate, formal microeconomic base for conventional macro models. This problem is aggregation issues. The conclusion emerging from the aggregation literature is that the conditions required for consistent aggregation are so rigid that constrained maximization at the individual level may have no macroeconomic implications. This presents a problem since the only way to solve the Lucas critique is to use optimizing underpinnings to go "behind demand and supply curves" (Sargent 1982), and to treat only the ultimate taste and technology parameters as policy-invariant. If aggregation issues prevent these individual optimizations from imposing any restrictions on macroeconomic relationships, the Lucas critique cannot be faced. Yet only a few commentators (for example, Geweke 1985) emphasize that ignoring aggregation issues can be as important as ignoring the Lucas critique.

Thus, we are on the horns of a dilemma. Economists should ignore neither aggregation problems nor optimizing underpinnings. Yet the current convention is, in essence, to ignore aggregation issues. The only justification for this approach must be an empirical one—that the predictions of the macro models, which are based on a "representative" agent, are not rejected by the data. (Some of these empirical issues are addressed in Chapter 11.)

Other aggregation issues concern macroeconomists' practice of lumping consumption goods and capital equipment into one commodity and grouping all nonmonetary paper assets as one aggregate called "bonds" or "equities." In the appendix of this book, we show that these conventions do not represent fundamental limitations of standard macroeconomics.

For the remainder of this book, we shall examine the macroeconomic implications of models that follow from the representative agent microeconomic considerations examined in this chapter.

CHAPTER 2

AGGREGATE DEMAND AND SUPPLY

2.1 INTRODUCTION

In this chapter, we shall analyze the standard aggregate demand and supply model of a closed economy. It is assumed that students are familiar with the graphic analysis of this model (the flexible-price *IS–LM* framework). Here we shall use an algebraic approach to derive and sign the basic policy multipliers. This exposition will make it possible for readers to appreciate the more technical methods used in economic journals and to relate these techniques to the simpler geometric approach stressed in intermediate-level treatments. We shall also explain the use of the correspondence principle and provide a formal analysis of uncertainty.

2.2 THE STRUCTURAL EQUATIONS

Our model is defined by the following structural equations:

$$Y = C + I + G; \tag{2.1}$$

$$C = C(Y); \tag{2.2}$$

$$I = I(Y, r); \tag{2.3}$$

$$M/P = L(Y, i); \tag{2.4}$$

$$\dot{P}/P = H[(Y - \bar{Y})/\bar{Y}] + \pi. \tag{2.5}$$

Equations 2.1 through 2.3 represent the familiar *IS* relationship. Aggregate demand is the sum of real consumption spending by households, C (which is a function of real income, Y), of real investment spending by firms, I (which depends on the levels of output and the real interest rate, r), and of an autonomous component of expenditure, real government spending, G. The real interest rate equals the nominal rate of interest, i, minus the expected inflation rate, π. Macroeconomists attempt to derive the qualitative effects of changes in exogenous variables on endogenous variables—such as the effect of changes in G on Y. Technically, the goal is to evaluate the sign of the multiplier dY/dG, where the differential symbol, d, indicates the change in each variable. The sign of these multipliers depends on the signs assumed for the partial derivatives of the behavioral functions of the economic agents. The customary assumptions (and notation) are

$$C_Y, I_Y > 0$$

and

$$I_r < 0.$$

The subscripts stand for partial derivatives; for example, $\partial I(Y, r)/\partial r = I_r$. The negative sign assumed for this response coefficient is simply an algebraic way of summarizing the presumption that the investment desired by firms lessens as borrowing costs rise.

In order to keep macroeconomic theorems as general as possible, analysts are loath to make any *quantitative* assumptions. The main exception—one almost always made—is that the marginal propensity to consume is assumed to be a positive fraction:

$$0 < C_Y < 1.$$

Equation 2.4 is a conventional *LM* relationship; tradeable asset markets are clearing when the real money supply, M/P—which is the ratio of the nominal money supply, M, to the price of goods, P—equals the quantity of real purchasing power demanded, L, which is a function of the level of output and of the nominal rate of interest, i. The sign assumptions are standard:

$$L_Y > 0; \qquad L_i < 0.$$

Equation 2.5, which is an expectations-augmented Phillips curve, is a summary of the aggregate supply side of the model. It is assumed that prices are fixed at an instant in time and that firms adjust the actual level of production to match aggregate demand at each point in time. This instant is referred to as the short run. The short run has Keynesian features: the price level is fixed and the national output is purely demand-determined (the aggregate supply curve is horizontal). Sometimes Keynesian models involve flexible goods prices but sticky money wages. For pedagogic simplicity in this chapter, we do not model the labor market explicitly and so treat equation 2.5 as a summary of the entire supply side of the economy. Thus, to define the Keynesian features of the system we have no alternative but to impose the nominal rigidity on goods prices. This approach is quite common.

The short run is not entirely Keynesian, since it is presumed that goods are produced directly for current sales, not for addition to inventory stocks. (Inventories do not exist in this standard model.) Also, in the long run, it is assumed that prices are completely flexible, so the economy achieves full employment of all resources. Given the production function, there is a particular level of national output associated with full employment. This "natural" rate of output is that level sustainable in full equilibrium; it is denoted by $\bar{Y}$. Between the short and the long run, prices are assumed to adjust gradually in a way that is intended to insure the elimination of temporary deviations of Y from its long-run sustainable level. The fact that H is a positive function of the output gap summarizes these features. Since the single argument in the H function would make an inconvenient subscript, we indicate the derivative with a prime:

$$H' > 0.$$

The other term in equation 2.5 is π, the expected inflation rate. In full equilibrium $Y = \bar{Y}$, so this equation simply says that the actual and the expected inflation rates eventually coincide. Since we take $\bar{Y}$ as an exogenous constant, the equation means that the full-equilibrium value for inflation is determined by demand-side considerations, as explained below.

To simplify the exposition in this and the next chapter, we ignore agents' expectations and set $\pi = 0$. (In later chapters, we replace this static expectations assumption with two alternatives: adaptive expectations in Chapter 4 and rational expectations in Chapters 5 and 6.) For now, with inflationary expectations set to zero, we have a single short-run Phillips curve and no difference between the real and the nominal interest rates.

The textbook Keynesian model (with fixed prices) can be achieved by assuming $H' = 0$; the textbook Classical model (with completely flexible prices and output fixed at a level that is independent of demand shocks) emerges when $H' \rightarrow \infty$. Rather than impose these limiting cases, we prefer the following interpretation: the Keynesian model applies in the short run (actually, the very instant that a shock occurs) no matter what the size of H', but the Classical model applies in the long run (actually, once infinite time has elapsed and $\dot{P}/P$ has asymptotically approached π). The size of H', which can be thought of as the steepness of the short-run Phillips curve, determines how rapidly the predictions of the Classical time frame come into play.

Given the central role of the H' parameter in the Keynesian-Classical controversy, it will be particularly important for us to discover, in later chapters, the macroeconomic implications of structural changes that alter the size of H'. Here, however, we take H' as fixed and explore the basic properties of this standard macro model.

Notice that our model has five equations, and five unknowns or endogenous variables. In the short run, they are Y, r, C, I, and $\dot{P}$, and we can use the system to determine how these variables respond to assumed changes in G, M, $\bar{Y}$, or P. In the long run, the endogenous variables are Y, r, C, I, and P. In the short run, P denotes the preexisting price level, the one that is given by history (as illustrated by the height of OA in Figure 2.1). When a shock occurs at time 0, all that can adjust is the right-hand time derivative of price at that point in time. This derivative is reflected in the model as the *slope* of the curve just to the right of point A, which is denoted by $\dot{P}$. Given that we are abstracting from underlying growth in this discussion and have set $\pi = 0$, the long run is *defined* by the condition that $\dot{P} = 0$. Thus, in the long run, $\dot{P}$ cannot be endogenous. In that time frame, it is P that is endogenous, since P is interpreted as the final equilibrium value of the price level, the one reached when all adjustment has taken place (height OB in Figure 2.1).

Figure 2.1   The Price Level and the Rate of Inflation

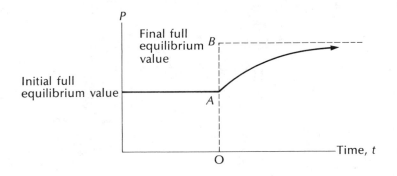

We can now proceed to reduce the five equations in five unknowns to one equation in one unknown, choosing whichever endogenous variable we wish to consider effects on. Suppose we concentrate on output and price responses. We can eliminate C and I immediately by substituting equations 2.2 and 2.3 into equation 2.1. However, algebraic substitution cannot go further unless we make some more specific assumptions about the general functions, $C(\cdot)$, $I(\cdot)$, $L(\cdot)$, and $H(\cdot)$. Since it is customary to limit analysis to "small" changes in the exogenous variables, we assume that all these functions are approximately linear. For example, consider the consumption function as illustrated in Figure 2.2. When income increases from Y_1 to Y_2, the actual consumption response is AB, but if a linear approximation is assumed the response is taken to be AD. So long as the change in Y is small, the latter presumed response will be approximately correct. The tangent to the actual consumption function is C_Y, so in equation form the approximation is

$$dC = C_Y \cdot dY.$$

Figure 2.2 Linear Approximations

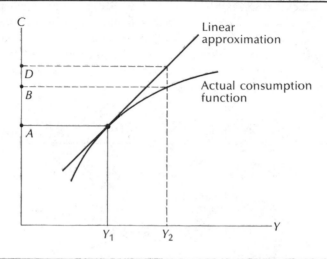

Thus, to obtain a full linear system, we rewrite the model in change form (that is, we take the total differential of all the structural equations). The result is

$$dY = C_Y\,dY + I_Y\,dY + I_r\,dr + dG; \tag{2.6}$$

$$L_Y\,dY + L_i\,dr = (1/P)\,dM - (M/P^2)\,dP; \tag{2.7}$$

$$(1/P)\,d\dot{P} - (\dot{P}/P^2)\,dP = (H'/\bar{Y})\,dY. \tag{2.8}$$

Notice that equation 2.7 was simplified by using the assumption that $d\pi = 0$. Equation 2.8 was simplified by using the same assumption as well as the stipulation that the natural rate of output is constant ($d\bar{Y} = 0$).

Equation 2.8 can be further simplified by realizing that the endogenous variables are now the *changes* in output, the interest rate, and prices (that is, either dY, dr, and $d\dot{P}$ in the short run or dY, dr, and dP in full equilibrium). The point of a linear approximation is to treat all coefficients of these differentials as *constants*. Since we assume that the system is never dramatically far away from its full equilibrium, these slope coefficients are evaluated at their full equilibrium values. The dP term in equation 2.8 can therefore be dropped, since its coefficient, $\dot{P}/P^2$, is zero in full equilibrium.

This approximation is not controversial as long as the system eventually converges to full equilibrium after any disturbance. The standard treatment is somewhat unsatisfactory, however, since this convergence is usually only established for the linearized version of the system (as shown below). In other words, only "local," not "global," stability analysis is undertaken. This limitation is another implication of our reluctance to specify particular functional forms for the behavioral equations.

2.3 SHORT-RUN ANALYSIS

Our equation system is recursive at a point in time; equations 2.6 and 2.7 determine dY and dr given exogenously specified values for dG and dM, and the predetermined level of dP. Once the value of dY is determined, it can be substituted into equation 2.8 to determine the change in $\dot{P}$.

If several policy multipliers are to be investigated, it is often helpful to rewrite the simultaneous part of the equation system in a matrix format, so that one can employ Cramer's Rule instead of numerous rounds of algebraic substitution. Here we rewrite equations 2.6 and 2.7 as

$$
\begin{bmatrix} 1 - C_Y - I_Y & -I_r \\ L_Y & L_i \end{bmatrix} \begin{bmatrix} dY \\ dr \end{bmatrix} = \begin{bmatrix} 1 & 0 & 0 \\ 0 & 1/P & -M/P^2 \end{bmatrix} \begin{bmatrix} dG \\ dM \\ dP \end{bmatrix}. \tag{2.9}
$$

Equation 2.9 is arranged so that the endogenous variables are on the left-hand side while the exogenous variables are on the right-hand side. Six multipliers can be derived immediately, each of them calculated as the ratio of two determinants. The denominator for all the multipliers is the determinant of the 2×2 matrix on the left-hand side—that is, $L_i(1 - C_Y - I_Y) + I_r L_Y$. The numerator for each multiplier—say, dY/dG—is the determinant of the matrix formed by replacing the column of coefficients for the endogenous variable of interest—in this case, dY—by the column of coefficients for the exogenous variable whose effects we are examining—in this case, dG. Hence, the numerator determinant for dY/dG is

$$
\begin{vmatrix} 1 & -I_r \\ 0 & L_i \end{vmatrix} = L_i,
$$

so the autonomous expenditure multiplier is

$$
\frac{dY}{dG} = \frac{L_i}{L_i(1 - C_Y - I_Y) + I_r L_Y}. \tag{2.10}
$$

The purpose of comparative static analysis is to determine the sign of multipliers such as this. However, this determination is impossible if we are prepared to assume only the restrictions noted earlier: $0 < C_Y < 1$; I_Y, L_Y, $H' > 0$; and I_r, $L_i < 0$. These restrictions are simply not sufficient to sign the denominator of the multiplier in equation 2.10.

Such an occurrence is common in macroeconomic analyses. Even in quite simple models (such as this one), researchers are often unable to sign the basic multipliers on the basis of the limited parameter assumptions that they are initially prepared to make. Yet since econometric methods do not yet permit widespread agreement on specific quantitative values for the structural parameters, model manipulators are loath to make more specific assumptions than are absolutely necessary. How can they solve this dilemma? Many economists regard the presumption of stability (that is, that given enough time, the economic system does converge to full equilibrium) as much less of a gamble than making particular numerical guesses about each individual parameter value. Moreover, the derivation of the full-equilibrium comparative static multipliers presumes stability. Thus, analysts prefer to acquire additional specific assumptions about the parameters by deriving the model's stability condition or conditions and then assuming that this condition or set of conditions holds. Using this "corresponding" convergence analysis to sign the multipliers of the equilibrium versions of the model (for both the short and the long run) is referred to as applying the correspondence principle.

The logic behind the use of the correspondence principle can be appreciated by comparing it to the use of second-order conditions in microeconomics. To resolve sign ambiguities in the behavioral responses in microeconomic analyses, we appeal to second-order conditions, which are already implicitly assumed as long as the behavior is being derived from first-order conditions. In both cases, economists are simply making some implicit assumptions explicit so that they can minimize sign ambiguities.

This analogy is somewhat strained, however, since second-order conditions have no necessary connection with dynamics. Indeed, there is more controversy regarding the correspondence principle in macroeconomics than about use of second-order conditions in microeconomics because in many of the former cases more than one plausible convergence analysis can be specified. The reason is that several slightly different versions of the model (especially its dynamics— in our case, equation 2.5) can be assumed. This sense of arbitrariness can be reduced by providing a clear microeconomic rationale for the model.

A more fundamental problem with the correspondence principle is that some economists (for example, Keynes) are not prepared to presume stability. Indeed, some of them can be viewed as arguing that this issue should be the fundamental focus of research (see Tobin 1975, 1980; and Hahn and Solow 1986). According to this approach, we should compare the stability conditions under alternative policy regimes, to see whether or not a particular policy is a built-in stabilizer. Thus, even though the stability conditions are not presumed to hold by all analysts, all approaches must evaluate what the conditions are. Thus, we now consider the stability analysis for our simple model.

2.4 CONVERGENCE OR STABILITY ANALYSIS

The derivation of at least the full equilibrium multipliers assumes that full equilibrium ($Y = \bar{Y}$) can be reached. What does this assumption involve? To answer this question, we must consider the dynamic adjustment equation 2.5 or 2.8 and derive the conditions under which convergence occurs.

From equation 2.8 we know that

$$d\dot{P}/dY = PH'/\bar{Y},$$

and from equation 2.9 we know that

$$\frac{dY}{dP} = \frac{-I_r M/P^2}{L_i(1 - C_Y - I_Y) + I_r L_Y} . \tag{2.11}$$

Combining these two results, we have

$$\frac{d\dot{P}}{dP} = \left(\frac{-I_r MH'}{P\bar{Y}}\right)\left(\frac{1}{L_i(1 - C_Y - I_Y) + I_r L_Y}\right). \tag{2.12}$$

Equation 2.12 has been derived on the assumption that there are no shocks to the exogenous variables. This assumption is appropriate because the whole point of this dynamic analysis is to see whether the system has forces that insure convergence to equilibrium *without* any assistance from policy.

Figure 2.3   The Stability Requirement

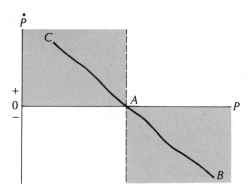

Figure 2.3 shows that $d\dot{P}/dP < 0$ is the necessary and sufficient condition for convergence. Suppose that the time change in P is related to its preexisting level, according to the relation shown by line CAB. A is the full equilibrium point, which is defined by the condition $\dot{P} = 0$. If P is below $0A$, convergence requires that P increase—that is, that $\dot{P}$ be positive. Similarly, if P is above $0A$, convergence requires that P decrease—that is, that $\dot{P}$ be negative. Thus, whenever

the observation point is to the left of the dashed line, $\dot{P}$ must be positive (and vice versa), so for convergence to occur, the observations must be on some line, such as CB, that passes through the two shaded regions and thus has a slope, $d\dot{P}/dP$, that is negative.

Equation 2.12 gives the expression for $d\dot{P}/dP$ for our model. This expression can be negative if and only if $L_i(1 - C_Y - I_Y) + I_r L_Y < 0$. Now that we have learned that this is the stability condition and that it is implicitly assumed when the full-equilibrium multipliers are calculated, internal consistency suggests that we use this condition to sign the denominator of all the multipliers, such as dY/dG. Hence, the model implies $dY/dG > 0$. Other multipliers can be signed in a similar fashion.

Graphically, there are at least two ways to appreciate why the stability condition is what it is. First, consider that since the aggregate demand curve is the summary of the IS and LM relationships, equation 2.11 gives the inverse of the slope of that aggregate demand schedule. The convergence requirement, $L_i(1 - C_Y - I_Y) + I_r L_Y < 0$, is the necessary and sufficient condition for the aggregate demand curve to be negatively sloped; as shown in Figure 2.4, convergence occurs only with such a slope. Only in that case do the price increases that stem from output's being greater than its long-run sustainable level lead to a dampening of the $Y - \bar{Y}$ gap.

Figure 2.4 The Convergence Requirement Shown with Aggregate Demand and Supply Curves

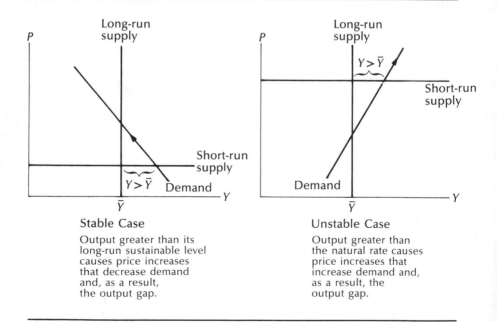

Stable Case

Output greater than its long-run sustainable level causes price increases that decrease demand and, as a result, the output gap.

Unstable Case

Output greater than the natural rate causes price increases that increase demand and, as a result, the output gap.

The other graphic approach for considering stability uses *IS–LM* curves. The slope expressions for these schedules follow immediately from equation 2.9, with changes in the exogenous variables set equal to zero. We have

$$\text{slope } IS = \frac{dr}{dY} = \frac{1 - C_Y - I_Y}{I_r} \gtreqless 0;$$

$$\text{slope } LM = \frac{dr}{dY} = \frac{-L_Y}{L_i} > 0$$

Figure 2.5 The Convergence Requirement Shown with *IS* and *LM* Schedules

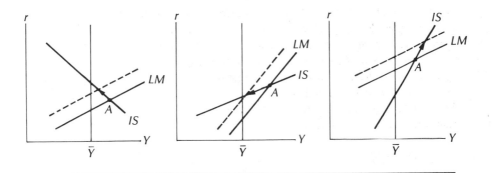

Because the *IS* curve can be positively or negatively sloped, the two curves can interact in three ways, which are shown in the three panels of Figure 2.5. In all three instances, assume that the economy starts from a point, such as *A*, at which actual output exceeds its long-run sustainable level. Given equation 2.5, this gap means that prices increase, and since rising prices shrink the real money supply, the *LM* curve must shift to the left (as shown by the dashed line in each case). Figure 2.5 makes it clear that convergence to $Y = \bar{Y}$ occurs only when slope *LM* > slope *IS*. (Note that in the left-hand panel this condition definitely holds, since slope *LM* > 0 and slope *IS* < 0.)

By substituting the slope expressions into this inequality, we have the necessary and sufficient condition for stability:

$$\frac{-L_Y}{L_i} > \frac{1 - C_Y - I_Y}{I_r}.$$

After transposing the $-L_Y/L_i$ term and multiplying the inequality through by $L_i I_r$, we can see that this graphic discussion has simply duplicated our algebraically derived stability condition:

$$L_i(1 - C_Y - I_Y) + I_r L_Y < 0.$$

In the end, then, instability is possible since aggregate demand may rise more per unit increase in aggregate supply than does aggregate supply itself. This situation occurs if the marginal propensities to spend as income increases $(C_Y + I_Y - I_r L_Y / L_i)$ exceed the amount by which aggregate supply increases with income (an amount which is unity). As noted, the aggregate respending propensity has three components: the direct income effect on households, C_Y; the direct income effect on firms, I_Y; and the indirect income effect on investment —rising income stimulates money demand $(L_Y > 0)$, pushing up interest rates $(L_i < 0)$ and so reducing investment $(I_r < 0)$.

2.5   FULL EQUILIBRIUM ANALYSIS

One purpose of stability analysis is to determine what theorists have implicitly assumed when deriving full equilibrium effects. Since we have just verified that convergence occurs when the standard slopes are assumed for the *IS* and *LM* curves, let us now derive the full equilibrium properties of our basic model.

Given our static-expectations simplification $(\pi = 0)$, full equilibrium obtains when $\dot{P} = 0$. Equation 2.5 implies that $Y = \bar{Y}$ in full equilibrium. As a result, the *IS* and *LM* relations determine the interest rate and the price level. So the matrix representation is set up as

$$\begin{bmatrix} 0 & -I_r \\ M/P^2 & L_i \end{bmatrix} \begin{bmatrix} dP \\ dr \end{bmatrix} = \begin{bmatrix} 1 & 0 \\ 0 & 1/P \end{bmatrix} \begin{bmatrix} dG \\ dM \end{bmatrix}. \tag{2.13}$$

The monetarist theory of inflation follows immediately from 2.13: $dP/P = dM/M$ (the percentage change in prices equals the percentage change in money). Since a great many economists stress the usefulness of this proposition in understanding long-run developments (see, for example, Lucas 1980b), and since this result obtains within the standard model only if stability is assumed, many analysts feel comfortable in explicitly using the convergence requirement to help eliminate sign ambiguities in *any* of the multipliers.

Incidentally, it is worth stressing that the full equilibrium properties of this model continue to reflect the quantity theory when the static-expectations simplification is dropped. In general, the full equilibrium condition is $\dot{P}/P = \pi$, so that $Y = \bar{Y}$. Then, as long as π is constant in full equilibrium, we have $d\pi = d\bar{Y} = 0$ and equations 2.13 can be used.

2.6   ALTERNATIVE GOVERNMENT POLICIES

Simple models of the sort we have analyzed can be used to investigate government policies in two ways. First, the autonomous expenditure and money supply variables can be considered exogenous instruments of the government. In this case, the comparative static multipliers that we derived represent conditional predictions concerning policy. For the second approach, the strategy is to presume that the government continuously adjusts one of its instruments—say, the money supply—and then to determine whether this ongoing reaction makes the system's stability condition more or less likely to be satisfied.

One dramatic form of making the money supply endogenous occurs when the central bank lets it be entirely demand-determined, so that interest rates can be pegged. This sort of behavior was prevalent in many Western countries before the mid-1970s, so it is interesting to determine whether this strategy makes the adjustment characteristics of the economy more or less desirable.

Before examining this issue, however, we must point out that an adequate analysis must satisfy two requirements: it must involve a model that captures all the important macroeconomic interactions (such as those between interest rates, expected inflation rates, and exchange rates); and it must define what is meant by "desirable" adjustment characteristics. Given the preliminary nature of the model examined in this chapter, our analysis cannot satisfy these requirements at this stage. As a result, we shall return to this policy issue in later chapters.

Nevertheless, even the oversimplified model is helpful in explaining the general nature of the method. We begin by recalling that with our static-expectations simplification, the real and nominal interest rates do not differ in this model. Thus, to examine this monetary policy, we simply consider the interest rate as an exogenous variable and the money supply as an endogenous one. So the matrix representation of *IS* and *LM* in the short run is

$$
\begin{bmatrix} 1 - C_Y - I_Y & 0 \\ L_Y & -1/P \end{bmatrix} \begin{bmatrix} dY \\ dM \end{bmatrix} = \begin{bmatrix} 1 & 0 & I_r \\ 0 & 1/P & -L_i \end{bmatrix} \begin{bmatrix} dG \\ dP \\ dr \end{bmatrix}. \tag{2.14}
$$

It follows that $dY/dP = 0$. Any change in the price level affects only nominal money demand, and since that is fully accommodated by the central bank, there is no need for Y or r to change to maintain portfolio equilibrium. Using equation 2.5 as before, the local stability condition is still

$$
\frac{d\dot{P}}{dP} = \left(\frac{d\dot{P}}{dY}\right)\left(\frac{dY}{dP}\right) = \frac{PH'}{\bar{Y}}\left(\frac{dY}{dP}\right) < 0.
$$

But in this policy regime, $dY/dP = 0$, so the convergence requirement is not met. The conclusion is that this pegged interest rate scheme should be avoided; it makes macroeconomic convergence break down, whereas stability is possible with an exogenous money supply.

Another way of appreciating why instability occurs with a pegged interest rate is to consider that full equilibrium cannot be consistently defined in this case. With r pegged by policy and Y equal to the exogenous value $\bar{Y}$ in full equilibrium, there is no endogenous variable that can keep the *IS* equation satisfied. Also, the *LM* relationship only prescribes a particular value of *real* balances; there are an infinity of combinations of the nominal money supply and the price level that can satisfy portfolio equilibrium. Sargent and Wallace (1975) and Sargent (1979, 92–95) argue against pegged interest rates on the grounds that full equilibrium is nonexistent and that nominal prices are indeterminant.

Notice that the present use of stability analysis differs from the application of the correspondence principle. In the latter, one assumes that the inherent stability of the economy is independent of policy and simply presumes that the convergence requirement is met. In contrast, the strategy here involves deriving the effect on the stability condition of an *ongoing* policy reaction to see if that effect is desirable or not.

2.7 SOME IMPLICATIONS OF UNCERTAINTY

At first thought, one is tempted to argue that autonomous expenditure is a more predictable tool than changes in the money supply for affecting aggregate demand. The former affects expenditure directly, while predicting the effects of changes in the money supply requires detailed knowledge of portfolio behavior and the response of investment to interest rates. However, this sort of reasoning implicitly introduces time lags, since the multipliers make clear that *all* structural parameters are involved in both the basic multipliers (dY/dG and dY/dM). Thus, if we are uncertain about the values of these structural parameters, we are unsure about both multipliers. If we wish to consider uncertainty, we should explicitly add it (and time lags, if desired) to the model.

Uncertainty about the slope coefficients is analyzed in Brainard (1967), while uncertainty in the form of additive disturbances is considered in Baumol (1961), Poole (1970), Boyer (1975), Smyth (1974), McCallum (1980), and many other recent papers. Smyth was among the first to consider the effects of discrete time lags and uncertainty together. We shall now review the analyses of Poole and Smyth.

Poole focuses his *fixed-price* analysis on the question of whether the central bank should peg the money supply or the interest rate. He assumes that unpredictable components of consumption and investment expenditure keep the position of the *IS* curve shifting back and forth and that similar stochastic shocks to money demand keep the *LM* curve moving too. The question of which monetary policy minimizes the variance of output about some average value can then be analyzed conveniently by considering each source of stochastic shocks independently.

First, consider all the unpredictability stemming from *IS* curve shifts between IS_1 and IS_2 in the left-hand panel of Figure 2.6. In this first case, we assume no uncertainty regarding money demand; if the money supply is pegged, the *LM* curve position is fixed, and the range of variation in output is between Y_1 and

Figure 2.6 Pegging Interest Rates and Pegging the Money Supply

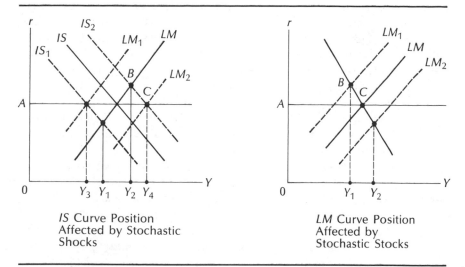

IS Curve Position
Affected by Stochastic
Shocks

LM Curve Position
Affected by
Stochastic Stocks

Y_2. A policy of pegging the interest rate only enlarges the output variations. For example, if the *IS* curve shifts out to position IS_2, there is pressure for the interest rate to rise to the level given by point *B*. To preclude this increase, the central bank must buy "bonds" (by issuing money) to raise bond prices and lower bond yields. This open-market operation must be large enough to move the *LM* curve to position LM_2, so that the observation point is *C*. The range of output variation with a pegged interest rate is between Y_3 and Y_4.

Now consider all the unpredictability stemming from *LM* curve shifts between LM_1 and LM_2 in the right-hand panel of Figure 2.6. Here we assume that the consumption and investment functions are known with certainty, but the position of the money demand function is not. With a pegged money supply, the central bank does nothing to counteract the shifts in the *LM* curve that follow from the stochastic shifts in the money demand curve, so the range of output variation is between Y_1 and Y_2. With a pegged interest rate policy, however, the central bank increases the money supply whenever there is pressure for interest rates to rise above $0A$ and decreases it whenever they would otherwise fall below $0A$. Thus, if money demand increases, shifting *LM* to position LM_1 so that interest rates would increase to the level given by point *B*, the central bank accommodates this increase in demand by supplying enough extra money to keep the *LM* curve from moving. The observation point stays at *C*, so this policy completely eliminates any output variation.

Poole concludes from these two cases that if there are large errors in predicting aggregate expenditures, the money supply should be pegged, while if there are large errors in predicting asset demands, the interest rate should be pegged. This analysis has been most influential. In the very short run, aggregate expenditures can be well predicted on the basis of the immediate past values, whereas financial asset markets can show significant short-run fluctuations. Given these facts, central banks choose to peg interest rates for a certain time interval but to adjust the level of the target interest rate periodically, depending on what the previous policy has meant for growth in the money supply. Since the mid-1970s, most Western central banks have dramatically shortened the time period for which the interest rate is pegged, as more attention has been paid to the growth in monetary aggregates. Hence, they are trying to peg the interest rate in the short run and the money supply in the longer run. In principle at least, this short-run policy makes sense in terms of Poole's analysis, and the long-run strategy is supported by our variable-price analysis above.

Of course, this analysis is not appropriate for discussing monetary policy in an open economy; it says nothing about exchange rates, so neither exchange rate expectations nor price expectations have had any role in the analysis. Poole's basic analysis has, however, been extended to these more complicated settings in many other studies (some of which are discussed in later chapters), so this method of analysis has had a significant impact on policy-making.

We now consider Smyth's analysis of additive uncertainty combined with discrete time lags. Smyth considers a one-period lag in the dependence of consumption on income and in the dependence of investment on income and the rate of interest. When his *fixed-price* linear *IS–LM* system is reduced to a single equation for national output, the result is

$$Y_t = \lambda Y_{t-1} + X + e_t, \tag{2.15}$$

where λ is a function of *IS–LM* slope parameters and X is a function of government expenditure and the money supply. The e is an error term (say, for the investment function) whose properties are assumed to be

$$E_t(e_{t+j}) = 0 \qquad \text{(mean value zero)};$$

$$E_t(e_{t+j} \cdot e_{t+h}) = \sigma_e^2, \text{ if } j = h \text{ (constant variance)};$$

$$= 0, \text{ if } j \neq h \text{ (no serial correlation)}.$$

E_t is the expectations operator based on information available at time t (and periods earlier).

In terms of our earlier notation, Smyth's summary coefficient λ equals $C_Y + I_Y - I_r L_Y / L_i$. C_Y is interpreted as the marginal propensity to consume, c, times one minus an income tax rate, $1 - k$; thus, $C_Y = c(1 - k)$. Simple inspection of the expression for λ verifies that it may be positive or negative. If λ is positive, a higher tax rate makes the value of λ smaller; if λ is negative, a higher tax rate makes the value of λ larger. All this is important in considering whether the tax system should be interpreted as a built-in stabilizer.

To examine the built-in stability issue, we begin by ignoring the error term. We can calculate both the one-period multiplier, $dY_t/dX = 1$, and the full equilibrium multiplier, $dY/dX = 1/(1 - \lambda)$, from equation 2.15. Full equilibrium is defined by the assumption that enough time has passed for $Y_t = Y_{t-1} = \ldots$ to be true. If we denote this full equilibrium value of Y by $\bar{Y}$, we can derive its expression from the deterministic version of equation 2.15: $\bar{Y} = X/(1 - \lambda)$. Using this definition, the deterministic version of equation 2.15 can be reexpressed in terms of deviations from full equilibrium: $Y_t - \bar{Y} = \lambda(Y_{t-1} - \bar{Y})$. Clearly, the deviations will disappear as time goes by only if $|\lambda| < 1$. We see, then, that the stability condition in a discrete-time model is a quantitative restriction, not just a qualitative one. Nevertheless, as with our earlier continuous-time analysis, full equilibrium effects are meaningful only if this condition is assumed.

Recall, however, that the analysis so far has omitted uncertainty—the e_t term. If we incorporate uncertainty, it is not clear that either the short-run or the long-run multipliers that we have just calculated are relevant. If we wish to discuss the built-in stability characteristics of the economy, we are expressing interest in the size of the variance of output, σ_Y^2.

The reduced form for σ_Y^2 can be calculated as follows. Take the expectations operator, E_t, through equation 2.15, using the assumption that $E(e) = 0$, to yield:

$$E(Y_t) = \lambda E(Y_{t-1}) + X.$$

When this relationship is subtracted from equation 2.15, and the result is squared, we have

$$[Y_t - E(Y_t)]^2 = \lambda^2[Y_{t-1} - E(Y_{t-1})]^2 + e_t^2 + 2\lambda e_t[Y_{t-1} - E(Y_{t-1})]. \tag{2.16}$$

The variance of Y is now calculated by taking the expectations operator through equation 2.16.

It is important to clarify the information set upon which this expectation is based. Two extreme assumptions are possible. The first is that expectations are based on $t - 1$ period information. If so, $E_{t-1}(Y_{t-1}) = Y_{t-1}$ and $\sigma_Y^2 = \sigma_e^2$. But this assumption is not appealing if we wish to consider the effects on the economy of a whole series of stochastic shocks buffeting the system through time (at any moment, the shocks from many periods continue to have some effect). To capture this *ongoing* uncertainty in the variance calculation, we need to assume that expectations for period t are based on information from period $t - j$, where j is much larger than one. The convention is to calculate the asymptotic variance by letting j approach infinity. In this case, both $[Y_t - E_{t-\infty}(Y_t)]^2$ and $[Y_{t-1} - E_{t-\infty}(Y_{t-1})]^2$ equal σ_Y^2, so equation 2.16 leads to $\sigma_Y^2 = \sigma_e^2/(1 - \lambda^2)$.

Thus, the relevant coefficient to consider is $1/(1 - \lambda^2)$—not the deterministic multiplier $1/(1 - \lambda)$. The coefficient that relates the variances is the only one that refers to the extent to which random shocks cumulate through the system —that is, to the built-in stability feature of the economy. Smyth shows that raising the tax rate must lower $1/(1 - \lambda)$ whether λ is positive or negative, but such a raise in the tax rate may raise or lower the more relevant reduced-form coefficient $1/(1 - \lambda^2)$. Increasing the tax rate decreases this coefficient if λ is positive but increases it if λ is negative. This result threatens the standard idea that the tax system acts as a built-in stabilizer.

This conclusion is interesting in itself because the question of stabilization policy is important. There is also a more general message. Simple intuition can be misleading when lags and consideration of uncertainty are involved. There appears to be no substitute for an explicit treatment of these factors.

2.8 CONCLUSIONS

We have now completed our explanation of basic macroeconomic methods by exploring the properties of a very standard model consisting of IS, LM, and Phillips curve relationships. In the next several chapters, we shall extend the model so that these methods can be used within a more complete system. This analysis will facilitate our evaluation of the fundamental differences between Keynesian and Classical attitudes toward the need for an ongoing stabilization policy.

CHAPTER 3

KEYNES
AND THE CLASSICS

3.1 INTRODUCTION

At the policy level, the hallmarks of Keynesian analysis are that involuntary unemployment can exist and that, without government assistance, any adjustment of the system back to full employment is likely to be slow and to involve cycles and overshoots. In its extreme form, the Keynesian view is that adjustment back to a full-employment equilibrium simply does not take place without policy assistance. This view can be defended by making either of the following points: (1) the economy has multiple equilibria, only one of which involves full employment; or (2) there is only one equilibrium, and it involves full employment, but the economic system is unstable without the assistance of policy, so it cannot reach full equilibrium on its own.

We shall consider the issue of multiple equilibria in Chapters 6 and 10. Here we focus on the question of general convergence. To simplify the exposition, we concentrate on stability versus outright instability, which is the extreme form of the issue, but we interpret any tendency toward outright instability as analytical support for the more general proposition that adjustment between full equilibria is protracted.

It is worth noting that this chapter and the next are closely related. One of our purposes here is to examine alternative specifications of the labor market, such as perfectly flexible money wages and perfectly fixed money wages, to clarify the causes of unemployment. Chapter 4 will present the next logical question: does increased money-wage flexibility lessen the amount of unemployment that follows from a decrease in aggregate demand? (Most economists presume that the answer is yes, but Keynes said probably no.) Thus, the two chapters taken together extend the basic macro model of Chapter 2 to allow for two important considerations that make macroeconomic convergence more problematic: firms' reactions to sticky prices and sales constraints and agents' variations in inflationary expectations.

3.2 THE LABOR MARKET WITH FLEXIBLE WAGES

Consider the following model of aggregate demand and supply:

$$Y = C[(1-k)Y] + I(i) + G; \tag{3.1}$$

$$L(Y, i) = M/P; \tag{3.2}$$

$$Y = F(N, K); \tag{3.3}$$

$$W = P \cdot F_N(N, K); \tag{3.4}$$

$$W(1-k) = P \cdot S(N). \tag{3.5}$$

Equations 3.1 and 3.2 are the *IS* and *LM* relationships; the symbols Y, C, i, G, M, and P are as defined in Chapter 2, while k stands for a proportional income tax rate. To avoid continued emphasis on points already discussed in Chapter 2, we now simplify by assuming that investment does not depend on output. The standard assumptions are that real government spending, G, and the nominal money supply, M, are exogenously determined. Equations 3.3, 3.4, and 3.5 are the production, labor demand, and labor supply functions, where N stands for employment.

We now allow for a positively sloped labor supply curve by assuming $S_N > 0$. We also assume that what workers care about is the after-tax real wage, $W(1-k)/P$. The price level is now an endogenous variable; that is, it can jump at a point in time. The framework is static: ongoing inflation and inflationary expectations are ignored, and there is no difference between the nominal and the real interest rates ($i = r$). (This chapter's analysis of variable prices will be extended in Chapters 4 to 6, where we shall add to the model first adaptive inflationary expectations and then rational inflationary expectations.)

In the present system, the five equations determine five endogenous variables: Y, N, i, P, and W. However, the system is not fully simultaneous. Equations 3.4 and 3.5 form a subset that can determine employment and the real wage, W/P. If W/P is eliminated by substitution, equations 3.4 and 3.5 become $F_N(N, K) = S(N)/(1-k)$. Since k and K are given exogenously, N is determined by this one equation, which is the labor market equilibrium condition. This equilibrium value of employment can then be substituted into the production function, equation 3.3, to determine output. Thus, this model involves what is called the Classical dichotomy: the key real variables (output and employment) are determined solely on the basis of aggregate supply relationships (the factor market relations and the production function), while the demand considerations (the *IS* and *LM* curves) determine the other variables (*i* and *P*) residually.

The model can be pictured in tems of aggregate demand and supply curves (in price-output space), so the term ''supply-side economics'' can be appreciated.

The aggregate demand curve comes from equations 3.1 and 3.2. Figure 3.1 gives the graphic derivation. The aggregate demand curve in the lower panel represents all those combinations of price and output that satisfy the demands for goods and assets. To check that this aggregate demand curve is negatively sloped, we take the total differential of the *IS* and *LM* equations, set the exogenous variable changes to zero, and solve for *dP/dY* after eliminating *di* by substitution. The result is

$$\begin{array}{l} \text{slope of} \\ \text{aggregate} \\ \text{demand} \end{array} = \frac{dP}{dY} = \frac{L_Y + L_i[(1 - C_{yd}(1 - k)]/I_i}{-M/P^2} < 0. \tag{3.6}$$

Figure 3.1 Derivation of the Aggregate Demand Schedule

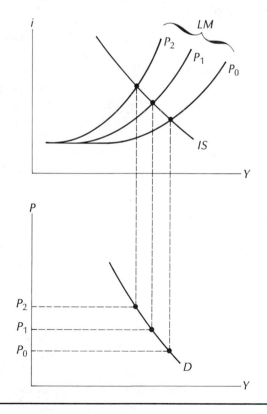

Figure 3.2 Aggregate Demand and Supply Schedules

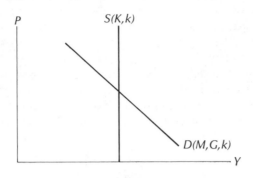

The aggregate supply curve is vertical, since P does not even enter the equation (*any* value of P, along with the labor market-clearing level of Y, satisfies these supply conditions). The summary picture, with shift variables listed in parentheses, is shown in Figure 3.2. The key policy implication is that the standard monetary and fiscal policy variables, G and M, involve price effects only. For example, complete crowding out follows increases in government spending (that is, output is not affected). The reason is that higher prices shrink the real value of the money supply so that interest rates are pushed up and preexisting private investment expenditures are reduced. Nevertheless, tax policy has a role to play in this model. A tax cut shifts both the supply and the demand curves to the right. Thus, output and employment must increase, although price may go up or down. Blinder (1973) formally derives the dP/dk multiplier and, considering plausible parameter values, argues that $dP/dk < 0$. Supply-side economists are those who favor models of this sort—those with the properties $dY/dG = dY/dM = 0$; $dY/dk < 0$.

This model, which is called the Classical system in intermediate texts, has a vertical aggregate supply curve but one that can be shifted by tax policy. A policy of balanced-budget reduction makes some macroeconomic sense here. Cuts in G and k may largely cancel each other in terms of affecting the position of the demand curve, but the lower tax rate shifts the aggregate supply curve to the right. Workers are willing to offer their services at a lower before-tax wage rate, so profit-maximizing firms are willing to hire more workers. Thus, according to this model, *both* higher output and lower prices can follow tax cuts.

This model also suggests that significantly reduced prices can be assured (without reduced output rates) if the money supply is reduced. Such a policy shifts the aggregate demand curve to the left but does not move the vertical aggregate supply curve.

In the early 1980s, several Western countries tried a policy package of tax cuts plus decreased levels of money supply growth; the motive for this policy package was, to a large extent, the belief that the Classical macro model has some short-run policy relevance. Such policies are controversial, however, because various analysts believe that the model ignores some key questions. Is the real world supply curve approximately vertical in the short run? Are labor supply elasticities large enough to lead to a significant shift in aggregate supply? Many economists doubt that these conditions are satisfied. Another key issue is the effect on macroeconomic convergence of the growing government debt that must accompany this combination policy of decreased reliance on taxation and money issue as methods of government finance. (This last issue is addressed in Chapter 7.)

Before leaving the textbook Classical model, let us review an alternative graphic exposition. In Figure 3.3, consider that the economy starts at point *A*. Then a decrease in government spending occurs. The initial effect is a leftward

Figure 3.3   The Classical Model

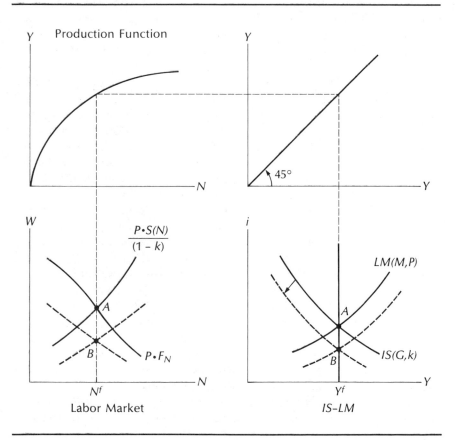

shift of the *IS* curve. Aggregate demand is given by the intersection of the original *LM* curve and the dashed *IS* curve. Aggregate supply is still Y^f. The excess supply of goods causes the price level to fall, which results in three shifts in the diagram: (1) labor demand shifts down (because of the decrease in the marginal revenue product of labor); (2) labor supply shifts down by the same proportionate amount as the decrease in the price level (because of workers' decreased money-wage claims); and (3) *LM* shifts to the right (because of the increase in the real money supply that is made possible by lower prices).

Both workers and firms care about real wages; had we drawn the labor market with the real wage on the vertical axis, neither the first nor the second shift would occur. These shifts occur because we must "correct" for having drawn the labor demand and supply curves with reference to the nominal wage.

The final observation point for the economy is *B* in both bottom panels of Figure 3.3. The economy avoids ever having a recession in actual output and employment since the shock is fully absorbed by the falling prices.

Many economists find this model unappealing for two reasons. First, they think they do observe recessions. Second, adjustment within this model involves firms that are perfectly happy to let inventories accumulate. A series of large decreases in aggregate demand would cause a dramatic increase in inventories, yet firms apparently never want to work them down since the model shows no layoffs.

This implicit build-up of inventories will be particularly acute if the economy is characterized by the phenomenon called a liquidity trap. This special case can be considered by letting the interest sensitivity of money demand become very large: $L_i \rightarrow -\infty$. Thus, the dashed *IS* curve in Figure 3.3 will intersect a horizontal range of the *LM* curve. This region of the *LM* curve does not shift as prices fall, so the intersection of *IS* and *LM* (which determines aggregate demand) will never return to the Y^f line. Thus, no consistent full equilibrium exists in this case.

Another way of appreciating the inconsistency that follows when $L_i \rightarrow -\infty$ is to consider what happens to the slope of the aggregate demand curve: it becomes vertical. (The reader can verify this fact by referring to equation 3.6.) Clearly, no well-defined equilibrium is possible if both the aggregate demand and supply curves are vertical. The Classical model can, however, be modified to avoid this problem by allowing the household consumption/savings decision to depend on the quantity of liquid assets available, a situation conveniently specified by making the consumption function $C[(1 - k)Y, M/P]$. (The second term in this function is referred to as the Pigou effect, which we discussed in Chapter 1 and shall examine again in Chapter 7.)

Macro models focusing on inventory fluctuations were very popular years ago (see, for example, Metzler 1941). Space limitations preclude our reviewing these analyses, but the reader is encouraged to consult Blinder (1981). Suffice it to say here that macroeconomic stability is problematic when firms try to work off large inventory holdings since periods of excess supply *must* be followed by periods of excess demand. Thus, it is very difficult to avoid overshoots when inventories are explicitly modeled.

What changes are required in the Classical model to make the system consistent with the existence of recessions and unemployment? By answering this question, we can clarify what most economists feel are the major assumptions behind Keynes's macroeconomic analysis. Keynes considered: (1) money-wage rigidity; (2) a model of generalized disequilibrium involving both money-wage and price rigidity; and (3) expectations effects that could destabilize the economy. The first and second points can be discussed in a static framework and so are analyzed in the remainder of this chapter. (The third point requires a dynamic analysis, which will be undertaken in Chapter 4.)

3.3   MONEY-WAGE RIGIDITY

Contracts, explicit or implicit, often fix money wages for a period of time. In Chapter 10, we shall consider what motivates these contracts. (The available literature points to such considerations as risk-sharing, deterrents to shirking on the job when information is incomplete, and the monopoly power of unions.) For the present, however, we shall presume the existence of fixed money-wage contracts and explore their macroeconomic implications.

On the assumption that money wages are fixed by contracts for the entire relevant short run, W is now taken as an exogenous variable stuck at value $\bar{W}$. Some further change in the model is required, however, since otherwise we would now have five equations in four unknowns—Y, N, i, and P.

Since the money wage cannot clear the labor market in this case, we must distinguish actual employment, N, labor demand, N^d, and labor supply, N^s, which are all equal only in equilibrium. When we considered discrepancies between labor demand and long-run labor supply in Chapter 1, we assumed that labor demand was always satisfied (and we shall return to this assumption later). To motivate this treatment more fully, we now consider an alternative assumption, which has attracted significant attention, but which has an unappealing implication. To appreciate this, we shall follow Patinkin (1965), Clower (1965) and Barro and Grossman (1971) and assume that employment equals the lesser of demand or supply: $N = \min(N^d, N^s)$.

Let us first consider a decrease in aggregate demand. Labor demand is less than labor supply, so $N = N^d$. Equation 3.4 needs no alteration, but equation 3.5 must be rewritten as: $\bar{W}(1 - k) = P \cdot S(N^s)$. The five endogenous variables are now Y, N, N^s, i, and P. Since N^s occurs nowhere in the model except in equation 3.5, that equation solves residually for N^s.

Figure 3.4 The Effects of Aggregate Demand Changes with Fixed Money Wages and Excess Labor Supply

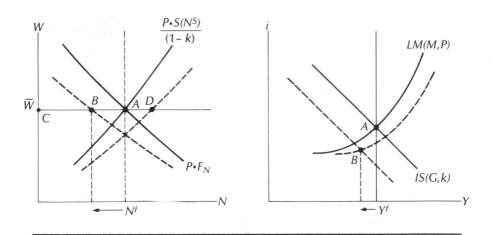

Figure 3.4 is a graphic representation of the results of a decrease in government spending. As before, we start from the observation point A and assume a decrease in government spending that moves the IS curve to the left. The resulting excess supply of goods causes price to decrease, with the same shifts in the labor demand, labor supply, and LM curves. The observation point becomes B in both panels of Figure 3.4. The unemployment rate, which was zero, is now BD/CD.

Unemployment has two components: layoffs, AB, plus increased participation in the labor force, AD. It appears that lack of labor market-clearing is the critical Keynesian assumption that generates unemployment in this model. Note that this unemployment can be reduced by *any* of the following policies: increasing government spending, increasing the money supply, or reducing the money wage (think of an exogenous decrease in wages accomplished by policy as the static equivalent of a wage guidelines policy). These policy statements can be proved by verifying that $dN/dG, dN/dM > 0$ and $dN/d\overline{W} < 0$.

Given the assumption that the short side of the labor market dominates in determining actual employment, we should expect the analysis to be quite different if aggregate demand increases. In this case, the IS curve shifts to the right and prices increase, so the labor demand, labor supply, and LM curves move as shown in Figure 3.5. The new observation point is B in both panels. (The results can be checked formally by changing equations 3.4 and 3.5 to $\overline{W} = PF_N(N^d, K)$ and $\overline{W}(1 - k) = PS(N)$ and deriving dN/dG.)

The surprising implication of this model (noted by Buiter and Lorie 1977) is that if the economy starts from a position of full employment, *any* change in aggregate demand—a decrease *or* an increase—must cause a fall in output and employment! Since most economists regard this proposition as rejected by "the

Figure 3.5 The Effects of Aggregate Demand Changes with Fixed Money Wages and Unfilled Vacancies

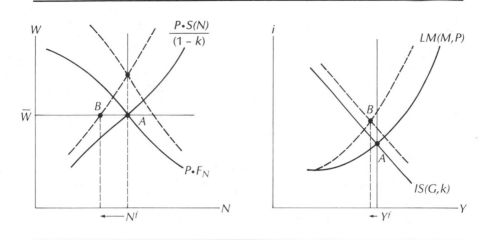

facts," they usually adopt one of two changes in the model. One of these options is to drop the assumption that the money wage is rigid in the upward direction; this approach is, however, inconsistent with the available microeconomic theories on wage rigidity (see Chapter 10). The other option is to drop the "short side of the market dominates" assumption in favor of the "labor demand is always satisfied" assumption. Empirical studies do suggest that existing contractual arrangements allow employers to determine employment levels residually.

Thus, we return to the "labor demand is satisfied" assumption, on which we relied in Chapter 1. With that assumption, the rigid money-wage model yields the following general conclusions:

1. Unemployment can exist only because the wage is "too high."
2. Unemployment can be lowered only if the level of real incomes of those already employed (the real wage) is reduced.
3. The level of the real wage must correlate inversely with the level of employment (that is, it must move contracyclically).

Intermediate textbooks call this model the Keynesian system. Many economists who regard themselves as Keynesians have a difficult time accepting these three propositions, however. They know that Keynes argued, in chapter 19 of *The General Theory*, that wage cuts might only worsen the Depression. They feel that unemployment stems from some kind of market failure, so it should be possible to help unemployed workers without hurting those already employed. Finally, they have observed that there is no strong contracyclical movement to the real wage; indeed, it sometimes increases when unemployment increases (see Geary and Kennan 1982).

3.4 MONEY-WAGE AND PRICE RIGIDITY: "GENERALIZED DISEQUILIBRIUM"

These inconsistencies between Keynesian beliefs on the one hand and the properties of the textbook Keynesian model on the other suggest that Keynesian economists must have developed other models that involve more fundamental departures from the Classical system. One of these developments is the generalization of the notion of disequilibrium to apply beyond the labor market, a concept pioneered by Barro and Grossman (1971) and Malinvaud (1977).

As noted in Chapters 1 and 2, it is common to analyze aggregate demand in isolation by assuming that the aggregate supply schedule is perfectly horizontal at a point in time. One way of defending this assumption is evident from the expression for the slope of the aggregate supply curve. In the fixed money-wage case, that slope is derived by taking the total differential of $Y = F(N, K)$ and $\bar{W} = PF_N(N, K)$. After setting the changes in exogenous variables equal to zero $(dK = d\bar{W} = 0)$ and eliminating dN by substitution, we have

$$\begin{matrix} \text{slope of} \\ \text{aggregate} \\ \text{supply} \end{matrix} = \frac{dP}{dY} = \frac{-PF_{NN}}{F_N^2} > 0.$$

This expression equals zero if $F_{NN} = 0$. To put the point verbally, the marginal product of labor is constant if labor and capital must be combined in fixed proportions.

This set of assumptions—rigid money wages and fixed-coefficient technology—is often appealed to in defending fixed-price models. (Note that these models are the opposite of supply-side economics since with a horizontal supply curve, output is completely demand-determined, not supply-determined.)

Another defense for price rigidity is simply the existence of long-term contracts fixing the money price of goods as well as factors. To use this interpretation, however, we must rederive the equations in the model that relate to firms, since if the goods market is not clearing, it may no longer be sensible for firms to set marginal revenue equal to marginal cost.

This situation is evident in Figure 3.6, which shows a perfectly competitive firm facing a sales constraint. If there were no sales constraint, the firm would operate at point A, with marginal revenue (which equals price) equal to marginal cost. Since marginal cost $= \bar{W}(dN/dY) = \bar{W}/F_N$, this is the assumption we have made throughout our analysis up to this point. But if the market price is fixed for a time (at $\bar{P}$) and aggregate demand falls so that all firms face a sales constraint (sales $\leqslant \tilde{Y}$), the firm will operate at point B. The marginal revenue schedule now has two components: $\bar{P}B$ and $\tilde{Y}D$ in Figure 3.6. Thus, marginal revenue and marginal cost diverge by amount BC.

Let us now formally reconsider the firm's reactions when it is in a situation

Figure 3.6 A Competitive Firm Facing a Sales Constraint

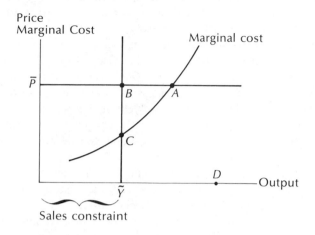

in which marginal cost does not equal marginal revenue. The revised theory of the firm is to maximize

$$\sum_{t=0}^{\infty} \left(\frac{1}{1+r}\right)^{t} [PF(N_t, K_t) - WN_t - P_I I_t - bP_I I_t^2]$$

subject to

$$I_t = K_{t+1} - (1 - \delta)K_t$$

and

$$F(N_t, K_t) \leq \tilde{Y}.$$

All the notation is as defined in Chapter 1; the only difference from the theory of the firm presented there is the sales constraint.

With fixed goods prices, no firm can sell more than $\tilde{Y}$, which is each individual's share of the lower level of national output that emerges after a decrease in aggregate demand. Since we are limiting our analysis to this decrease in demand, we can assume that the constraint is binding as an equality—that is, that firms have become cost-minimizers for the predetermined level of output, $\tilde{Y}$. Following the same solution procedure we used in section 1.2, we obtain the revised investment function:

$$I = \frac{1}{2b} \left[\frac{F_K(W/P)}{F_N(r + \delta)} - 1 \right]. \tag{3.7}$$

The revised labor demand condition is simply the inverse of the production function (since at any point in time, the capital stock is determined by history and the level of output is demand-determined by the sales constraint). The model now has two key differences from what has been used thus far in the text. First, labor demand is now independent of the real wage, so any reduction in the real wage should not help in raising employment. Second, the real wage is now a shift variable for the *IS* curve, so wage cuts can decrease aggregate demand and thereby lower employment. (The second point is explained below.)

These properties can be verified formally by noting that the model becomes simply equations 3.1 to 3.3 but with W and P exogenous and with the revised investment function replacing $I(i)$. The three endogenous variables are Y, i, and N, with N solved residually by equation 3.3.

The model is presented graphically in Figure 3.7. The initial observation point is A in both the goods and labor markets. Assume a decrease in government expenditure. The demand for goods curve moves left so firms can only sell $\tilde{Y}$; the labor demand curve becomes the $\tilde{N}$ line, and the observation point moves to point B in both diagrams. Unemployment clearly exists. Can it be eliminated? Increases in M or G would shift the demand for goods back, so these policies would still work. But what about a wage cut? If the $\bar{W}$ line shifts down, all that happens is that income is redistributed from labor to capitalists (as shown by the shaded rectangle). If capitalists have a smaller marginal propensity to consume than workers, the demand for goods shifts further to the left, leading to further declines in $\tilde{Y}$ and $\tilde{N}$. The demand for goods shifts to the left in any event, however, since given the modified investment function (equation 3.7), the lower wage reduces investment. Thus, wage cuts actually make unemployment worse.

Figure 3.7 The Effects of Falling Demand with Fixed Wages and Prices

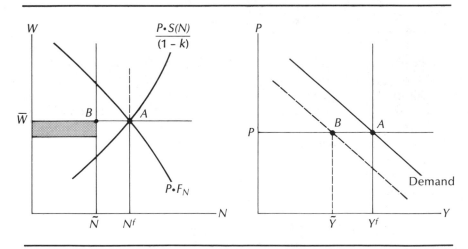

Keynesians find this generalized model appealing since activist aggregate demand policy can still successfully cure recessions while wage cuts cannot. Thus the unemployed can be helped without taking from workers who are already employed (that is, without having to lower the real wage). However, the prediction that wage cuts lead to lower employment requires the assumption that prices do not fall as wages do. In Figure 3.7, the reader can verify that if *both* the $\bar{W}$ and $\bar{P}$ lines shift down (so that the real wage remains constant), output and employment must increase. The falling price allows point B to shift down the dashed aggregate demand curve, so $\tilde{Y}$ increases. Thus, with a less binding sales constraint, the position of the $\tilde{N}$ line shifts to the right.

Many economists are not comfortable with the assumption that goods prices are *more* sticky than money wages. This discomfort forces them to downplay the significance of the prediction that wage cuts could worsen a recession, at least as shown in generalized disequilibrium models of the sort just summarized. For this reason, we do not pursue these models further in this text. (For a brief but excellent survey of this literature, we refer the reader to Stoneman 1979.)

3.5 CONCLUSIONS

In this chapter we have reviewed Keynesian and Classical interpretations of the goods and labor markets. We have established, among other points, that unemployment can exist only in the presence of some stickiness in money wages. Appreciation of this fact naturally leads to a question: should we advocate increased wage flexibility so as to avoid at least some unemployment? There are two general responses. First, one can say that private agents must have adopted the institution of temporarily rigid wages (contracts) for a reason and that reason must be understood before one can be confident that increasing wage flexibility is "good." (The microeconomic theories of wage rigidity are considered in Chapter 10.) Second, one can presume that the microeconomic costs of increased flexibility would not be large and, therefore, directly proceed with the macroeconomic analysis of whether the built-in stability of the overall economy is enhanced by wage flexibility. In section 3.4, we reviewed one argument against this possibility. The model of generalized equilibrium supports the proposition that wage cuts could worsen a recession. In the next chapter, we shall reconsider another mechanism—expectations—whose presence may increase this concern.

CHAPTER 4

EXPECTATIONS AND THE DESIRABILITY OF WAGE AND PRICE FLEXIBILITY

4.1 INTRODUCTION

Turning from considerations of generalized goods and labor market disequilibrium, we shall now focus on the fact that wage decreases can lead to a general *expectation* of falling demand for firms' products. In fact, this expectations effect was the mechanism that Keynes stressed when he argued that increased wage flexibility would not be desirable (1936, Chap. 19).

To pursue this approach, however, we must go beyond considering a once-and-for-all change in the price *level* (as in the last chapter), and examine determinants of the inflation/deflation *rate*. We must also replace our simple rule of static expectations with an explicit hypothesis about how expectations are formed. For much of this chapter, we assume adaptive expectations. Although this hypothesis has some appealing properties and is used in a vast amount of the writings of mainstream macroeconomics of the 1960s and 1970s, it does involve economic agents' making systematic forecast errors. The assumption that represents the polar opposite case is that agents make no forecast errors, systematic or otherwise—an assumption known in the literature as perfect foresight. For balance, then, we shall introduce perfect foresight analysis near the end of this chapter.

Throughout, the entire focus is on the following two questions. Can inflationary or deflationary expectations create macroeconomic instability? When these features are part of a model, can increased wage flexibility be a bad thing for macroeconomic adjustment?

4.2 ADAPTIVE EXPECTATIONS

We consider the following macro model:

$$Y = C[(1 - k)Y] + I(i - \pi) + G; \tag{4.1}$$

$$M/P = L(Y, i); \tag{4.2}$$

$$\frac{\dot{P}}{P} = f \cdot \left(\frac{Y - \bar{Y}}{\bar{Y}} \right) + \pi; \tag{4.3}$$

$$\dot{\pi} = \lambda(\dot{P}/P - \pi). \tag{4.4}$$

The notation and the *IS* and *LM* relationships are the same as those already used; π stands for the expected inflation rate. In the two previous chapters, we set it to zero and ignored it (the static expectations assumption); now it is used to define the real interest rate, $i - \pi$, in the investment function. Notice that π is here the rate that agents expect for actual inflation. Our theory for the expectations-augmented Phillips curve, given in Chapter 1, suggested that it should involve the expected *equilibrium* inflation rate, not the expectation of the actual inflation rate. Nevertheless, we have defined π as the latter here, since this practice was common until 1980. It is useful to compare the more modern analyses below with what was mainstream macroeconomics for a long time. Equation 4.4, which is explained a little later, stipulates how expectations are revised.

Consider first equations 4.1 through 4.3 alone. This three-equation system determines Y, i, and $\dot{P}$ for given values of $G, k, M, \bar{Y}$, and π and the preexisting level of P. P is exogenous in the short run, so the model is very Keynesian with a horizontal aggregate supply curve. Y is interpreted as demand and supply, and $\bar{Y}$ is the level of output that is sustainable in the long run (the natural rate). Wage contracts fix the level of the money wage and, therefore, the price at a point in time (as explained in section 1.4), but the contracts give employers the freedom to hire whatever quantity of labor they desire. If this quantity involves a point off the aggregate labor supply schedule, wages and, therefore, prices adjust through time. We define the long run as having the property that actual and expected inflation are equal. In this case, $Y = \bar{Y}$, so the aggregate supply curve is vertical at the natural rate value, and the model is fully Classical in full equilibrium.

Figure 4.1 The Effects of Inflationary Expectations on Interest Rates

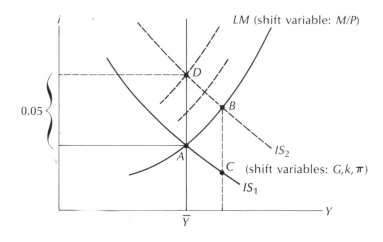

Before explicitly examining equation 4.4, which makes inflationary expectations endogenous, we shall consider the distinction between nominal and real interest rates as well as the effects of an exogenous increase in inflationary expectations. Investment depends on the real interest rate, but the *IS* and *LM* curves are usually drawn with the nominal interest rate on the axis. As a result, we must shift the *IS* curve whenever π changes. From equation 4.1, we have $di/d\pi = 1$ if $dG = dk = dY = 0$, so the *IS* curve shifts up by the exact increase in π. Figure 4.1 shows the effects of an exogenous increase in π. IS_1 is drawn for $\pi = 0$. When π increase to 0.05, the curve shifts up to IS_2, and the observation point moves from A to B (because aggregate demand is given by the intersection of *IS* and *LM*, and at a point in time, this model assumes that output is entirely demand-determined). By comparing points A and B, we see that the nominal interest rate rises but not by the full amount of the increase in inflationary expectations. The real interest rate falls, as given by the height of point C. At point B, output is greater than its long-run sustainable level, so given equation 4.3, price must increase. This rise decreases the real money supply, so the *LM* curve shifts left, and in the end the observation point coincides with point D. Eventually, then, the nominal interest rate does rise by the full amount of the increase in inflationary expectations. But as long as parameter *f* is fairly small, a long time lag is involved. (It should not be surprising, then, that although inflation accelerated in the early 1970s, nominal interest rates did not rise dramatically until later in the decade.)

Now consider a contractionary monetary policy, with the economy starting at point D. This policy is supposed to lower nominal interest rates by recessing the economy enough to lower inflationary expectations, and it will do so eventually in this model. But until π is reduced, IS_2 is the relevant IS curve, so the leftward shift in LM means even higher nominal interest rates for the early part of the adjustment period. We have seen a recent example of this phenomenon, too. When governments made monetary policy contractionary in the early 1980s, both nominal and real interest rates went very high.

It seems that this model is rich enough to account for the observed simultaneous fluctuations in output, inflation, and the real and nominal interest rate. Thus, it will be particularly instructive to consider the convergence or stability condition for this model. Much of the Keynes versus Classic debate concerns establishing the conditions under which the covergence requirement is or is not met.

Before considering the built-in stability properties of this model, however, we must formally endogenize π and so must provide a motivation for equation 4.4. The adaptive expectations hypothesis is often called the error-learning model, since it specifies that the change in the agent's forecast is equal to a fraction of the previous forecast error. For discrete time, this hypothesis can be written as

$$\pi - \pi_{-1} = \lambda \left[\left(\frac{\Delta P}{P} \right)_{-1} - \pi_{-1} \right]$$

where

$$0 < \lambda < 1,$$

the subscripts standing for lagged time periods.

An alternative interpretation of this hypothesis can be seen if it is rewritten for several time periods:

$$\pi = (1 - \lambda)\pi_{-1} + \lambda(\Delta P/P)_{-1},$$

$$\pi_{-1} = (1 - \lambda)\pi_{-2} + \lambda(\Delta P/P)_{-2}, \ldots,$$

so that successive substitution leads to

$$\pi = \lambda \left[\left(\frac{\Delta P}{P} \right)_{-1} + (1 - \lambda) \left(\frac{\Delta P}{P} \right)_{-2} + (1 - \lambda)^2 \left(\frac{\Delta P}{P} \right)_{-3} + \ldots \right]. \qquad (4.5)$$

This last formulation of the hypothesis states that π is a weighted average of past actual values, with less weight given to the more distant past. The weights decline geometrically. Both the error-adjustment and the weighted-average interpretations suggest a certain plausibility for the adaptive expectations hypothesis, as does its long-run consistency property. If actual inflation eventually settled at some constant value, x, surely π should be x too, at least eventually. It is reassuring to see that when $(\Delta P/P)_{-1} = (\Delta P/P)_{-2} = \ldots x$ is substituted in equation 4.5, π does equal x.

Figure 4.2   Adaptive Expectations

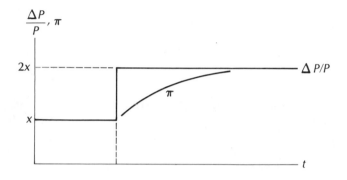

Nevertheless, the adaptive expectations hypothesis has some unappealing properties, too. One is that long-run consistency does not imply short-run consistency. In general, adaptive expectations involve *systematic* forecast errors by agents. For example, if actual inflation jumps from x to $2x$ and stays at $2x$ indefinitely, π as defined by equation 4.5 will underpredict actual inflation *throughout* the adjustment period in the manner shown in Figure 4.2. Another unappealing feature of this forecasting rule is that only past observations matter in it. Announcements concerning the future values of key variables, such as the money supply, are precluded from having any effect on expectations.

The appeal of the rational expectations hypothesis is that it does not involve these shortcomings. Nevertheless, many economists, especially many involved with empirical work, continue to rely on the adaptive scheme, so we shall explore its macroeconomic implications. We do so by adding equation 4.4 to the model, since this equation defines the continuous-time version of the error adjustment hypothesis. (Once the rational expectations assumption is explained in the next chapter, we shall be able to explain why using the adaptive hypothesis as part of empirical studies can raise the likelihood of a researcher's model fitting the facts.)

4.3 INFLATIONARY EXPECTATIONS AND THE MONETARY INSTRUMENT QUESTION

A useful means of understanding this model is to compare macroeconomic stability under two alternative monetary policies: a pegged nominal interest rate and a pegged money supply. Consider first Figure 4.3, in which the central bank pegs the interest rate at $\bar{i}$, which is its "natural" rate. The natural interest rate is the value determined by "productivity and thrift"—the intersection of the $\bar{Y}$ line with the IS curve drawn for $\pi = 0$. Suppose the central bank does not realize that the marginal propensity to consume increases, so the IS curve shifts to IS_2. There is pressure for the economy to move from point A to point B, but the central bank precludes such a shift by buying bonds. This action raises bond prices, which keeps interest rates down at $\bar{i}$ by moving the LM curve to LM_2. So the new observation point is C. But C cannot be a long-run equilibrium, since $Y > \bar{Y}$. According to equation 4.3, inflation occurs, and given equation 4.4, expected inflation also goes up. The increase in π shifts the IS curve to IS_3. There is pressure to move to point D, but the central bank again increases the money supply to peg the interest rate, so the observation point is now E. We see that there is ever-accelerating inflation and that the system is unstable. Friedman (1968) uses this analysis to argue against a pegged interest rate policy.

Figure 4.3   Instability with Pegged Interest Rates

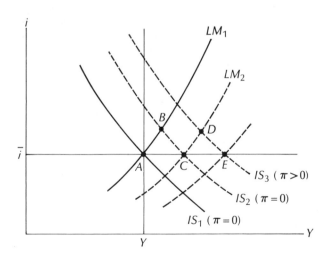

Figure 4.4   The Stability Question with a Monetarist Policy

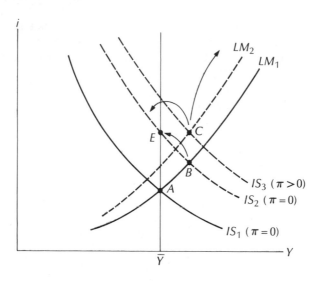

Now consider Figure 4.4 to see the implications of a fixed nominal money stock. As before, the economy is originally at point A when the marginal propensity to consume increases, making the IS curve shift to IS_2. With no response from the central bank, the observation point moves to B, but this position cannot be sustained since $Y > \bar{Y}$. According to equations 4.3 and 4.4, both actual and expected inflation increase. The actual price increases reduce the gap between Y and $\bar{Y}$ by shifting the LM curve to the left, but the expected price increases widen it by shifting the IS curve to the right. The observation point moves to a point, such as C, that may be closer to or further away from the $\bar{Y}$ line than was point B. The new full equilibrium point is E, which has both output and the interest rate at their natural levels (given by $\bar{Y}$, and the intersection of the $\bar{Y}$ line and the now-relevant IS curve with $\pi = 0$). The three arrows in the diagram indicate that the economy may or may not converge to this equilibrium (and the adjustment path may or may not involve cycles). Friedman concludes that since stability is at least possible in this case (and that since possible stability is better than definite instability), pegging the money supply is better than pegging the interest rate. It is interesting that most Western central banks reacted to the accelerating inflation of the early 1970s by shifting away from a pegged interest rate policy.

4.4 CAGAN'S CONVERGENCE REQUIREMENT

When conjecturing about the need for an interventionist stabilization policy, it is instructive to derive the formal stability condition under the pegged money policy. This derivation is most conveniently performed as follows. From the total differential of equations 4.1 and 4.2, we have

$$\frac{dY}{d(M/P)} = \frac{I_r}{\Delta}$$

$$\frac{dY}{d\pi} = \frac{-I_r L_i}{\Delta}$$

where $\Delta = L_i[1 - C_{Y^d}(1 - k)] + I_r L_Y$.

These results mean that the percentage change in output—$(dy = dY/Y)$—equals $I_r M / \Delta PY$ times the percentage change in the money supply—$d(m - p)$—plus $-I_r L_i / \Delta Y$ times the actual change in π. Thus, for given values of the exogenous variables (G and k), equations 4.1 and 4.2 imply

$$dy = \theta(dm - dp) + \psi d\pi,$$

where $\theta = I_r M / \Delta PY$ and $\psi = -I_r L_i / \Delta Y$. For simplicity we assume a functional form for the aggregate demand schedule so that it is linear in the logs of output and the money supply and in the level of expected inflation. Thus we have essentially the same log-linear summary of *IS* and *LM* that we used in section 1.4:

$$y = \theta(m - p) + \psi \pi. \tag{4.6}$$

As noted above, we simplify here by dropping exogenous variables that are not involved in this convergence analysis. Equation 4.6 is a compact summary of the temporary equilibrium part of the model (*IS–LM*).

In logarithmic terms, the dynamic equations 4.3 and 4.4 are

$$\dot{p} = f(y - \bar{y}) + \pi; \tag{4.7}$$

$$\dot{\pi} = \lambda(\dot{p} - \pi). \tag{4.8}$$

We now summarize this system as two differential equations in π and y. Substituting equation 4.7 into equation 4.8 eliminates $\dot{p}$ and gives us the first line of the matrix. Differentiating equation 4.6 with respect to time, we get

$$\dot{y} = \theta(\dot{m} - \pi) + f(\psi \lambda - \theta)(y - \bar{y}), \tag{4.9}$$

and this equation forms the second line in the matrix:

$$\begin{bmatrix} \dot{\pi} \\ \dot{y} \end{bmatrix} = \begin{bmatrix} 0 & \lambda f \\ -\theta & f(\psi \lambda - \theta) \end{bmatrix} \begin{bmatrix} \pi \\ y \end{bmatrix} + \text{exogenous terms.}$$

Full equilibrium is defined by $\dot{\pi} = \dot{y} = 0$ (which was represented by points A and E in Figure 4.4). When $\dot{\pi} = 0$, equation 4.8 implies that actual and expected inflation are equal. When $\dot{p} = \pi$, equation 4.7 implies that the actual and natural output rates are equal. When $\dot{y} = 0$ and $y = \bar{y}$, equation 4.9 implies that $\dot{p} = \pi = \dot{m}$, which means that when the economy is in full equilibrium, inflation is a "purely monetary phenomenon." However, since the model does involve simultaneous fluctuations in output and inflation during the short-run adjustment period, inflation is not "always and everywhere a monetary phenomenon." (The quoted phrases are due to Friedman.)

The necessary and sufficient conditions for stability are that the determinant of the 2×2 matrix be positive and that the trace be negative. These conditions are $\theta \lambda f > 0$, which is necessarily satisfied, and $f(\psi \lambda - \theta) < 0$, which may or may not be satisfied. The latter conditon is the algebraic counterpart of the several possible arrows shown in Figure 4.4. In the graph, we saw that convergence exists if the stabilizing effect of actual inflation is more powerful than the destabilizing effect of expected inflation. The actual inflation effect works through the real money supply, so a high value of coefficient θ, the money multiplier on aggregate demand, makes stability more likely. But the higher λ, the coefficient of expectations revision, and the higher ψ, the effect of expected inflation on aggregate demand, the less likely it is that the stability condition will be met. Thus, it makes intuitive sense that the convergence requirement is that $\theta > \lambda \psi$.

Other ways exist for appreciating the reason for this convergence requirement. An inflation in money prices requires an excess supply of money. How can higher prices make the excess supply even bigger, so that inflation accelerates? This phenomenon is possible if the increase in actual prices shrinks the real money supply more slowly than the increase in expected inflation raises the nominal interest rate and so shrinks money demand. Another way of appreciating the stability requirement is to consider the goods market. A rise in prices shrinks the real money supply and raises borrowing costs so that an "excess demand" gap can be eliminated. But higher prices lead to higher inflationary expectations, which lower the real burden of any nominal interest rate charges. If expected inflation rises more rapidly than the nominal interest rate, the "excess demand" gap will be widened.

All of these phenomena can be considered in the deflationary direction, and this provides a rationale to support Keynesian worries that a noninterventionist authority can leave the economy with protracted (ever-widening) depression and deflation.

We can express the stability condition in a more particular form by using the definitions of θ and ψ and the definition of the interest elasticity of money demand, $e = -L_i i / (M/P)$. The stability condition becomes

$$e\lambda / \bar{i} < 1. \tag{4.10}$$

This condition is sometimes referred to as the Cagan convergence condition, since Cagan (1956) was the first to derive it (in a model of hyperinflation). Before considering whether this condition is likely to be met, notice that the stability issue is not affected by the size of $C_{Yd}, k, L_Y, I_r,$ or f. All these parameters affect the size of both the M/P and the π multipliers to the same extent, so they cannot affect their relative size.

We now consider condition 4.10 in two separate situations: an ongoing inflation, such as that of the 1970s, and a deep depression, such as that of the 1930s. In a period of inflation, the equilibrium nominal interest rate, $\bar{i}$, is high, a situation that contributes to the satisfaction of condition 4.10. Conversely, the extremely low interest rates of a deep depression make it very difficult for condition 4.10 to be satisfied. (For a discussion of how alternative functional forms for the money demand function can affect this argument, see Yarrow 1977.) The interest elasticity of money demand also seems to depend on the level of interest rates. When inflation and interest rates are high, agents tend to economize on money holdings as much as feasible, and the remaining interest elasticity, e, is estimated to be quite low, a situation that contributes to satisfying condition 4.10, as Johnson (1977) notes. In deep depressions, on the other hand, agents are so fearful of default on nonmonetary assets that the interest elasticity of money demand can be much higher. At the limit, this argument is presented as the liquidity trap: $e \rightarrow \infty$. As e moves in this way, condition 4.10 cannot be satisfied. Thus, this model represents a compact system that fully allows for Keynes's worry that wage and price decreases could only worsen the Depression, through expectational effects. At the same time, however, the model does not suggest that instability must always occur. Indeed, macroeconomists can appeal to this one simplified model, and consistently argue that government intervention was justified in the 1930s (to avoid instability or at least protracted adjustment problems) but was not required in the 1970s (to avoid hyperinflation). Since any scientist wants a single, simple model to "explain" a host of diverse situations, it is easy to see why this model represented mainstream macroeconomics before the rational expectations revolution.

Before concluding, it is worth emphasizing that this model does not support the Keynesian proposition that an increase in the degree of wage flexibility can worsen the characteristics of macroeconomic adjustment. Increased wage flexibility is considered by examining the implications of a steeper short-run Phillips curve—that is, a larger value for parameter f. As has been shown, the likelihood of instability is independent of the value of f. It can also easily be shown that the likelihood of a cyclical approach, rather than an asymptotic adjustment, to full equilibrium is also independent of f. All that a larger f means is that adjustment is faster, whether that adjustment is along a stable or an unstable path. In the end, then, the only thing that this model provides for those with Keynesian priors is that it shows instability to be a serious issue, especially in deflationary situations.

4.5 PERFECT FORESIGHT

We now examine the same model except that we now replace the hypothesis of adaptive inflationary expectations with the assumption of perfect foresight. Some Keynesians regard this alternative hypothesis as unappealing (perhaps because it sounds so unrealistic). For this reason, it is most interesting that we shall find that an increased degree of wage flexibility *can* worsen the macroeconomy's adjustment properties in this case. Thus, the Keynesian policy presumption finds its strongest analytical support within a model that involves what some regard as an un-Keynesian expectational hypothesis.

In this case, the actual inflation rate is involved in specifying the real interest rate in the investment function, $I = I(i - \dot{P}/P)$, so the log-linear summary of the *IS–LM* part of the model becomes

$$y = \phi g + \theta(m - p) + \psi \dot{p}, \tag{4.11}$$

instead of equation 4.6.

The aggregate supply summary is taken directly from Chapter 1 (equation 1.4) since we assume that agents forecast the equilibrium inflation rate, $\dot{p}$, perfectly as $\dot{m}$:

$$\dot{p} = f \cdot (y - \bar{y}) + \dot{m}.\text{*} \tag{4.12}$$

It is important that the theory behind the aggregate supply function given in Chapter 1 supports the proposition that what belongs in the Phillips curve equation is expected $\dot{p}$, not expected p. If it were the latter, and we assumed perfect foresight, the supply function would reduce to $y = \bar{y}$, so the model would preclude even temporary output gaps. Such a model would have to be rejected. In the analysis below, we rely on the way in which f is related to the underlying demand and supply parameters as derived in Chapter 1 (equation 1.6), which we repeat here for convenience:

$$f = 1/(\psi + \theta/a). \tag{4.13}$$

The effect of a change in autonomous expenditure on output is calculated by substituting equation 4.12 into equation 4.11 to eliminate $\dot{p}$:

$$y = \left(\frac{1}{1 - \psi f}\right)[\phi g + \theta(m - p) + \psi \dot{m} - \psi f \bar{y}]; \tag{4.14}$$

$$dy/dg = \phi/(1 - \psi f). \tag{4.15}$$

---

*The reader can verify that the equilibrium inflation rate, $\dot{p}$, is $\dot{m}$. We can use equation 4.14 below to define $\bar{p}$ as that value of p that makes $y = \bar{y}$:

$$(1 - \psi f)\bar{y} = \phi g + \theta(m - \bar{p}) + \psi \dot{m} - \psi f \bar{y}.$$

Assuming $\dot{g} = \dot{\bar{y}} = \ddot{m} = 0$, the time derivative of this equation yields $\dot{\bar{p}} = \dot{m}$.

The stability of the economy is assessed by taking the time derivative of equation 4.14 and using equation 4.12 to eliminate $\dot{p}$. Assuming $\dot{g} = \dot{\bar{y}} = \dot{m} = 0$, the result is

$$\dot{y} = \left(\frac{-f\theta}{1 - \psi f}\right)(y - \bar{y}). \tag{4.16}$$

The system is stable only if $1 - \psi f > 0$, a restriction sufficient to guarantee that the expenditure multiplier has its conventional sign: $dy/dg > 0$. This restriction (which we assume) is the familiar requirement that the income sensitivity of investment not be "too large." In this case, the income sensitivity comes indirectly through the dependence of investment on the expected (equals actual) rate of inflation, and through the dependence of inflation on the output gap.

We are now in a position to assess whether increased wage flexibility leads to more desirable responses to aggregate demand shocks. We established in Chapter 1 that the flexibility of wages increases with increases in the size of a. From equation 4.13, $\partial f/\partial a > 0$, so increased wage flexibility makes the slope of the short-run Phillips curve steeper (as we were presuming earlier in this chapter). Then, from equation 4.15, we obtain

$$\frac{\partial(dy/dg)}{\partial f} = \frac{\phi\psi}{(1 - \psi f)^2} > 0,$$

which means that a given drop in aggregate demand causes a *bigger* temporary recession when wages are more flexible.

The logic of this result runs as follows. Given that aggregate demand depends on both autonomous expenditure and inflationary expectations, which are perfectly anticipated, a decrease in autonomous expenditure has both a direct and an indirect effect. The direct effect leads to lower output. The indirect effect follows from the fact that agents realize that the fall-off in output will reduce inflation; other things being equal, this decrease raises the real interest rate, so firms reduce the investment component of aggregate demand. With increased wage and price flexibility, this secondary effect is larger than it would be otherwise. So the Keynesian proposition that increased wage flexibility is "bad" (in the sense that it increases the temporary output deviation) is supported by the hypothesis of perfect foresight.

Increased wage flexibility is not all "bad" in this model, however. The speed with which the temporary recession is eliminated is proportional to the absolute value of the coefficient in equation 4.16. Since $\partial[f\theta/(1 - \psi f)]/\partial f = \theta/(1 - \psi f)^2 > 0$, increased wage flexibility must speed up the elimination of output disturbances.

In brief, increased wage flexibility makes the impact multiplier less appealing, but it makes adjustment speed more favorable. These results provide at least partial analytical support for the Keynesian proposition that increased wage flexibility may not help the built-in stability properties of the economy. (Similar analytical support is given by DeLong and Summers 1986, Howitt 1986c, and Fleming 1987.) This result is particularly important since policy analysts are now considering ways to stimulate the adoption of schemes such as profit-sharing and shorter wage contracts. One motive for encouraging these institutional changes is a desire to increase wage flexibility, which their proponents presume would be "good."

4.6 CONCLUSIONS

In this chapter we have examined the effects of inflationary expectations on the convergence properties of the economy, and we have allowed for two hypotheses concerning inflationary expectations. These hypotheses represent opposite polar cases in the sense that adaptive expectations involves agents' making systematic forecast errors, while perfect foresight involves their making no errors, systematic or otherwise. Perhaps a more appealing intermediate assumption is to model uncertainty so that agents make forecast errors, but not systematic ones. This is the rational expectations case, which we shall examine in the next two chapters. It turns out that the results largely duplicate those of the analysis involving perfect foresight.

The second task for the coming chapters on expectations is extending the analysis to allow for nonstatic expectations for other endogenous variables. After all, it is not particularly compelling to argue that agents should not be assumed to make systematic errors in forecasting inflation rates, while accepting the idea that they make systematic errors in forecasting interest rates and output levels.

CHAPTER 5

RATIONAL
EXPECTATIONS
AND THE
LUCAS CRITIQUE

5.1 INTRODUCTION

Lucas (1972) started the rational expectations revolution in macroeconomics, but only after Sargent and Wallace (1975; 1976) used the hypothesis in their work on optimal monetary policy did the idea really attract widespread attention. Thus, we begin our summary of this literature with a description of their model. Unfortunately, much of the attention in the papers that followed was focused on the "policy irrelevance" result obtained by Sargent and Wallace: that systematic aggregate demand policy has no effect on real variables even in the short run. One purpose of our survey is to show that this result does not hinge on the assumption of rational expectations at all and, in fact, is not robust. Stabilization policy questions remain legitimate and have nontrivial answers when one assumes that agents have rational expectations.

The second and more substantive purpose of this chapter and the next is to permit an explanation of a series of issues that now occupy center stage in macroeconomic analyses: the Lucas critique of standard methods of estimation and simulation (which is discussed in this chapter) and nonuniqueness problems, the time inconsistency of "optimal" government policies, and the effects of policies expected in the future (all three of which are considered in Chapter 6). The assumption of rational expectations forces all these issues to be considered in a way that insures that private agents understand how policy changes the rules required for private optimization. Thus, the analyst can distinguish between anticipated and unanticipated policies without having to rely on a mechanistic forecasting scheme, such as adaptive expectations, that is independent of the forces governing the actual value of the variable forecast.

At the most general level, the hypothesis of rational expectations means that economic agents forecast in such a way as to minimize forecast errors (squared deviations between actual and expected values), subject to the information and decision-making costs (constraints) that confront them. Thus, the assumption of rational expectations is just the assumption that people do the best they can under the circumstances, in forecasting activities as in other areas. It does not mean that people make no forecast errors; it simply means that such errors have no serial correlation, no *systematic* component.

It seems impossible for an economist to object to the general proposition of rational expectations. The hypothesis becomes controversial, however, when strong assumptions are made concerning the constraints. Thus far in macro-economics, the particular assumptions made in this regard are that decision-making costs are zero and that agents have perfect knowledge about the structure of the economy except for certain additive disturbance terms. Under these conditions, rational expectations can be defined as

$$p_t^e = E_{t-1}(p_t).$$

where p_t^e is the agents' expectations for the log of price, and $E_{t-1}(p_t)$ is the mathematical expectation of p_t, which we, as model manipulators, can calculate. The subscript for expectations, E, signifies that they are conditional on information available at the end of period $t - 1$. This expectations hypothesis is an extension of the standard "as if" methodology (for example, predicting consumer choices on the basis of assuming that households behave as if they drew a set of indifference curves and looked for tangencies). In this case, the hypothesis is that private agents in the economy have enough knowledge of how the system works that we can assume that they forecast *as if* they formally derived the reduced-form equation for each endogenous variable and used these equations in forming their expectations of the endogenous variables.

5.2 STATIC AND RATIONAL EXPECTATIONS COMPARED

Some of the implications of switching to rational expectations are illustrated by the following model, which follows Sargent/Wallace (1976) very closely:

$$y = \delta y_{-1} + \beta(p - p^e) + u; \tag{5.1}$$

$$y = \theta(m - p) + v; \tag{5.2}$$

$$m = \bar{m} + \gamma y_{-1}; \tag{5.3}$$

$$p^e = 0; \tag{5.4a}$$

$$p^e = E_{-1}(p). \tag{5.4b}$$

As before, lower-case letters indicate logarithms, and units are chosen so that the natural output rate, $\bar{y}$, equals zero. The subscript -1 denotes the previous time period. Before analyzing the model, we shall discuss each equation in turn.

Equation 5.1 is the aggregate supply function, which states that the deviation of output from its natural value depends on inertia factors (the previous output gap, y_{-1}), the unanticipated change in the price of goods, and a stochastic error term, u, that has a zero mean, constant variance, σ_u^2, and no serial correlation. One interpretation of this aggregate supply function is simply that it is an inverted expectations-augmented Phillips curve that has been combined with the standard marginal-cost/marginal-revenue identity (such as we considered in Chapter 1). For example, when the Phillips curve

$$w - w_{-1} = f \cdot (n - \bar{n}) + p^e - p_{-1}$$

is combined with the first difference of the labor demand function,

$$w = p + ln(1 - \alpha) + y - n,$$

and the production function,

$$y = \alpha lnK + (1 - \alpha)n,$$

we have:

$$(p - p_{-1}) = \left(\frac{f + \alpha}{1 - \alpha}\right)(y - \bar{y}) - \left(\frac{\alpha}{1 - \alpha}\right)(y_{-1} - \bar{y}) + (p^e - p_{-1}),$$

which is precisely equation 5.1, as long as $\bar{y} = 0$, $\delta = \alpha/(\alpha + f)$, $\beta = (1 - \alpha)/(\alpha + f)$, and an error term is added. Note that δ is a fraction, a fact that is convenient since, as we shall see, it turns out to be the stability condition for this model. With this Keynesian interpretation of the aggregate supply function, deviations of output from its natural rate value (zero) occur because households are temporarily off their long-run labor supply schedules.

There is also an alternative, Classical interpretation of this supply function that is due to Lucas (1973). Assume that wages are set every period so that the labor market is clearing at all times. Also assume that production takes place at isolated points, which Lucas refers to as islands. Both the firms and the households on each island are fully acquainted with economic life there; in particular, they know the selling price of the good that they jointly produce. Thus, using our earlier notation, the wage is set equal to $P_i F_N$, where P_i is price of good i (the one produced on that island). Neither firms nor households know everything about economic activity on the other islands. Nevertheless, households need to make a forecast about these events since they must know the general cost of living if they are to calculate real wages from their point of view. Hence, they agree to wages set at $P^e S(N)$, where P^e is the expectation of the average of prices over all islands (which can be formed by agents residing on any island). Adding up all these labor market-clearing conditions on each island (assuming constant returns to scale to avoid aggregation problems), and defining P as the average of all the P_is, we have: $W = PF_N = P^eS(N)$ or $P/P^e = S(N)/F_N$. This equation can be simplified using log-linear functional forms: $Y = F(N, K) = N^{1-\alpha}K^\alpha$ (so $F_N = (1 - \alpha)K^\alpha N^{-\alpha}$ and $S(N) = DN^d$ where $0 < \alpha < 1$ and $d > 0$. With these specific functional forms, the basic market-clearing condition becomes

$$\frac{P}{P^e} = \frac{DN^{\alpha+d}}{(1 - \alpha)K^\alpha}.$$

The Walrasian "auctioneer" insures that prices are set to reflect this relationship. By taking logs, we have

$$p - p^e = ln\left(\frac{D}{(1 - \alpha)K^\alpha}\right) + (\alpha + d)n. \tag{5.5}$$

Now define $\bar{n}$ as that value of the log of employment that occurs when agents make no expectational errors. Setting $p = p^e$ in equation 5.5 then yields the expression for $\bar{n}$. When this definition of $\bar{n}$ is subtracted from equation 5.5 and the result is simplified by using $y - \bar{y} = (n - \bar{n})(1 - \alpha)$, which follows directly from the production function, we have

$$p - p^e = \left(\frac{\alpha + d}{1 - \alpha}\right)(y - \bar{y}).$$

This equation is the same as equation 5.1 of the model except for the lack of an error term and of the lagged output-gap term. The lagged y term can be explained if we assume adjustment costs for labor so that the marginal product of labor is a function of both the current and the lagged level of employment. Thus, equation 5.1 has a perfectly flexible wage interpretation as well, and Classicals, therefore, refer to it not as an expectations-agumented Phillips curve but as a Lucas supply function.

The lagged output term in equation 5.1 is important since when rational expectations are assumed (equation 5.4b), equation 5.1 implies that the output gap would be a random variable with *no serial correlation* if δ were zero. The reason is that the assumption of rational expectations means no systematic errors are made in forecasting; thus, the forecast error, $p - p^e$, is not serially correlated. Clearly, however, the facts are that the output-gap time-series has a high degree of serial correlation, so δ must be assumed to be nonzero. In the Keynesian interpretation of equation 5.1, this assumption follows automatically, but in the Classical interpretation it requires nonlinear adjustment costs for employment, which we have not explicitly modeled here.

Before proceeding with the analysis of our model, we draw attention to one refinement of the Classical interpretation of the aggregate supply function, a refinement known as the signal extraction problem. Households are attempting to forecast the general price level, and since they can observe their own island price, p_i, they can rely on the historically given relationship between it and the overall price index to make a better forecast than one based only on previous economy-wide information (that is, the one we denoted by p^e). They can be thought of as running a regression using past data:

$$(p - p^e) = j(p_i - p^e).$$

If the variance of p_i is very high relative to that of p, the special knowledge of p_i is nearly worthless for making predictions, and the correlation coefficient, j, will be estimated to be close to zero. On the other hand, if the variance of p_i is not large, knowledge of the individual island price is valuable for making predictions of the overall index and parameter j will be estimated to be close to unity. In general, agents should forecast the (log of the) overall price level as a weighted average of p^e, expectations based only on previous information that is available economy-wide, and of p_i: $(1 - j)p^e + jp_i$. Thus, the more sophisticated version of the Lucas supply function for an individual island is

$$[p_i - (1 - j)p^e - jp_i] = \left(\frac{\alpha + d}{1 - \alpha}\right)(y - \bar{y}_i),$$

so in the aggregate,

$$(p - p^e) = \frac{\alpha + d}{(1 - \alpha)(1 - j)}(y - \bar{y}).$$

In this version, the steepness of the short-run supply curve is not exogenous but depends on the variability of prices across sectors (islands). Lucas (1973) has tested and found support for this hypothesis, but for our macroeconomic policy analysis, we simply proceed with the simpler equation 5.1, taking the coefficients to be constants.

Incidentally, there is another (different) aggregate supply function that is attributed to Lucas—one that involves all households' having the same information set. In that set up, workers are trying to forecast future real wages and to compare their forecast to today's real wage. The idea is that households will choose to work more only when the compensation for the foregone leisure is high or is expected to be high. This model of the intertemporal substitution of labor implies that recessions simply reflect a voluntary and temporary withdrawal of labor services. Recessions occur because workers expect higher real wages in the future, so they plan to work more then and less in the present period.

Most economists feel that the estimates of the wage elasticity of labor supply are simply too small to interpret business cycles in this way. That is, it does not seem possible for slides up and down a steep labor supply schedule to yield the large variations in employment and the small cyclical variations in the real wage that they think they observe. We shall discuss the likely empirical validity of the intertemporal labor substitution model in Chapter 11. We mention it here simply to insure that the reader can appreciate the difference between the two supply functions that are attributed to Lucas in the literature.

To distinguish the two hypotheses we shall use the following phrases: the intertemporal labor substitution model and the monetary misperceptions model.

The second phrase refers to the discussion of separate islands, in which agents cannot know in advance why the price on their island has increased. It may be because their product's relative price has increased (in which case they should increase supply), or it may be because the whole economy is undergoing general inflation (in which case they should not increase supply). Sargent and Wallace examine the monetary misperceptions hypothesis. Since Minford and Peel (1983) show that policy irrelevance does not follow when the intertemporal labor sub-stitution hypothesis is used, and since we wish to guide the reader through this policy irrelevance debate, we shall focus on the monetary misperceptions approach here. This ends our rather extended aside on alternative aggregate supply func-tions; we shall now return to an examination of the model defined by equations 5.1 to 5.4.

Equation 5.2 is the reduced form of an *IS–LM* model in which the *LM* curve is assumed to be vertical—that is, $M/P = Y^{1/\theta}$. This special case is taken so that the *IS* curve can be neglected (it just solves residually for the interest rate). It is convenient to make the *IS* curve irrelevant to price and output determination in our initial derivations, so that we can ignore investment and interest rates. Without this simplification, we would be forced to distinguish the real and nominal interest rates, so a $p_{t+1}^e - p_t$ would enter the aggregate demand side of the analysis. (We consider this complication in Chapter 6.) In equation 5.2, v is another stochastic shock that has the same properties as u and is not correlated with u.

Equation 5.3 is the monetary policy reaction function. Parameter γ indicates the authorities' degree of "leaning against the wind." Friedman has advised that γ be 0, while activists want it to be negative. What does this model say about this "rules-versus-discretion" debate in stabilization policy?

As a base for comparison, we first consider the case of static expectations. If agents expect a constant price level (at value unity), they expect the logarithm of price to be zero (that is, equation 5.4a holds). To examine output effects, we derive the reduced form for y by substituting equation 5.3 into equation 5.2 to eliminate m and equation 5.2 into equation 5.1 to eliminate p. The result is

$$y = \left(\frac{\delta + \beta\gamma}{1 + \beta/\theta}\right)y_{-1} + \left(\frac{\beta\bar{m}}{1 + \beta/\theta}\right) + \frac{u + (\beta/\theta)v}{1 + \beta/\theta}. \tag{5.6}$$

If the authority wants this equation to approximate the assumed ideal ($y = 0$ for all time periods), it must set $\bar{m} = 0$ and $\gamma = -\delta/\beta$. These settings will minimize the asymptotic variance of output at

$$\sigma_y^2 = \frac{\sigma_u^2 + (\beta/\theta)^2\sigma_v^2}{(1 + \beta/\theta)^2}$$

since the lagged dependent variable will be removed from operating through government policy.

This model fully supports the policy advice of the activists since it is a

Figure 5.1   Aggregate Supply and Demand with Static Expectations

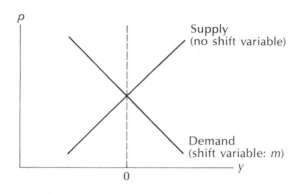

Keynesian macro model in the textbook sense of having an aggregate supply curve with a positive slope (equal to $1/\beta$), as shown in Figure 5.1. The position of the supply curve is independent of monetary policy. A particular value of the average value of the money supply, $\bar{m}$, is required to make the demand curve intersect with the supply curve at the $y = 0$ point on average. By setting $\gamma = -\delta/\beta$, the authorities can continuously adjust the position of the demand curve so that the variance of y is minimized.

Now let us consider rational expectations, by replacing equation 5.4a with equation 5.4b. Once this relationship is substituted in equation 5.1, the three-equation system contains four endogenous variables: $y, p, E(p)$, and m. To derive the reduced form for y, we must, therefore, generate additional relationships between the variables by taking the expectations operator through all three equations. (Remember that this operator has an implicit -1 subscript, meaning that agents are assumed to know everything up to and including that period. They also know δ, β, θ, and γ with certainty; all they do not know is the current observations on u and v.)

Taking the expectations operator through equations 5.1 to 5.3, after substituting equation 5.4b into equation 5.1, we have

$$E(y) = \delta E(y_{-1}) + \beta\{E(p) - E[E(p)]\} + E(u) = \delta y_{-1}; \qquad (5.1a)$$

$$E(y) = \theta[E(m) - E(p)]; \qquad (5.2a)$$

$$E(m) = \bar{m} + \gamma y_{-1}. \qquad (5.3a)$$

Subtracting equation 5.2a from equation 5.2, we have

$$y = E(y) + \theta[m - E(m)] - \theta[p - E(p)] + v. \qquad (5.2b)$$

The reduced form for y can be obtained by replacing the terms on the right-hand side of equation 5.2b; we use equation 5.1a to eliminate $E(y)$, the difference between equations 5.3 and 5.3a to eliminate $m - E(m)$, and equation 5.1 to eliminate $p - E(p)$. The result is

$$y = \delta y_{-1} + \frac{(\theta/\beta)u + v}{1 + \theta/\beta}. \tag{5.7}$$

Neither of the policy parameters, $\bar{m}$ and γ, appears in this solution equation, so they cannot affect the asymptotic variance of output. Analysts who use this model say policy is irrelevant because there is no optimal value for either parameter. The reason for this is evident from equation 5.2b: money matters only to the extent that agents did not forecast its value perfectly (money enters in terms of the $m - E(m)$ derivation). Thus, the rules-versus-discretionary-policy debate is not an issue for this model. Activist policy does not have even a short-run effect, unless it is random (and such a situation would only increase the variance of output). It should be emphasized, however, that Friedman's suggestion of setting $\gamma = 0$ receives no more support from this model than does the activist strategy of setting $\gamma < 0$.

To understand this result of policy irrelevance, it is necessary to derive the reduced form for p^e. To do this, substitute equation 5.2 into equation 5.1 to eliminate y, obtaining

$$p = \frac{1}{\beta + \theta}(\theta m - \delta y_{-1} + \beta p^e + v - u). \tag{5.8}$$

Now take the expectations operator through equation 5.8, use $p^e = E(p)$, and collect the p^e terms:

$$p^e = E(m) - \frac{\delta}{\theta}y_{-1}. \tag{5.9}$$

Equation 5.2 shows that the aggregate demand curve shifts up one-for-one with increases in the money supply. The position of the short-run aggregate supply schedule depends on p^e, and according to equation 5.9, p^e shifts up one-for-one with increases in the expected money supply even in the impact period. Thus, when money increases, both the demand and supply curves in Figure 5.2 shift up by the same amount, and the observation point goes straight from A to B *without* going, via the arrow, to the right of the $y = 0$ line.

Since a similar phenomenon follows a decrease in the money supply, this model predicts that no prolonged regression (a period involving $y < 0$) will follow an anti-inflation policy that is properly announced and that agents believe will be in place. Many analysts conclude that the recession of the early 1980s provided sufficient real-world evidence to reject this model. This interpretation is not universal, however. For example, Sargent (1986) argues that although the contractionary monetary policy of most Western economies in the early 1980s was well-announced, it was not credible for agents to expect that policy to last, given the inability or unwillingness of governments to cut their large budget deficits significantly.

Figure 5.2 Aggregate Supply and Demand with Rational Expectations

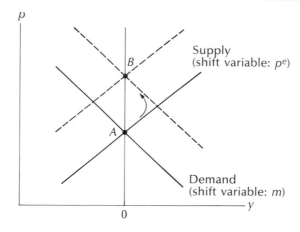

Whether or not this specific model is particularly applicable, we shall explain below that this "policy irrelevance" result is quite model-specific. We shall consider a series of models, all involving rational expectations but each using slightly different aggregate demand or supply functions. Policy does matter in almost all these other cases, so in retrospect it is unfortunate that the Sargent/ Wallace work has stimulated so much interest in the policy irrelevance question, particularly since, according to the interviews presented in Klamer (1984), this was not their intention. They were simply trying to illustrate how sensitive the answer to a basic policy question can be to alternative expectations assumptions.

5.3   THE LUCAS CRITIQUE

It should be obvious that the hypothesis of rational expectations per se is not threatened by the 1980s' experience of disinflation policy. The issue of lasting significance, which is well-illustrated in the Sargent/Wallace study, is the Lucas critique. It faults the standard method by which applied economists use estimated equations to generate counterfactual predictions.

To see the problem involved in standard simulation methodology, subtract p^e from both sides of equation 5.8, and substitute equation 5.9 in the right-hand side of the result to yield

$$(p - p^e) = \frac{\theta}{\beta + \theta}[m - E(m)] + \frac{1}{\beta + \theta}(v - u). \tag{5.10}$$

When equation 5.10 is substituted into equation 5.1, the result is

$$y = \delta y_{-1} + \phi(m - m^e) + \frac{\beta}{\beta + \theta}v + \frac{\theta}{\beta + \theta}u, \tag{5.11}$$

where $\phi = \beta\theta/(\beta + \theta)$ is a function of the private agents' reaction coefficients, β and θ, but *not* of the policymakers' reaction coefficients, $\bar{m}$ and γ. (Incidently, Sargent and Wallace start their analysis, which involves both static and rational expectations, with equation 5.11 instead of equation 5.1. We have just shown that the derivation of the former from a standard macroeconomic base requires the assumption of rational expectations.)

Standard econometric practice involves estimating models in which the endogenous variables are related to their own lagged values and the values of the exogenous variables. In our example, this practice involves running the following regression:

$$y = \alpha_0 + \alpha_1 y_{-1} + \alpha_2 m. \tag{5.12}$$

The estimated αs are interpreted as behavioral constants, which are then used to compute dynamic multipliers for all sorts of time paths for the money supply. The αs are not changed when the various possible monetary policies are considered.

There is nothing wrong with this practice if the static expectations model is true. In this case, equations 5.1 and 5.2 imply

$$y = \left(\frac{\delta}{1 + \beta/\theta}\right) y_{-1} + \left(\frac{\beta}{1 + \beta/\theta}\right) m + \text{error term}. \tag{5.13}$$

By interpreting regression 5.12 in terms of equation 5.13, we see that $\alpha_0 = 0$, $\alpha_1 = \delta/(1 + \beta/\theta)$, and $\alpha_2 = \beta(1 + \beta/\theta)$. It is quite permissible to assume that the αs are policy-invariant, since they are not functions of γ.

But there *is* something inherently inconsistent with standard simulation methodology if the rational expectations model is true. If we substitute equation 5.3a into equation 5.11, the result is

$$y = -\phi\bar{m} + (\delta - \phi\gamma)y_{-1} + \phi m + \text{error term}. \tag{5.14}$$

When regression 5.12 is interpreted in terms of equation 5.14, we see that $\alpha_0 = -\phi\bar{m}$, $\alpha_1 = \delta - \phi\gamma$, and $\alpha_2 = \phi$. Clearly, in this case, neither α_0 nor α_1 can be policy-invariant since both are functions of the policy parameters, $\bar{m}$ and γ, which *must* change if we consider alternative policies.

To perform logically consistent counterfactual simulations, we require estimates of the policy-invariant parameters, δ and ϕ. Yet as just noted, knowledge of the αs does not allow us to identify δ separately from the policy parameters. The three interpretation relationships given in the previous paragraph represent three equations in four unknowns—$\delta, \phi, \bar{m}$, and γ. To recover δ separately, we must estimate *both* equations 5.14 and 5.3, subject to cross-equation overidentifying restrictions (since there are five reduced-form coefficients estimated to determine the four structural parameters). If this simultaneous estimation approach is not adopted, more than one estimate of some of the structural parameters emerge. Running regression 5.12 yields three estimated coefficients: a constant and coefficients for the y_{-1} and m terms. According to the interpretation relationships given above, the coefficient of m is an estimate of ϕ, and the constant is an estimate of $-\phi\bar{m}$. Using the ϕ estimate from the m coefficient, one can obtain an estimate for $\bar{m}$. But when the policy reaction function (equation 5.3) is estimated, the constant term obtained gives *another* estimate of $\bar{m}$. The simultaneous estimation procedure with cross-equation restrictions insures a unique estimate for each structural parameter, such as $\bar{m}$, since the relationships between the reduced-form coefficients that follow from the theory are imposed during estimation. (For a specific example of this estimation procedure, used in a highly aggregative macro model, see Taylor 1979a.)

This critique of standard estimation/simulation methods holds for all rational expectations models (and is, therefore, much more fundamental than the model-specific prediction of policy irrelevance). The discussion in the previous two paragraphs indicates how to get around the critique. To recap, analysts must use a systems method of estimation, one that can impose the cross-equation restrictions involved in the theory, to obtain estimates of the private sector's reaction coefficients (in our model, parameters δ, β, and θ). These parameters can be taken as independent of policy. Alternative policies can then be investigated consistently by assuming different values of the policymakers' parameters (in our model, $\bar{m}$ and γ). Thus, the critique is answered by acknowledging that reduced-form parameters are functions of *both* private-sector reaction coefficients and the behavior parameters of the authorities (so the reduced-form coefficients vary with changes in policy); and by obtaining separate estimates of the *structural* parameters.

This answer to the critique of standard policy analysis is adequate as long as the private sector's reaction coefficients are themselves assumed to be policy-invariant. But in Chapter 1 we emphasized that, from a strict microeconomic perspective, the only true behavioral constants are the taste and technology parameters. The structural equations in a macro model are the first-order conditions that follow from a constrained maximization involving tastes, technology, *and* market constraints. Policy works by changing the market constraints facing individuals. In principle, therefore, many of the private-sector reaction coefficients can change with alternative policies, even though tastes and technology stay constant. The previous few paragraphs ignored this broader application of the Lucas critique. The only way to avoid it is to start each macroeconomic analysis with the microeconomic underpinnings (for example, as we did at the end of Chapter 1 when we allowed the steepness of the short-run Phillips curve to vary with the degree to which interest rate variations were resisted by the monetary authority).

5.4 STICKY WAGES AND PRICES

The main reason aggregate demand policy does not matter for real output in the Sargent/Wallace model is that it includes wages flexible enough to fully insulate output and employment from demand shocks. (It is true that their model involves wages that are set before the aggregate price level is fully known, but the monetary authority has to base its setting of the money supply on the same limited information.)

The Sargent/Wallace model also involves goods prices that are not fixed during the impact period. Let us now consider prices that are fully fixed at a point in time. One might expect that this assumption would add enough Keynesian flavor to the specification of aggregate supply so that the policy irrelevance result would no longer obtain.

The most natural specification of sticky prices is the discrete-time version of the expectations-augmented Phillips curve considered in earlier chapters:

$$p - p_{-1} = f \cdot (y_{-1} - \bar{y}) + E_{-1}(\bar{p}) - \bar{p}_{-1}.$$

This relationship simplifies to:

$$p - E(\bar{p}) = fy_{-1} + p_{-1} - \bar{p}_{-1}. \tag{5.15}$$

Clearly, equation 5.15 makes the price level fully determined by occurences of the previous time period. We now replace equation 5.1 by equation 5.15 and investigate policy relevance. (For a fuller analysis of this case, see McCallum 1980.) Equation 5.2 is used to define $\bar{p}$, the log of the price level that would make output equal its natural rate value (zero):

$$0 = \theta(m - \bar{p}) + v.$$

The lagged value of this relationship is used to eliminate $\bar{p}_{-1}$ from equation 5.15. Also, through this relationship, we take the expectations operator based on the previous period's information set, obtaining $E(\bar{p}) = m$. Then, if equation 5.2 and $E(\bar{p}) = m$ are substituted into equation 5.15, we have the solution equation for output:

$$y = (1 - \theta f)y_{-1} + v. \tag{5.16}$$

Since $\bar{m}$ and γ do not appear, policy still does not matter. We conclude that price stickiness per se is not sufficient to overturn the proposition of policy irrelevance.

What turns out to be required is price stickiness for more than one period. The reason is that policy can do something for private agents only if the time interval between changes in policy setting is shorter than the time interval between adjustments made by the private agents concerning their nominal variable.

Taylor's (1979b) model involves two-period wage contracts. Half the population signs them in each period; as a result, at any point in time half the agents are constrained in setting their nominal variable, while the monetary authority faces no such constraint. Let us see why a predictable monetary policy has real effects in this model, even with the assumption of rational expectations. (We postpone until Chapter 10 a consideration of theories about why agents may choose to constrain themselves by long-term nominal contracts.)

Let x_t be the logarithm of the wage set in period t for the next two periods. Assuming for simplicity a constant marginal product of labor, there is a constant mark-up of prices over wages—$P = (1/F_N)W$—so the terms wages and prices can be used interchangeably. The overall price index is

$$p_t = 0.5(x_t + x_{t-1}). \tag{5.17}$$

As before, wage settlements depend on expected prices and the expected gaps between actual output and its long-run sustainable level. But this case requires two observations on each of these variables since the wage is being set for two periods. Let us assume that

$$x_t = 0.5[p_t^e + p_{t+1}^e + f(hy_t^e + (1-h)y_{t+1}^e)] + u_t. \tag{5.18}$$

(Notice that our specification is based on the hypothesis that workers care about the *real* value of their *own* wages. This treatment differs slightly from Taylor's; he hypothesizes that workers care about their *relative* wage position, so x_{t-1} and x_{t+1}^e appear in equation 5.18 in place of the $p_t^e + p_{t+1}^e$ terms. This difference is not important, however, since none of the conclusions depend on this variation in the model's specification.)

Equations 5.17 and 5.18 represent the revised aggregate supply function when two-period overlapping contracts are involved. (Actually, a literal two-period extension of an expectations-augmented Phillips curve would involve expected inflation rates, not expected price levels as in equation 5.18. However, none of the results depend on this difference, so to avoid a much more complicated analysis, we follow Taylor's specification involving levels.) The aggregate demand relationships are similar to those of Sargent/Wallace:

$$y_t = \theta(m_t - p_t) + v_t; \tag{5.2}$$

$$m_t = \gamma p_t^e. \tag{5.19}$$

The private sector's demand relationship is exactly the same as the one we used before. The policy reaction function is different, but not in any substantive way. For simplicity we set $\bar{m}$ (which appeared in our earlier policy reaction function) equal to zero. Before, the authority was reacting to variations in the lagged output gap; now, it is reacting to the expectation of the current price level. But since the expectations are based on previous-period information, there is no fundamental difference between Taylor's and Sargent/Wallace's specifications of policy reaction.

Since we are assuming rational expectations, the e superscript stands for the expectations operator conditional on $t-1$ information: $p_t^e = E_{t-1}(p_t)$ and $p_{t+1}^e = E_{t-1}(p_{t+1})$. The object of the exercise is to show that the policy parameter, γ, is involved in the solution equation for y_t. If it is, we can determine whether the authority should "lean against the wind" ($\gamma < 0$), "accommodate" ($\gamma > 0$), or follow the monetarist approach ($\gamma = 0$).

Using equations 5.17, 5.2, and 5.19 and the expectations operator, we derive a set of expressions to be substituted into equation 5.18:

$$p_t^e = 0.5(x_t^e + x_{t-1});$$

$$p_{t+1}^e = 0.5(x_{t+1}^e + x_t^e);$$

$$y_t^e = 0.5\theta(\gamma - 1)(x_t^e + x_{t-1});$$

$$y_{t+1}^e = 0.5\theta(\gamma - 1)(x_{t+1}^e + x_t^e).$$

Substituting these expressions into equation 5.18 and taking the expectations operator through, we obtain the reduced form for x^e:

$$[f\theta(\gamma - 1)(1 - h) + 1]x_{t+1}^e + [f\theta(\gamma - 1) - 2]x_t^e$$
$$+ [f\theta(\gamma - 1)h + 1]x_{t-1}^e = 0. \quad (5.20)$$

Since the model is linear, all the endogenous variables have time paths with the same characteristics. Thus, we can restrict our attention to showing that the policy parameter, γ, enters the solution equation for x^e instead of for y.

To obtain the explicit solution from equation 5.20, we must introduce a trial solution. In Chapter 1, we discussed the familiar phenomenon of compound interest to justify the appropriate form for the trial solution of a difference equation. Here we can use $x_t^e = A\lambda^t$. When this trial solution is substituted into equation 5.20, the characteristic equation, which determines λ, is obtained:

$$[f\theta(\gamma - 1)(1 - h) + 1]\lambda^2 + [f\theta(\gamma - 1) - 2]\lambda$$
$$+ [f\theta(\gamma - 1)h + 1] = 0. \quad (5.21)$$

Since we are dealing with a second-order difference equation, two values of the characteristic root, λ, are possible; the general form of the solution is

$$x_t^e = A_1\lambda_1^t + A_2\lambda_2^t.$$

The values for λ_1 and λ_2 are found from equation 5.21, and a restriction on the As can be determined from the fact that history will determine the initial value, x_0^e. Setting $t = 0$ in the solution equation, we have

$$x_0^e = A_1 + A_2.$$

But this restriction leaves an infinity of combinations of values for A_1 and A_2 that will satisfy the model as it has been specified thus far. To obtain a unique solution equation for x_t^e (and therefore for y_t), some additional arbitrary restriction must be imposed.

Taylor ''solves'' this indeterminacy problem by following the profession's propensity to reject unstable outcomes. But to do this he must restrict his attention to numerical values of the parameters f, θ, γ, and h that insure that one of the λ values exceeds one in absolute value. If such a characteristic root, say, λ_2, is allowed to have influence, the model would be unstable. To avoid this situation, Taylor's additional restriction is to set $A_2 = 0$; thus, he obtains a unique and stable solution: $x_t^e = x_0^e \cdot \lambda_1^t$. Given Taylor's willingness to confine attention to particular ranges of parameter values, his procedure involves nothing more than the standard rejection of unstable outcomes. (We shall discuss this nonuniqueness problem much more fully in the next chapter.)

No matter which additional restriction is imposed, equation 5.21 shows that both values for the characteristic root, λ, depend on the policy parameter, γ. Thus, policy "matters" in this model despite the hypothesis of rational expectations. This phenomenon occurs because the monetary authority can fully adjust its nominal instrument each period, but the private agents cannot adjust everyone's money wage each period. Prices are stickier than the money supply. The nonuniqueness problem we have encountered means, however, that there is little point in deriving an optimal value for γ (the value that would minimize the asymptotic variance of output).

5.5   CONCLUSIONS

The purpose of this chapter has been to introduce the solution techniques required when macro models involve the assumption that agents understand the ongoing rule underlying government policy. An increasing number of analysts are uneasy about not assuming rational expectations because any other approach involves the implicit assumption that agents are continually surprised by policymakers' actions. Surely if a stabilization policy is supposed to be good for private agents, the proof that it is so should not depend on the assumption that the agents do not understand the policy.

We have explained how to derive rational expectations solutions and have emphasized two issues. One is the Lucas critique of standard econometric and simulation methods, a challenge that is a fundamental contribution of the literature on rational expectations. The other is the policy-relevance debate, which the rational expectations hypothesis does not prejudge in any way. Those who lean toward a policy rule that involves feedback do not need to fear a model that assumes rational expectations. Indeed, in Chapter 6, we shall show that strong support for certain rather Keynesian policy proposals can come from a rational expectations analysis.

More ground must be covered, however, before the reader is ready to analyze more complicated macroeconomic structures involving rational expectations. The models of this chapter were simplified in many ways. For example, aggregate demand was independent of expected inflation, and inflation was the only endogenous variable for which the rational expectations hypothesis was evoked. Also, a discouraging element of arbitrariness entered the last few pages of the chapter, in the form of the nonuniqueness problem. It is to these issues that we shall turn in the next chapter.

CHAPTER 6

RATIONAL EXPECTATIONS: CURRENT CONTROVERSIES

6.1   INTRODUCTION

The purpose of this chapter is to extend the coverage of rational expectations models in several important directions. First, we shall discuss the credibility of macroeconomic policy in order to explain what has come to be called the time-inconsistency problem. Next we shall explore the implications of alternative information sets by allowing agents to have some current information about the stochastic elements in the economy while making their current decisions. In section 6.4, we shall return to the nonuniqueness problem that was introduced at the end of the last chapter. We shall continue in the next section to an analysis in which agents have rational expectations for all endogenous variables, not just for prices. We shall also consider the announcement effects of future stabilization policies. We shall conclude, in section 6.6, with some remarks on the alternative reactions different economists have had to recent developments.

6.2   TIME INCONSISTENCY

Taylor's model of rational expectations and sticky wages, which was discussed in the last chapter, can be used to introduce an argument for stabilization policy rules that do not involve feedback, an issue that has received much emphasis in recent years. Disinflation in Taylor's model requires a contractionary monetary policy, and even if it is perfectly announced in advance, a temporary recession must occur. Suppose that this fact leads the government to decide that the optimal policy for the present is to avoid disinflation policy. An apparent alternative is for the government to announce a future contractionary monetary policy. If agents believe that the government will implement this policy, they should set lower wages and prices as contracts come up for renewal during the interval between the policy announcement and its implementation. However, the agents know that if they do not set lower prices, the government will face the same dilemma in the future that it faces now. As a result, the policy announcement (the promised future monetary contraction) is not credible: the authorities' current decision to postpone contraction implies that they may not deliver on its promise in the future. The only dynamically consistent—that is, credible—plan is one that leaves the authorities no freedom to react to developments in the future. As Kydland and Prescott (1977, 627) put the problem, discretionary policy can be suboptimal because "There is no mechanism to induce future policy makers to take into consideration the effect of their policy, via the expectations mechanism, upon current decisions of agents."

This argument can be clarified by referring to Figure 6.1, where *AC* is the natural rate of output line on which, according to models such as Taylor's, all points that are sustainable in the long run must lie. Also shown are two members of the family of short-run Phillips curves and a set of indifference curves that represent the basis for the authorities' stabilization policy choices. They regard higher output as "good" but higher inflation as "bad," so indifference curve

Figure 6.1   The Superiority of Stabilization Rules without Feedback

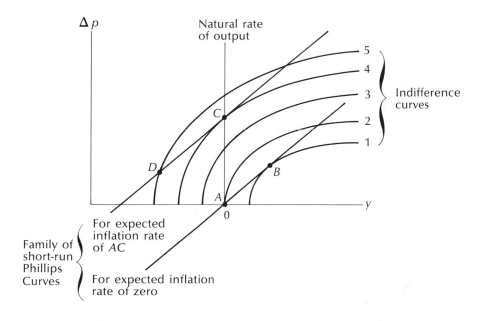

1 represents higher utility than indifference curve 5. (We assume that the indifference curves are parabolas so their slopes are undefined as they hit the horizontal axis.)

To consider a policy problem such as that of the early 1980s, assume that the economy is initially at point C, which is sustainable. There is no short-run temptation for an activist authority to intervene since any moves must be along the given short-run Phillips curve (line DC), and only lower levels of utility can result. A longer-run reason for intervention does exist, however, since higher utility can be had at lower steady-state inflation levels. Policymakers can—and those of the early 1980s did—deliberately accept for the short run the lower utility of moving to a point such as D for a long enough period to have the resulting recession decrease the underlying inflation rate. Eventually the expected inflation rate can be worked down to zero, so the relevant short-run trade-off is line AB and the sustainable point A can be reached. (A point such as D is not sustainable since it involves actual inflation less than expected inflation.) Since point A lies on indifference curve 2, the eventual achievement is higher utility.

This costly transition to achieve point A is wasted, however, if the authorities are committed to continued intervention once the economy gets there. The temptation is to stimulate demand to move to point B, thereby increasing utility to indifference curve 1. But this shift forces agents to revise their inflationary expectations upward, so the observation point must track back up to point C.

We can summarize as follows. Only the outcome represented by point C is sustainable for interventionist policymakers (who always try to go to the tangency of an indifference curve with the short-run Phillips curve). But all points on the natural rate of output line are sustainable for noninterventionist policymakers. If they try for the tangency of an indifference curve with this long-run constraint, they pick point A, which involves higher utility than C. Thus, even though aggregate demand policies "matter" in the short run in Taylor's model, this reasoning suggests that a policy of nonintervention is preferred.

This argument for rules over discretion has many other applications in everyday life. For example, both students and professors would be better off if there were no final examinations. Yet students seem to need the incentive of the exam to work properly. Thus, one's first thought is that the optimal policy would be a discretionary one in which the professor promises an exam and then, near the end of term, breaks that promise. This way the students would work and learn but would avoid the trauma of the exam, and the professor would avoid the marking. The problem is that students can anticipate such a broken promise (especially if there is a history of this behavior), so we opt for a "rules without feedback" approach—exams no matter what. Most participants regard this policy as the best one. (For further discussion of this issue, see Fischer 1980a.)

It is worth emphasizing that our demonstration of the superiority of rules over discretion leaves open the question of which rules are "good" and which are "bad." In terms of Figure 6.1 for example, once dynamic and/or stochastic elements are considered, it is perfectly legitimate to investigate whether a once-

and-for-all institutional change that leads, for example, to a steeper or a flatter short-run Phillips curve is desirable or not. In other words, investigations of alternative structural changes and their effects on the built-in stability properties of the economy are not analyses of discretionary policies.

6.3 ALTERNATIVE INFORMATION SETS

In Chapter 5, we examined a model in which aggregate demand policy had effects, despite the assumption of rational expectations, because wages were set by staggered contracts. We shall now show that policy can have real effects even in a model that does not include staggered contracts. The reason is that agents will surely have *some* current information on the error terms when making some of·their decisions in the present time period. There is a class of endogenous variables—asset prices—for which agents have information on a continuous basis, and this information can be used to deduce some information concerning current shocks. The signal extraction procedure involved was outlined in section 5.2, pages 68–69, and is explained more fully in Minford and Peel (1983). Rather than delve into the extent of algebra required to solve the signal extraction problem in a full model, however, we shall illustrate the implications of having some current information available by analyzing the following model, which is due to Sargent (1973) and Turnovsky (1980):

$$y_t = \beta[p_t - E_{t-1}(p_t)] + u_t; \tag{6.1}$$

$$y_t = \theta(m_t - p_t) + \psi[E_t(p_{t+1}) - p_t)] + v_t; \tag{6.2}$$

$$m_t = \gamma y_{t-1}. \tag{6.3}$$

The notation is the same as that used in Chapter 5. Equation 6.1 defines aggregate supply, equation 6.2 aggregate demand, and equation 6.3 the monetary policy reaction function.

   This system resembles the Sargent/Wallace model discussed in the last chapter, but it is simplified in that the lagged output term has been dropped from the aggregate supply function and the intercept has been dropped from the policy reaction function. However, this system is also an extension of Sargent/Wallace's since aggregate demand here depends on expected inflation, not just on the money supply. The extension involves letting the *LM* curve be positively sloped. Expected inflation could be defined as $E_{t-1}(p_{t+1} - p_t)$, an appropriate expression if agents made decisions about their demands for goods and assets at the same time they agree to a money wage. Here, as in the original Sargent/Wallace model, we assume that agents do not have knowledge of the current disturbances while agreeing to a wage. If we had included that alternative definition of expected inflation, we would have found that policy still did not matter (as shown by McCallum 1980). Instead of assuming that agents have no current-period information when making demand decisions, we consider the opposite polar case in equation 6.2 by assuming that agents have all the t-period information by the time they are forecasting inflation to make their decisions on the demands for goods and assets. By comparing such polar cases we can demonstrate the fundamental importance of alternative information-set assumptions for the properties of rational expectations models.

As in Chapter 5, our goal is to derive the solution equation for y_t and to determine whether γ enters this equation. The problem with simply proceeding with the usual substitutions, however, is that we need an expression for $E_t(p_{t+1})$. It can be had by writing the equation for p_t forward one period in time and taking the expectations operator through, but this just introduces an $E_t(p_{t+2})$ term. We can go through this set of infinite forward substitutions, as Sargent (1973) does, but it is easier to use the undetermined coefficient method. Simple inspection of the model indicates that the solution equations for y_t and p_t should involve only y_{t-1}, u_t, and v_t, since these are the only predetermined variables in the system. Thus, we can posit trial solutions whose right-hand sides involve only these three variables. We assume the following reduced forms:

$$y_t = h_1 y_{t-1} + h_2 u_t + h_3 v_t; \tag{6.4}$$

$$p_t = g_1 y_{t-1} + g_2 u_t + g_3 v_t. \tag{6.5}$$

It turns out that if we include additional lags in these trial solutions (for example, if we add y_{t-2}, u_{t-1}, or v_{t-1} terms to equations 6.4 and 6.5), more than one rational expectations solution for the model is obtained. McCallum (1983) suggests that analysts avoid this nonuniqueness problem by including in the trial solutions only the minimal set of state variables that is warranted by considering the structure of the basic model. The idea is that only "fundamentals" ought to matter. (We shall discuss this and other aspects of the nonuniqueness problem in the next section.)

At this stage the h and g parameters in equations 6.4 and 6.5 are entirely arbitrary. The remaining task is to combine equations 6.4 and 6.5 with 6.1 through 6.3 so that the hs and gs can be explicitly defined in terms of the ultimate structural parameters: θ, ψ, β, and γ. The key question for the policy relevance debate is whether any of the hs depend on γ.

Taking $E_{t-1}(\cdot)$ through equation 6.5 yields

$$E_{t-1}(p_t) = g_1 y_{t-1}. \tag{6.5a}$$

Taking $E_t(\cdot)$ through equation 6.5 written forward one period in time and using equation 6.4 yields

$$E_t(p_{t+1}) = g_1 h_1 y_{t-1} + g_1 h_2 u_t + g_1 h_3 v_t. \tag{6.5b}$$

Substituting equations 6.5 and 6.5a into equation 6.1 yields

$$y_t = \beta(g_2 u_t + g_3 v_t) + u_t. \tag{6.6}$$

We now have two versions of the reduced form for y_t: equations 6.4 and 6.6.

For these equations to be the same, we know that

$$h_1 = 0; \tag{6.7a}$$

$$h_2 = \beta g_2 + 1; \tag{6.7b}$$

$$h_3 = \beta g_3. \tag{6.7c}$$

Further identifying restrictions are derived as follows. Substitute equations 6.3, 6.5, and 6.5b into equation 6.2 to eliminate m_t, p_t, and $E_t(p_{t+1})$; then compare the result to equation 6.4. As before, for internal consistency the coefficients in these equations must be the same. The restrictions are

$$g_1 = \left(\frac{\theta}{\theta + \psi} \right) \gamma; \tag{6.8a}$$

$$1 + \beta g_2 = \theta g_2 + \psi g_1 h_2 - g_2 \psi; \tag{6.8b}$$

$$\beta g_3 = \theta g_3 + \psi g_1 h_3 - \psi g_3 + 1. \tag{6.8c}$$

Equations 6.7b, 6.7c, 6.8b, and 6.8c can be used to express h_2, h_3, g_2, and g_3 as functions of the private agents' reaction coefficients, θ, ψ, and β, and of g_1. Since, according to equation 6.8a, g_1 depends on the policy parameter γ, all the reduced-form parameters except h_1 are functions of policy. Thus, the time path of output *is* affected by predictable monetary policy.

The reasoning behind this result runs as follows. The positions of both the aggregate demand and supply schedules depend on expectations. But these expectations are based on *different* information sets. Thus, when the money supply changes, the demand and the short-run supply curves shift by different vertical distances. More fundamentally, the nature of monetary policy, even though it is predictable, affects the extent to which expected inflation responds to shocks. As a result, policy affects the way in which aggregate demand responds to shocks.

Enough has been said to justify the conclusion that the hypothesis of rational expectations, even without considerations of sticky wages or prices, in no way threatens the relevance of stabilization policy. The policy-irrelevance conclusion does not even hold in the original Sargent/Wallace framework if the policy variable is allowed to have direct supply-side effects. For example, by adding to these models a standard tax function—$T_t = ky_t$, where k is the tax rate—it can be shown that k affects the time path of output deviations. If the tax function were interpreted as a policy reaction function, it would seem inappropriate to be specifying that the authority has better access to information than private agents. But the tax function is not a reaction function. It simply reflects the fact that taxes are deducted at source and, therefore, respond to current income.

The lasting contribution of the rational expectations approach is not the policy-relevance debate. It is that this approach makes analysts examine the effects of government policy in a way that is consistent with agents' understanding how policy changes the rules required for private optimization. By doing so, it forces us to focus on policy rules and, therefore, to distinguish the effects of unanticipated policies from anticipated ones. The logic of the rational expectations approach requires that policy be framed in terms of an ongoing rule, not as a one-time change in the policy instrument. Therefore, the proper focus of policy analysis is on the ongoing or built-in stability properties of the economy.

6.4 PROBLEMS OF NONUNIQUENESS

So far, the generality of our rational expectations analysis has been limited by a problem of nonuniqueness on two occasions. We first encountered this issue when discussing Taylor's model of staggered or overlapping money-wage contracts, near the end of Chapter 5. The second encounter was in the section just completed on alternative assumptions about the information available when forecasts are made. In each of these cases, we referred to a procedure for eliminating the nonuniqueness. Let us now explore these procedures and others more fully.

Taylor avoids nonuniqueness by limiting his attention to parameter values that make one of the characteristic roots of the model lead to stability and the other to instability. He then employs standard correspondence-principle reasoning: since outright instability does not seem to be observed in the real world, the stable characteristic root must be the only one that operates. Essentially, one of the mathematical solutions to the model is deemed economically inadmissible.

The problem with this procedure is that it is not always plausible to limit attention to situations in which the number of initial conditions that can be set arbitrarily (to eliminate the effects of a characteristic root) just equals the number of unstable characteristic roots. Often both values for the characteristic root imply stability (indeed, this situation exists for a wide range of quite acceptable values for the underlying structural parameters of Taylor's model).

Some suggestions have been made for a general solution to this problem of nonuniqueness. For instance, Taylor (1977) suggests assuming that agents choose (and, therefore, analysts should pick) the solution that involves the smallest variance for a particular endogenous variable. But for which endogenous variable and over what time horizon should this rule be applied? McCallum (1983) proposes rejecting rational expectations solutions if the reduced-form coefficients are not continuous functions of the structural parameters. Scarth (1985) suggests a simple extension of the correspondence principle for second-order discrete-time systems: since two-period sawtooth cycles are not observed, the admissible characteristic root must be positive.

All this arbitrariness is quite unappealing, and analysts hope that the frequency with which we are confronted by problems of nonuniqueness may decrease as model builders provide more explicit microeconomic underpinnings (so we can impose more structural restrictions on the macro model). Nevertheless, as McCallum (1983) argues, the vexing problem of nonuniqueness will remain, and many economists find it an unappealing feature of the rational expectations hypothesis.

After all, that hypothesis was introduced in an attempt to reduce the number of arbitrary assumptions made in macroeconomics; it is unfortunate that implementing it requires invoking some arbitrary solution of the problem of nonuniqueness.

Economic "Fundamentals" and the Nonuniqueness Problem

In our discussion of alternative information sets, we noted that nonuniqueness problems can be minimized if the assumed trial solutions involve the minimal set of state variables consistent with economic "fundamentals." Even this method of limiting the problem has qualified appeal, however, since it is possible that allowing "nonfundamentals" to replace "fundamentals" in a trial solution can reduce the asymptotic variance for *all* the endogenous variables.

This proposition can be demonstrated by considering an extension of McCallum's (1980) model of costly output adjustment that is presented in his survey on rational expectations and stabilization policy. (This system is very similar to the model of costly wage adjustment that we examined in section 1.4.)

In McCallum's model, firms face prohibitive costs if their selling price is not set before each period begins or if they do not produce whatever is required to meet demand during the period. They also incur finite costs whenever output differs from its natural level and whenever output is changed by an amount that differs from the change in the natural level. If units are chosen so that the logarithm of the natural rate is zero, the ith firm's cost function is

$$\delta_1[E_{t-1}(y_t^i)]^2 + \delta_2[E_{t-1}(y_t^i) - y_{t-1}^i]^2, \tag{6.9}$$

which is minimized subject to the firm's perception of the demand for its product:

$$E_{t-1}(y_t^i) = -\eta[p_t^i - E_{t-1}(p_t^*)], \tag{6.10}$$

where p^* is the logarithm of the going market price and η is the individual demand elasticity (which cancels out of the analysis below). The constraint states that firms lose (gain) sales if their price exceeds (is less than) this going price. When the constraint and a lagged version of it are substituted into the quadratic cost function, the firm's price adjustment rule is derived by setting the derivative with respect to p_t^i equal to zero. Since all firms are assumed to be alike, the aggregate price-setting rule is

$$p_t - E_{t-1}(p_t^*) = (1 - \phi)(p_{t-1} - p_{t-1}^*), \tag{6.11}$$

where ϕ is a technology parameter that depends on the relative size of the adjustment costs compared to the costs of producing at a level other than the natural rate: $\phi = \delta_1/(\delta_1 + \delta_2)$.

As in the traditional analysis, aggregate demand here is a function of the money supply and an exogenous disturbance:

$$y_t = \theta(\bar{m} - p_t) + v_t. \tag{6.12}$$

We can simplify the model (although we do not have to do so for our analysis) by assuming that the money supply is constant, so the steady-state inflation rate is zero. Units are chosen so that the logarithm of the money supply, $\bar{m}$, is zero.

To close the model, we must define what individual sellers consider when forecasting the going market price, p^*. We consider two alternatives:

1. Agents expect the going market price to be $\bar{p}$, which is the value of price that would make current aggregate output equal its steady-state value (zero). Thus, $p_t^* = \bar{p}_t = (1/\theta)v_t$ since this is the value of price that makes y_t equal 0 in equation 6.12.
2. Agents expect the going market price to equal its long-run average or steady-state value (zero). Thus, $p_t^* = 0$.

McCallum does not discuss options; he simply assumes the first case. But there is nothing more implausible about the second option since either rule is rational for an individual as long as all other individuals forecast their average opinion of market price in the same way.

We are stressing the existence of two options for defining p^*, each of which involves the rational expectations hypothesis, so that we have a simplified example through which we can emphasize what is called the average opinion problem. This problem (which is examined in Frydman and Phelps 1984), creates a non-uniqueness issue that cannot be resolved by focusing on fundamentals. If we cannot define average opinion unambiguously, we cannot define fundamentals.

Let us examine each case in turn. If we adopt the first definition, $p^* = \bar{p}$, which is McCallum's case, we use equation 6.12 to obtain expressions for $p_t - E_{t-1}(\bar{p}_t)$ and $p_{t-1} - \bar{p}_{t-1}$, which are then substituted into equation 6.11. The result is $y_t = (1 - \phi)y_{t-1} + v_t$. The reduced form for price can now be solved from equation 6.12: $p_t = [-(1 - \phi)/\theta]y_{t-1}$. The asymptotic variances for output and price level follow:

$$\sigma_y^2 = \frac{1}{1 - (1 - \phi)^2}\sigma_v^2;$$

$$\sigma_p^2 = [(1 - \phi)/\theta]^2\sigma_y^2.$$

(6.13)

If we use the second definition, $p^* = 0$, equation 6.11 becomes $p_t = (1 - \theta)p_{t-1}$. The current and lagged versions of the aggregate demand function (equation 6.12) are used to replace the price variables with output, and the resulting reduced forms are $y_t = (1 - \phi)y_{t-1} + v_t - (1 - \phi)v_{t-1}$ and $p_t = [(1 - \phi)/\theta](v_{t-1} - y_{t-1})$.

Since both the current and lagged values of the disturbance term are involved in the output reduced form, the derivation of the asymptotic variance is slightly more complicated than that given in Chapter 1. If we square both sides of the output reduced form, we get

$$y_t^2 = (1 - \phi)^2 y_{t-1}^2 + v_t^2 + (1 - \phi)^2 v_{t-1}^2 + 2(1 - \phi)y_{t-1}v_t$$
$$- 2(1 - \phi)v_t v_{t-1} - 2(1 - \phi)^2 y_{t-1}v_{t-1}.$$

The $y_{t-1}v_{t-1}$ term in this equation can be replaced by $(1 - \phi)y_{t-2}v_{t-1} + v_{t-1}^2 - (1 - \phi)v_{t-1}v_{t-2}$. Then, when the expectations operator is brought through, we have

$$\sigma_y^2 = (1 - \phi)^2\sigma_y^2 + \sigma_v^2 + (1 - \phi)^2\sigma_v^2 - 2(1 - \phi)^2\sigma_v^2$$

since $E(y_{t-1}v_t) = E(v_t v_{t-1}) = 0$. This formula simplifies, so the final expressions for the asymptotic variance are:

$$\sigma_y^2 = \sigma_v^2; \tag{6.14}$$

$$\sigma_p^2 = [(1 - \phi)/\theta]^2(\sigma_y^2 - \sigma_v^2) = 0.$$

Comparing equations 6.13 and 6.14, we see that the variance for both variables is less when $p^* = 0$.

This result can be interpreted in two ways. One response involves treating McCallum's presumption that $p^* = \bar{p}$ as an inherent part of the model. From that point of view, private agents must be described as paying attention to "nonfundamentals" if they put any weight on the value zero (instead of $\bar{p}$) while forecasting the going market price. Taylor (1977) shows that more than one stable solution can exist in rational expectations models when such "nonfundamentals" are considered. But in his examples, the involvement of "nonfundamentals" leads to higher variances, so there is clearly some appeal to his proposal that these solutions be rejected. In our example, however, the involvement of "nonfundamentals" lowers the variances, so Taylor's proposal seems to call for the rejection of the "fundamental" solution, which is the one analyzed by McCallum.

The other response we can make to all of this is to regard both solutions as economically admissible. The fact that the economy has settled on the $\bar{p}$ solution is then interpreted simply as an arbitrary outcome that followed some unspecified initial condition. If this view is taken, a clear role for policy emerges. If a government policy can induce agents to focus their attention on a new possibility for the average opinion, that policy can switch the economy to a preferred long-run equilibrium.

The policy that comes to mind here is a tax-based incomes policy, one in which the authorities use the tax system to induce agents to pay attention to the value zero when forecasting p^*. Each agent will realize that others will so behave if we add to the individual cost function of equation 6.9 a third component,

$$\delta_3[(p_t^i - p_{t-1}^i) - (0 - p_{t-1}^i)]E_{t-1}(y_t^i),$$

a term stipulating that the firm can expect to pay a tax (or receive a subsidy) that will be proportional to its scale of output, y_t^i and for which the tax rate will depend on the gap between the inflation in the firm's price and the guideline rate (which is defined as part of the incomes policy).

The standard presumption that agents choose the minimum variance solution is arbitrary, since most models contain no decentralized mechanism that could induce agents to select that solution (or, indeed, any other). That problem of arbitrariness is eliminated in this incomes policy model; the tax/subsidy incentive is the otherwise missing decentralized incentive.

We do not want to downplay the significance of the regime switch that this policy could effect. Nevertheless, we devote the remainder of this section to analyzing an incomes policy that does not move the economy away from an original equilibrium involving $p^* = \bar{p}$ to one involving $p^* = 0$. Such a tax-based incomes policy can be defined by adding the third component to the firm's cost function and deriving the way in which the policy affects the aggregate supply function. By using equation 6.10 and setting the derivative of the cost function with respect to p_t^i at zero, we get equation 6.11 (with $p^* = \bar{p}$), except $1 - \phi$ now equals $\delta_2/(\delta_1 + \delta_2 - \delta_3/\eta)$ instead of $\delta_2/(\delta_1 + \delta_2)$. This result unambiguously raises the variances for both output and price, so the incomes policy is not recommended. Thus, according to this model, the desirability of an incomes policy very much depends on whether it causes the regime shift or not.

We do not suggest that this analysis can be used to reach a final verdict on tax-based incomes policies. But we have shown two things. First, the rational expectations approach can provide significant support for such a non-Classical policy proposal as tax-based incomes policy (since the policy can effect a regime switch by changing all agents' perception of average opinion). Second, we need further work on how to resolve nonuniqueness problems in rational expectations models.

6.5 ANNOUNCEMENT EFFECTS

Thus far, our analyses have been restrictive in that we have invoked the rational expectations hypothesis for *only one* of the endogenous variables. It is difficult to motivate a model that involves static expectations for output and the interest rate but rational expectations for goods prices. If it seems unrealistic to assume that agents make systematic errors in forecasting prices, is it not similarly unacceptable to assume that they make systematic errors in forecasting output and interest rate levels? We shall eliminate this unappealing asymmetry in the analysis of this section. In addition, we shall emphasize the announcement effects of future policies.

To illustrate the current effects of future policies, it is convenient to abstract entirely from supply-side complications and concentrate on an aggregate demand model with fixed goods prices. Price expectations are still an issue in this context, however, since equity prices vary. Sensible agents should not expect equity prices to stay constant—that is, they should not expect interest rates and output levels to stay constant—if actual equity prices (which depend on output levels and interest rates) vary in a predictable way within the model, as they do in the following system:

$$Y = aq + bY + G; \tag{6.15}$$

$$r = cY - lM; \tag{6.16}$$

$$r = \frac{jY + \dot{q}}{q}. \tag{6.17}$$

In examining this system, which is a simplification of Blanchard's (1981) model, we shall follow Blanchard and use a continuous-time deterministic analysis so that rational expectations and perfect foresight mean the same thing. (It is useful to review such issues as the nonuniqueness problem in this slightly different context.)

Equation 6.15 is a standard *IS* equation: aggregate demand (which equals output, Y) depends positively on output (because of consumption), the price of equities (Tobin's valuation ratio), q (because of investment), and autonomous expenditure, G. It is assumed that b, the propensity to consume, is a fraction. Blanchard's version of this equation is $\dot{Y} = \sigma(aq + bY + G - Y)$, which states that output adjusts sluggishly to clear excess demand in the goods market, leaving him to deal with a set of two differential equations. For simplicity, we shall first consider $\sigma \rightarrow \infty$, which (since inventories are assumed away) means that national output can jump instantaneously to clear the goods market and we have only one differential equation.

Equation 6.16 is the *LM* relationship: the interest rate depends positively on output and negatively on the money supply. Equation 6.17 defines the two components of the yield on equities: (1) "dividend" income, which equals the marginal product of capital expressed as a proportion of the equity investment, and (2) capital gains on holding equities. (The second term should be the expected capital gains, but with no error terms, the assumption of rational expectations is equivalent to an assumption of perfect foresight; thus, we can use actual capital gains in equation 6.17.)

Assuming a Cobb-Douglas production function, $Y = K^{\alpha}N^{1-\alpha}$, the marginal product of capital is $\alpha Y/K$. Parameter j in equation 6.17 can then be interpreted as α/K. Another interpretation is had by rearranging equation 6.17 to $q = (jY + \dot{q})/r$, which says that the price of equities must equal the present value of the stream of marginal product of capital payments and capital gains. The standard fixed-price *IS–LM* model assumes that expected changes in q are zero; this model continues to assume fixed goods prices but assumes that expected changes in equity prices equal the actual changes.

It is important to realize that asset prices here are not pinned down by history or any accumulation identity. They can jump at a point in time, a feature that leaves the model's initial conditions to be determined endogenously. One way of appreciating the implications of this feature of endogenous initial conditions is to count equations and unknowns. There are three equations to determine four variables: Y, r, q, and $\dot{q}$. Thus, an infinity of solutions are possible. To remove this underdeterminacy, analysts must impose some additional restriction. The standard assumption is that the initial level of asset prices adjusts so that the economy avoids any instability that might otherwise occur. Agents are assumed to behave as if they have held a general meeting and agreed to have the initial value of q jump to the level that avoids macroeconomic instability. No decentralized incentive mechanism that induces individual agents to behave in this manner is ever specified. However, the solution procedure can be appreciated by considering two points: (1) *some* decision rule is needed for choosing among the infinity of perfect-foresight solutions; and (2) analysts feel that instability is not generally observed in actual economies.

We begin our analysis for this model by deriving the stability condition. After eliminating Y and r by substitution, we have

$$\frac{d\dot{q}}{dq} = \frac{\bar{r}(1-b) - a(j - \bar{q}c)}{1-b}, \tag{6.18}$$

where the bars indicate full equilibrium values. If the numerator in equation 6.18 is negative, the system is stable, so all the infinity of solutions involve convergence to the full equilibrium (defined by $\dot{q} = 0$). Several of these possible solutions are shown in Figure 6.2. The numbered points indicate a few of the infinity of possible starting points, and the arrows show the corresponding time paths for q following a change in one of the exogenous variables.

Since convergence is involved in all the time paths, there is no obvious criterion for ruling out all but one of them. On the other hand, if the numerator in equation

Figure 6.2 The Infinity of Stable Perfect-Foresight Paths

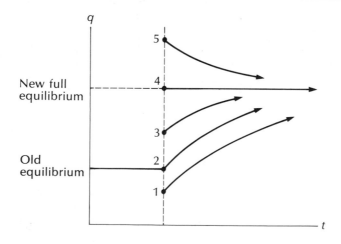

Figure 6.3   The Infinity of Unstable Perfect-Foresight Paths

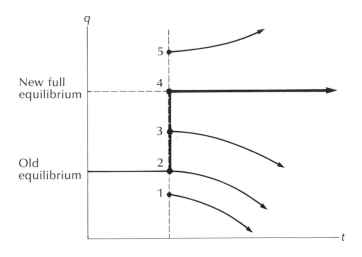

6.18 is positive, all the infinity of solutions except one involve departure from full equilibrium; the exception shows an immediate jump to full equilibrium (the heavy line in Figure 6.3). Thus, if the numerator in equation 6.18 is positive, the nonuniqueness problem can be solved by appealing to the proposition that instability is not observed. Because analysts want to use the presumption of convergence to avoid nonuniqueness problems, they presume the right-hand side of equation 6.18 is positive. Given this presumption, instability would obtain if it were not for the endogenous character of the initial condition, and this instability can be avoided by assuming that q jumps instantaneously. Since only one differential equation is involved, the jump must make $\dot{q} = 0$ immediately, so the only characteristic root (which involves instability) cannot operate. Analysts regard this avoidance of instability as the least arbitrary criterion for choosing among the infinity of starting values for q; if the model were not inherently unstable, this criterion would be lost. Thus, we assume $\bar{r}(1 - b) - a(j - \bar{q}c) > 0$ and proceed to evaluate the multipliers on the assumption that $\dot{q} = 0$. (These multipliers could initially be interpreted as the long-run or full-equilibrium effects, but given that q jumps instantaneously to make $\dot{q} = 0$, they are also the impact effects.) They are

$$\frac{dY}{dG} = \frac{\bar{r}}{\bar{r}(1 - b) - a(j - \bar{q}c)};$$
$$\frac{dY}{dM} = \frac{al\bar{q}}{\bar{r}(1 - b) - a(j - \bar{q}c)}.$$

Notice that both these multipliers have their conventional positive sign only if the denominators are positive, which is what we have just assumed.

Let us summarize the discussion. The correspondence principle is still involved in models involving perfect foresight (the deterministic analogue of rational expectations). The sign of the comparative static multipliers is determined by the sign restriction imposed by considering dynamics. What differs is the criterion for choosing that sign restriction. In our earlier macro models, which involved backward-looking expectations, initial conditions were given; the most severe problem facing analysts was the possibility of instability, which the sign restriction was chosen to preclude. In contrast, modern macroeconomists, with models involving forward-looking expectations, must choose initial conditions. Since this choice can be made so as to avoid instability, the possibility of instability is no longer the sole issue. In addition, analysts find the nonuniqueness of equilibrium an equally severe problem, so they choose the sign restriction that avoids this issue in what seems to be the least arbitrary method.

This methodology is easily followed as long as the number of unstable characteristic roots in the dynamic model just equals the number of endogenous variables that are free to jump (as in the model we are discussing). In general, however, this approach cannot avoid nonuniqueness if the number of free initial conditions exceeds the number of unstable characteristic roots (as we saw earlier in discussing Taylor's model), and there is no well-defined solution at all if the number of unstable roots exceeds the number of jump variables or free initial conditions. (Scarth's 1980 analysis of bond-financed deficits with fully flexible prices provides an example of the latter case. For a general discussion of these issues, see Blanchard and Kahn 1980.)

Having rationalized a unique outcome for this particular model, let us now investigate the policy multipliers graphically. From equation 6.15, the slope of the *IS* curve is $dq/dY = (1 - b)/a > 0$. Increases in *G* shift this schedule to the right, and all observations occur on this schedule. The *LM* curve is derived from equations 6.16 and 6.17 after the interest rate is eliminated by substitution. The *LM* curve is the $\dot{q} = 0$ locus, and since the differential of this equation implies $d\dot{q}/dq > 0$ (for a given *Y* and *M*), all points above the *LM* curve involve *q*'s rising, and all points below the *LM* curve involve *q*'s falling.

The slope of the *LM* curve is $dq/dY = (j - \bar{q}c)/\bar{r}$, which can be positive or negative. The reasoning behind this ambiguity runs as follows. An increase in output has two effects on the value of stocks. The direct effect is a rise in the marginal product of capital, and stock prices should increase to reflect this higher profit. This effect is captured by the *j* term in the expression for the slope of *LM*. The indirect effect of raising output on stock prices follows from an increase in the transactions demand for money, which pushes up the interest rate. The higher interest rate means that the expected profit incomes are discounted more heavily than before, so the willingness to acquire this income stream is reduced. This downward pressure on *q* is captured by the $\bar{q}c$ term in the slope expression. To have convenient labels for the two possible signs for expression $(j - \bar{q}c)$, Blanchard (1981) calls the $(j - \bar{q}c) > 0$ case the "good news" case (since output increases are regarded as good news by the stock market) and $(j - \bar{q}c) < 0$ the "bad news" case, labels we shall use here. Notice that whatever the slope of the *LM* curve, it shifts up when the money supply increases.

Figure 6.4 *IS* and *LM* Schedules for the Perfect-Foresight Model

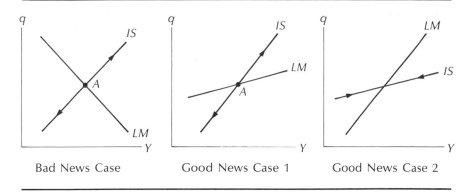

Bad News Case   Good News Case 1   Good News Case 2

This model involves three possible ways of drawing the *IS* and *LM* schedules, as shown in Figure 6.4, where the law of motion is shown by the arrows on the *IS* curve in each case. We have already ruled out the second good news case since it involves stability. The $\bar{r}(1 - b) - a(j - \bar{q}c) > 0$ condition can be manipulated to read that slope *IS* must be greater than slope *LM*. Since q can jump to any value initially and Y jumps accordingly to keep the observation point on the *IS* curve, all points on the *IS* curve are legitimate candidates for the initial observation point, no matter what the change in G or M. To have some basis for choosing among these possibilities, we confine our attention to the unstable cases, so the economy settles at point A immediately.

The multipliers we calculated above represent the effects of monetary and fiscal policies that have been unanticipated. (For the bad news case, they are shown graphically in Figure 6.5.) Now let us consider anticipated policies—

Figure 6.5 Unanticipated Policies in the Perfect-Foresight Model: The Bad News Case

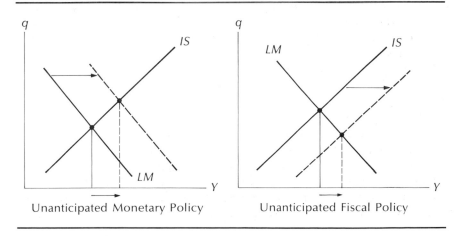

Unanticipated Monetary Policy   Unanticipated Fiscal Policy

Figure 6.6 Anticipated Monetary Policy in the Perfect-Foresight Model: The Bad News Case

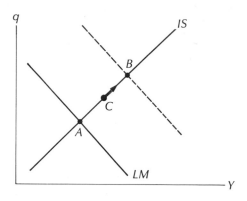

that is, ones that are announced today but will not be implemented until some time in the future. For the bad news case, the effects of a future monetary policy are shown in Figure 6.6. The initial observation point is A; once the policy is actually in place, the economy will be at point B. But the very announcement of the policy will have some effect. Knowing that output will be higher and that interest rates will be lower, agents calculate an increased present value of the profit income stream, and for this reason equity prices should go up immediately, though not by the full steady-state amount. The higher q stimulates investment, so Y must also jump upward. Thus, the economy moves immediately to some point such as C. Then, since point A remains the full-equilibrium point until the policy is actually implemented, the economy starts tracking along the IS curve away from point C, apparently on an unstable course. However, the position of point C is determined so that the economy will have just arrived at point B when the policy is actually implemented; all motion stops at that point in time. To summarize: the observation point goes from point A to point C immediately upon announcement of the policy and then slides gradually from C to B as the implementation date approaches. Nothing actually happens to q and Y right at the implementation date.

This analysis illustrates that causality tests in economics can be very misleading. In this scenario, it is the money supply change that causes the boom in the stock market and the increase in output. However, analysts who define causality in the Granger fashion—essentially, as what happens first—would incorrectly conclude that the boom in the stock market causes the increases in output and the money supply, and it would be incorrectly decided that the monetary authority was behaving in an accommodating way.

Now let us consider a fiscal policy that is anticipated for the future, again assuming the bad news case. The effects are shown in Figure 6.7. Once the fiscal policy is actually implemented in the future, the observation point will be

Figure 6.7   Anticipated Fiscal Policy in the Perfect-Foresight Model: The Bad News Case

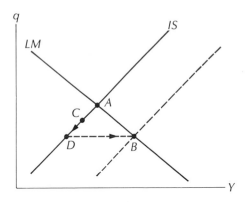

B. But even as the policy is announced, it has an effect on the stock market. With output known to be going higher in the future, stock prices tend to go up now (as the future higher incomes are capitalized). In this bad news case, however, this effect is dominated by the fact that agents know that future interest rates will be higher too. The higher discount rates cause the present value of profit incomes to fall, and since this effect dominates, *q* must fall (not rise). Thus, on the announcement of the future policy, the observation point immediately jumps from point *A* to point *C*. Then, since point *A* is still the full-equilibrium point until the policy is actually implemented, the economy starts tracking along the *IS* curve from point *C* toward point *D*. The position of point *C* is determined so that the economy will have just arrived at point *D* on the policy implementation date, when the observation point jumps to *B*. To summarize: the observation point goes from *A* to *C* immediately upon announcement, slides gradually from *C* to *D* as the implementation date approaches, and then jumps from *D* to *B* on the implementation date.

  Notice that anticipated fiscal policy can have perverse short-run effects in this model. In the bad news case, the government's promise of future fiscal expansion leads in the short run to more than complete crowding out, even though money demand is a function of the interest rate. These perverse effects might actually be helpful in certain situations—say, the dilemma facing many policymakers in the late 1980s.) *If* an announcement of future government expenditure cuts is believed, the model says it is possible for such a policy promise both to bring down the deficit in the future and to raise employment now! This possibility is certainly interesting. But the general and much more important message of this section is simply that with forward-looking agents, analysts must be very careful to distinguish unanticipated from anticipated government policies.

  Before closing this section, let us see how the analysis can be extended to a situation involving two dynamic processes. Following Blanchard (1981) we now assume that changes in the level of output clear the goods market not in instantaneous jumps but through gradual adjustment in response to imbalances between aggregate demand and supply. To model this situation, we replace equation 6.15 with

$$\dot{Y} = \sigma(aq + bY + G - Y); \qquad \sigma > 0. \tag{6.19}$$

The observation point is now generally off the *IS* curve, which has the interpretation of the $\dot{Y} = 0$ locus. From equation 6.19, $\partial\dot{Y}/\partial q = \sigma a > 0$, so points above the *IS* curve involve rising output, and points below it falling output. As before, the laws of motion for q come from equations 6.16 and 6.17. All these forces for motion are summarized in Figure 6.8 (again for the bad news case). The fact that all the vertical arrows show forces pushing the observation point away from the *LM* curve is the graphic depiction of the unstable characteristic root discussed above. The fact that all the horizontal arrows show forces pushing the observation point toward the *IS* curve illustrates that the second characteristic root in this second-order dynamic system is stable.

It is convenient that one root is stable and one unstable because with output now adjusting sluggishly *through* time, there is only one jump variable: q. Figure 6.8 shows that, in general, if an arbitrary starting point is chosen, the economy will not converge to the full equilibrium point, E. The saddle path, shown by the line SS, connects all those initial conditions from which the economy will converge to E. As before, analysts assume that the initial value of q is determined by the requirement that the economy avoid instability; in this case, that means being on the saddle path.

Figure 6.8   Derivation of the Saddle Path

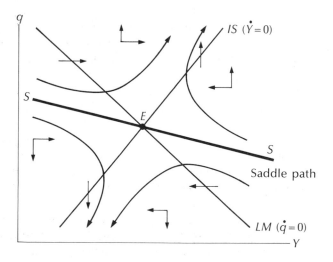

An example can clarify the reasoning. Suppose an unanticipated increase in the money supply occurs, as illustrated in Figure 6.9 (for the bad news case). The economy was initially at point A and will eventually be at point B. The impact-period response is dictated by two considerations: (1) with sluggishly adjusting output, the initial point must be somewhere on the vertical line passing through A; and (2) to avoid instability, q must jump so as to place the observation point somewhere on the new saddle path. The only point that satisfies both these requirements is C. The response is an instantaneous move from A to C and then a gradual (actually, an infinitely long) move from C to B. Thus, we see that short-run effects differ from long-run effects, even for unanticipated policies, when higher-order dynamics are involved.

Figure 6.9 Unanticipated Monetary Policy with Sluggishly Adjusting Output: The Bad News Case

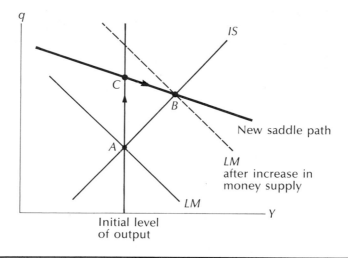

It is useful to be able to calculate impact effects of this sort formally, rather than simply illustrating them geometrically. (However, since this discussion is somewhat messy, some readers may prefer to skip to the conclusion of this chapter.) Very briefly, the mechanics are as follows. By reexpressing equations 6.16, 6.17, and 6.19 in terms of deviations from full equilibrium we have

$$(\dot{Y}\,\dot{q})' = A[(Y - \bar{Y})(q - \bar{q})]', \tag{6.20}$$

where

$$A = \begin{bmatrix} \sigma(b-1) & \sigma a \\ (\bar{q}c - j) & \bar{r} \end{bmatrix}.$$

When we considered second-order differential equation systems like this one in Chapter 3, we noted that the stability conditions are determinant $A > 0$ and trace $A < 0$. It is now worth considering why these conditions are required. The characteristic equation underlying equation 6.20 is given by $|-A + \lambda I| = 0$ or $(\lambda - z_1)(\lambda - z_2) = 0$, where the zs stand for the two possible values of the characteristic root, λ. The characteristic equation can be reexpressed as $\lambda^2 - (z_1 + z_2)\lambda + z_1 z_2 = 0$ or $\lambda^2 - (\text{trace } A)\lambda + (\text{determinant } A) = 0$, since the trace of A is the sum of these roots and the determinant of A is their product. Stability requires that both roots be negative, since the form of the solution for differential equations is $q_t = \bar{q} + B_1 e^{z_1 t} + B_2 e^{z_2 t}$. If both zs must be negative, their sum must be negative and their product positive. But in the present model, where the initial value for equity prices is chosen to avoid instability, nonuniqueness requires that the system have a saddle path—that is, that one root be negative and the other positive. Therefore, the product of the roots (the determinant of A) must be negative, which requires that $\bar{r}(1 - b) - a(j - \bar{q}c) > 0$, as we assumed in the simpler model.

Let us take z_2 as the positive (unstable) root. The initial jump in q to place the system on the saddle path means that B_2 is set to zero, so once on that path the dynamics are described by the stable laws of motion: $q_t = \bar{q} + B_1 e^{z_1 t}$ and $Y_t = \bar{Y} + C_1 e^{z_1 t}$. But given the linear approximation involved in taking deviations from full equilibrium, C_1 must be proportional to B_1 on the saddle path. Assuming $B_1 = nC_1$, then, motion along the saddle path must obey the rule that the two deviations from equilibrium have to be proportional:

$$(q - \bar{q}) = n(Y - \bar{Y}). \tag{6.21}$$

It turns out that n and the positive root, z_2, can be solved from

$$[n - 1][-A + z_2 I] = [0 \ 0] \tag{6.22}$$

(see Dixit 1980). As noted before, z_2 can also be solved (along with z_1) from $|-A + \lambda I| = 0$.

Once the expression for n is known, calculating the impact effects, such as dq/dG, from equation 6.21 is straightforward:

$$\frac{dq}{dG} = \frac{d\bar{q}}{dG} + n\left(0 - \frac{d\bar{Y}}{dG}\right). \tag{6.23}$$

The impact effect on q is simply a weighted average of the full-equilibrium effects (which we calculated earlier), since the assumption of sluggish adjustment of output precludes any impact effect on Y.

With knowledge of these techniques, readers can also calculate how institutional changes affect the speed of adjustment along the saddle path. This methodology is important for assessing whether changes in policy rules contribute to the built-in stability properties of the economy.

6.6 CONCLUSIONS

If we do not assume rational expectations or perfect foresight, our macroeconomic analyses must be restricted to policies that agents do not fully understand. With rational expectations or perfect foresight added, our examination of government policy assumes that agents fully understand both the present and future implications of any new policy rule. Faced with this bold option, of alternative assumptions concerning agents' knowledge, an increasing number of analysts feel compelled to assume rational expectations (or perfect foresight). It is a strong, polar-case assumption, but it seems to many less arbitrary than the available alternatives.

It was for this reason that we have devoted this chapter to extending the reader's understanding of rational expectations models. We have discussed several important topics: time inconsistency, announcement effects, and the implications of alternative assumptions about information availability. We have allowed for rational expectations for all the endogenous variables. Finally, we have shown that some parts of this approach still involve a discouraging element of arbitrariness, which is reflected in, for example, nonuniqueness problems and the lack of any decentralized incentive mechanism to motivate jumps onto saddle paths. Progress requires that practitioners be aware of both the existing solution methods and the controversies.

Some economists have misgivings about the rational expectations revolution that are more generally based than those focused on solution methods. They agree that macroeconomics should have a good microeconomic basis, in the sense that agents should be assumed to avoid doing things that are obviously against their self-interest. But these economists see the recent literature as pushing this general notion too far. It is not that they believe no researchers should pursue what has become the mainstream line of inquiry; rather, they think that those researchers should not insist their approach is the only way. For example, say the dissenters, without serious consideration of aggregation issues, how can formal optimization models predict anything about what might be "rational" for agents in a "real" economy?

Another concern is that the standard methodology cannot handle what Knight (1921) calls fundamental uncertainty. Decision-makers constantly confront uncertainties that—in contrast to risks—cannot be treated mathematically by using repeated samples. (For example, the uncertainty about nuclear war is not that some percentage of the next number of wars will involve nuclear weapons. One would be enough.) A group called the Post-Keynesians argue that by paying insufficient attention to these issues, the mainstream New Keynesians may be backing the wrong horse in the sense that they have embraced the rational expectations methodology and continued to emphasize temporary wage rigidity as central to Keynes, rather than taking uncertainty as the fundamental Keynesian issue.

CHAPTER 7

INTRINSIC DYNAMICS

7.1 INTRODUCTION

The analysis in previous chapters has involved both stock variables, such as the quantities of capital and money, and flow variables, such as the rate of investment spending and the government budget deficit (government spending minus taxes). But it has not included the accumulation identities that necessarily relate these stock and flow variables through time as parts of the macro models. Yet by definition, net investment is the time rate of change of the capital stock. Similarly, the time rate of change in the money supply and the quantity of government bonds outstanding is necessarily equal to the size of the government budget deficit (as long as we are dealing with a closed economy in which there is no gift-giving or stealing between the government and private agents). The purpose of this chapter is to introduce the reader to the implications of the intrinsic dynamics that follow from such accumulation identities.

We shall, however, limit our discussion to the government financing constraint, continuing to neglect the investment/capital stock accumulation identity. We proceed with this limitation for two reasons. First, the study of deficit financing has produced a vast literature that is highly topical at this time of record levels of budget deficits and government debt. Most of this literature relies on the common simplifying assumptions that investment is a small proportion of the capital stock but a significant proportion of the level of national income. With these assumptions, investment can be modeled as an important component of aggregate demand and the model's time interval can be presumed to be short enough for the supply-side effect of investment (the increase in the capital stock) to be roughly zero. Since we wish to survey this literature, we must follow the hypotheses customarily involved. (Strictly speaking, of course, these simplifying assumptions of short-run macro theory represent a mis-specification, which is entirely unacceptable for long-run analyses of economic growth. But many analysts view this problem as representing a second-order effect for issues of *short-run* stabilization policy.)

Our second reason for limiting discussion to the government financing constraint is the desire for pedagogic simplicity. That we can maintain the simplifying limitation without reaching misleading conclusions is suggested by the work of several authors who explicitly consider both the government financing constraint and the capital stock accumulation identity, combining short-run stabilization questions with longer-run growth considerations in one full model. (For examples, see Turnovsky 1977 and Shah 1984. Blackhouse 1981 ignores the government debt accumulation identity, but he explains that the fixed-price *IS–LM* model can be viewed as a temporary equilibrium of the standard Neoclassical growth model and that these two models are linked through time via the capital stock accumulation identity.) Fortunately, these studies show that the results of the simpler stabilization policy models, which ignore the capital stock dynamics, are not overturned in the extended analyses.

Discussions of the government financing constraint often focus on the fact that budget deficits are largely financed by issuing interest-bearing bonds. Many observers now worry that the government's commitment to pay interest on these bonds in the future will lead to an ever-increasing budget deficit. Whether this concern is warranted is the focus of this chapter's analysis.

Unfortunately, the standard macro models we have examined thus far give no role to government bonds. Thus, before the analysis can proceed, we must consider in some detail how and under what circumstances government bonds should be included within conventional macroeconomics. The debate on this issue, which is called the Ricardian equivalence controversy, will be discussed in section 7.2. After clarifying how bonds can be modeled, we analyze both aggregate demand aspects of deficit financing (section 7.3) and aggregate supply considerations (section 7.4). We shall conclude by emphasizing the distinction between the feasibility of bond-financed budget deficits and the desirability of this policy. Since a monetarist policy stance presumes the desirability of bond-financed deficits and our analysis questions it, this chapter's material has direct policy relevance.

7.2 THE RICARDIAN EQUIVALENCE CONTROVERSY

The standard fixed-price *IS–LM* model involves no role for government bonds. The demand for liquidity—money demand—is specified to be independent of the private sector's bond holdings. Also, asset accumulation—that is, savings and, therefore, consumption—is specified to be independent of the quantity of liquid assets already accumulated. Finally, the definition of disposable income for private agents does not include interest payments on government bonds. Should these features of standard aggregate demand theory be regarded as short-comings, or can they be defended?

Before we can answer this question, we need some notation that allows us to define the number of bonds outstanding, the amount of interest payment involved, and the market value of bonds. In general, the price of a bond equals the present value, PV, of the stream of payments that the ticket allows its owner. Thus,

$$\text{bond price} = \frac{1}{1+r} + \frac{1}{(1+r)^2} + \cdots$$

if each bond is a consol—a promise to pay one dollar per year forever. This formula can be simplified as

$$\text{bond price} = \frac{1}{1+r} + \frac{1}{(1+r)^2} + \cdots = \frac{1/(1+r)}{1 - 1/(1+r)} = 1/r.$$

Prices and yields are related inversely for any bond. Consols are convenient for analysis since they involve the simplest possible formula for inverse variation: yield $= r$; price $= 1/r$. Thus, if B is the number of bonds outstanding, the total interest payments equal B and the market value of bonds is $(1/r)B$.

With this background and the assumption that goods prices are constant, we can specify the government financing constraint as

$$G + B = T + \dot{M} + \left(\frac{1}{r}\right)\dot{B}. \tag{7.1}$$

This identity precludes stealing and gift-giving between the public and private sectors, as well as the purchase of private bonds by the government, by stipulating that the uses of government funds—spending on goods, G, and interest payment on public debt, B—be just covered by the sources of government funds—taxation, T; high-powered money issue, $\dot{M}$; and bond issue, $(1/r)\dot{B}$. $\dot{M}$ and $\dot{B}$ stand for the number of new tickets issued per unit of time, and $1/r$ is the price of each bond sold.

The presence of this financing constraint in a macro model means that *one* of the policy variables cannot be set exogenously; its value must be determined residually by the setting of the other policy instruments, the outcome of the economy, and the need to satisfy the financing constraint. Standard *IS–LM* analysis that does not involve equation 7.1 can be defended in the following manner. The money supply, the level of government spending, and the tax rate are set exogenously, so the endogenous policy variable whose time path is governed by equation 7.1 is B. If interest is limited to macro variables other than bonds, the equation can be ignored, so long as the positions of the *IS* and *LM* schedules are independent of the amount of government bonds outstanding.

The assumption that private decisions are unaffected by the quantity of government bonds outstanding is called Ricardian equivalence. In this view, agents are assumed to exclude bonds from their wealth. Bonds are seen both as a promise of future interest payments from the government and as an implicit promise of future taxes that the government will need to levy to pay that interest. It is assumed that members of the public use the same discount rate to calculate the present value of both the interest receipts and the tax obligations. It is also assumed that the public have an infinite planning horizon or—what amounts to the same thing (see Barro 1974)—that agents make bequests to their heirs in an overlapping-generations framework. These assumptions mean that government bonds represent both an asset and a liability of the same value. The two features cancel each other off in the definition of private sector wealth, so private decisions concerning asset allocations, *LM*, and asset accumulations, *IS*, should be unaffected by bonds.

The Ricardian equivalence hypothesis can be clarified by referring to Figure 7.1. For simplicity, the diagram refers to a planning horizon with only two periods: the present (measured on the horizontal axis) and the future (measured on the vertical axis). Suppose the agent's income sequence is expected to be Y_1^d today, and Y_2^d tomorrow. This endowment point is given by point A in the diagram. If the individual can borrow and lend at a given interest rate, r, his consumption possibilities are limited by the straight line through A, which has a slope of $-(1 + r)$. The end points of this constraint are points $[Y_1^d + Y_2^d/(1 + r), 0]$, which represents the maximum the individual can consume

Figure 7.1   Ricardian Equivalence

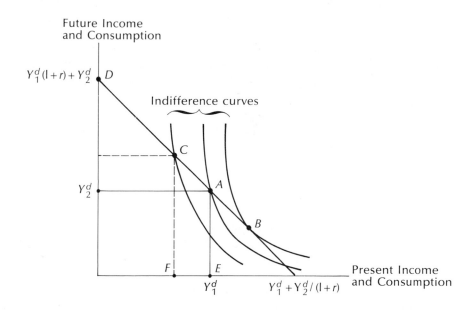

in the first period, and $[0, Y_1^d(1 + r) + Y_2^d]$, which represents the maximum amount of consumption in the second period. As an example, we show an indifference curve tangent to this constraint at point B, where this individual is borrowing against future income to permit current consumption to exceed present income.

What happens if the government raises taxes today to retire some government bonds? If Ricardian equivalence exists, agents do not feel that their consumption possibilities are affected at all. They regard this policy as one of substituting current taxes for future taxes of the same present value. Of course, the government policy changes the endowment point—from A to some point such as C—but the present value of the overall stream of income (the position of the intertemporal budget constraint) is not affected. Agents still choose to consume the amounts given by point B. They simply have to do more borrowing than they did before the increase in present-period taxes.

Many theorists find Ricardian equivalence an unappealing hypothesis because it assumes that no agent is constrained by liquidity, a situation that seems inconsistent with observations. Many individuals must pay a higher rate of interest when they borrow than they receive when they lend. This difference is thought to occur mainly because quite a number of individuals possess only human wealth—that is, the present value of their expected future labor income. Lending institutions find human wealth a bad form of collateral: slavery laws preclude a person's passing the ownership rights to his labor income to another individual, and there are enforcement problems in any event. If the borrowing rate is higher than the lending rate, the intertemporal budget constraint has a kink at the endowment point. To illustrate this issue in a dramatic way, we consider an individual who is deemed such a bad risk that he cannot borrow at all. The initial budget constraint for this individual is line DAE; after an increase in current taxes (which retires some bonds and, therefore, cuts future taxes), the budget constraint is DCF. The liquidity-constrained individual is originally at a corner solution (point A) and moves to a similar outcome at point C. A similar analysis would hold true for a current-tax cut. Thus, for a liquidity-constrained individual, the issuing of government bonds that allow the government to reduce current taxes *does* raise current consumption expenditures.

Generally, it seems sensible to follow the suggestions of Friedman (1956; 1957) to let both the propensity to consume out of broadly defined wealth and the proportion of broadly defined wealth that is held as money depend on the ratio of liquid assets to total wealth. For the standard *IS–LM* model that involves static expectations concerning income, this can be accomplished by letting: (1) consumption depend positively both on disposable income, Y^d (since that is the expected yield on broadly defined wealth), and on liquid assets—money and bonds, $A = M + B/r$; and (2) money demand depend positively on both total output, Y, and liquid assets, A. This form is convenient for our purposes here since it allows us to suppress the liquid asset and disposable income effects of government bonds in order to examine Ricardian equivalence as a special case.

To see how the expression for disposable income is affected by the Ricardian equivalence issue, we follow McCallum (1978) and Sargent (1979) and define disposable income as consumption services enjoyed plus agents' change in wealth. Consumption services are defined as private spending, C, plus proportion j of government spending, G, which is the fraction that private agents find useful. If we assume Ricardian equivalence, bonds are not included in wealth, so it is simply (high-powered) money plus capital, $M + K$. Taking the time derivative of this wealth definition and noting the capital stock accumulation identity, $I = \dot{K} + \delta K$, we have disposable income defined as $Y^d = C + jG + I - \delta K + \dot{M}$. Simplifying this equation with the goods market identity, $Y = C + I + G$, we have $Y^d = Y - \delta K - (1 - j)G + \dot{M}$. It is common to consider bond-financed deficits—so $\dot{M} = 0$—and to assume implicitly that all government expenditure is wasted—$j = 0$. Thus, $Y^d = Y - \delta K - G$; in other words, disposable income equals net national income minus what the government spends (not what the government calls taxes). Whether one regards government spending as wasted or not, the key point to realize here is that disposable income is unaffected by either conventionally defined taxes or government bonds.

If Ricardian equivalence is not assumed, however, wealth is defined as the sum of money, capital, and government bonds, $M + K + B/r$. Taking the time derivative of this expression and combining it with $I = \dot{K} + \delta K$, $Y = C + I + G$, and the same conceptual definition as before, the expression for disposable income becomes $Y^d = Y - \delta K - (1 - j)G + \dot{M} + (1/r)\dot{B} - (B/r^2)\dot{r}$. This expression can be simplified by assuming static expectations (when agents are forecasting disposable income, they expect no capital gains or losses and assume $\dot{r} = 0$) and government expenditure that is entirely wasted ($j = 0$). Finally, we use the government financing constraint, and the equation for disposable income becomes $Y^d = Y - \delta K + B - T$. Ricardian equivalence is considered the special case that occurs when the B and T terms are replaced by G (and the liquid asset effects of bonds on consumption and money demand are suppressed).

7.3 FINANCING BUDGET DEFICITS: AGGREGATE DEMAND CONSIDERATIONS

Let us set up a basic model for examining the financing of budget deficits:

$$G + B = k(Y + B) + \dot{M} + \left(\frac{1}{r}\right)\dot{B}; \tag{7.1}$$

$$Y = C(Y^d, A) + I(r) + G; \tag{7.2}$$

$$Y^d = (1 - k)(Y + B); \tag{7.3}$$

$$A = M + B/r; \tag{7.4}$$

$$M = L(r, Y, A). \tag{7.5}$$

Blinder and Solow (1973) analyze this system, which involves the assumption of fixed goods prices—that is, a horizontal aggregate supply curve. (We shall extend this model in sections 7.4 and 7.5 to allow for flexible prices.)

The government budget constraint has already been explained. Its presence means that no single government expenditure multiplier can exist. The constraint makes the model necessarily dynamic, so we consider both the impact period and the full equilibrium, the latter being defined by the existence of a balanced budget. The other four equations define the *IS* and *LM* relationships, using notation defined earlier. Notice, however, that the inclusion of interest payments on government debt, B, in the definition of disposable income adds government transfer payments to the model. The restrictions on the derivatives that have not appeared before are $C_A \geq 0$ and $0 \leq L_A < 1$. Constraining L_A to a fraction means that both money and bonds are "normal" assets. Ricardian equivalence can be imposed by setting $C_A = L_A = 0$ and removing B from equation 7.3.

It is possible to finance an increase in government spending in three basic ways: (1) with a balanced budget (the tax rate is endogenous in the model); (2) by money issue (the money supply is endogenous); and (3) through bond issue (the bond stock is endogenous). Of course, various combinations of tax, money, and bond finance are possible, but we restrict our formal analysis to the polar cases.

Before analyzing how macroeconomic stability is affected by the method of deficit financing, we must clarify the existence of separate Walras's law considerations for both the stock and the flow aspects of the model. This explanation will also help any reader who is wondering why we are highlighting the government's financing constraint without giving similar stress to the private sector's flow budget constraint.

The latter relationship can be expressed as

private disposable income	−	total private expenditures	+	private sector's capital gains	=	change in private sector's wealth

Using our symbols, this condition is

$$Y^d - C - I + \text{gains} = \dot{A}.$$

Substituting in equation 7.3 and the time derivative of equation 7.4, we have

$$Y + B - T - C - I + \text{gains} = \dot{M} + \left(\frac{1}{r}\right)\dot{B} - \left(\frac{B}{r^2}\right)\dot{r}.$$

Since the final term is the expression for capital gains on bonds and since, from equation 7.2, $Y = C + I + G$, this private sector's accumulation identity reduces to equation 7.1. Thus, by including in the model the *stock* liquid asset constraint on the private sector (equation 7.4) and the money market-clearing condition (equation 7.5), the bond market-clearing condition is implied. And by including the *flow* accumulation identity for the private sector and the definitions of Y and Y^d, the government sector's accumulation identity (equation 7.1) is implied.

We wish to compare the stability conditions for two versions of this model: one involving money-financed budget deficits, and one involving bond-financed deficits. To derive the stability conditions, it is convenient to summarize the static part of the model by summary equations for Y and r as functions of the variables that are predetermined at any point of time. These summary equations can be derived by linearizing equations 7.2 through 7.5—that is, by taking the total differential and substituting down to either Y or r on the left-hand side (from the four-equation system solving for Y, Y^d, r, and A). Let the following equations stand for these summary relationships, which define temporary equilibrium:

$$Y = F(G, k, M, B); \tag{7.6}$$

$$r = H(G, k, M, B). \tag{7.7}$$

The derivatives of these functions are the symbols for the impact period multipliers. It is left for the reader to derive these multipliers and to verify that

$$\frac{dY}{dG} = F_G > 0; \qquad \frac{dr}{dG} = H_G > 0; \qquad \frac{dY}{dk} = F_k < 0; \qquad \frac{dr}{dk} = H_k < 0;$$

$$\frac{dY}{dM} = F_M > 0; \qquad \frac{dr}{dM} = H_M \gtreqless 0; \qquad \frac{dY}{dB} = F_B \gtreqless 0; \qquad \frac{dr}{dB} = H_B > 0.$$

All these multiplier results can be verified by the standard graphic analysis of a static *IS–LM* system. For example, a tax hike shifts the *IS* curve down to the left, so both output and interest rate fall: $F_k, H_k, < 0$. The only noteworthy effects are those that involve an ambiguous sign: H_M and F_B. A money supply increase has an ambiguous effect on the interest rate since, with the liquid asset effect in the consumption function, both the *IS* and *LM* curves shift; the *LM* curve moves to the right as usual (as long as $L_A < 1$), and the *IS* curve moves up.

The other ambiguous effect is that of bonds on aggregate demand. If we wish to consider Ricardian equivalence, we simply set $F_B = 0$. But without that assumption, there is uncertainty because raising the level of bonds shifts both the *IS* and *LM* curves upward. With more bonds, household consumption spending rises, both because an increased proportion of wealth is in a liquid form and because transfer payments (interest payments on the public debt) go up. The shift in the consumption function moves the *IS* curve up (or out). The *LM* curve shifts up (or to the left) when more government bonds are issued. The portfolio effect stems from the fact that when agents have additional liquid assets to distribute between money and bond holdings, the demand for both assets increases. If agents receive all their additional liquid assets in the form of bonds (because that is what the government issues), their demand for money increases and portfolio equilibrium can obtain only at a higher interest rate.

Notice that when the government issues either money or bonds to cover a budget deficit, the model is necessarily dynamic since the time rate of change in either money or bonds is involved in equation 7.1. Thus, multipliers such as dY/dG are an entire time path. For convenience, however, we limit our analysis to derivation of the two extremes: the impact result and the long-run multiplier.

The impact multiplier gives the response of Y at the very instant government expenditure increases—before any time has passed to allow the government to actually issue either money or bonds. For this instant, then, the multiplier is the same under either method of future financing, and only the static equations are required for its derivation. Thus, $dY/dG = F_G$ for both cases. Impact-period analysis is required, however, to derive the stability conditions: $d\dot{M}/dM < 0$ in the money-financed case, and $d\dot{B}/dB < 0$ in the bond-financed case.

Case (1): Money-Financed Deficits

For money-financed deficits, the compact version of the model is:

$$Y = F(G, k, M, B);$$

$$G + B = k(Y + B) + \dot{M};$$

and the two endogenous variables are output and the money supply. Specifically, the two equations determine Y and $\dot{M}$ in the impact period, when G is increased, and the level of M is interpreted as the preexisting money stock, which is given by history. The system can be solved sequentially, and the interesting results are $dY/dG = F_G > 0$ and $d\dot{M}/dM = -kF_M < 0$. The second result shows that the model is definitely stable (without further assumptions about the structural parameters). As time passes following the increase in government spending, the budget must eventually become balanced again. Thus, it is legitimate to calculate the long-run multiplier.

To do so, we use the long-run version of the model, which is

$$Y = F(G, k, M, B);$$

$$G + B = k(Y + B);$$

and the endogenous variables are Y and M. Within this time frame, M is now interpreted as the resulting level of the money supply that occurs after the budget deficit returns to zero. $\dot{M}$ is now exogenously set to zero to define full equilibrium. The model is again recursive, but this time it is the government budget constraint that solves for Y. Then, given this value for Y, we can solve the first equation for M. From the budget identity, $dY/dG = 1/k$, so the government expenditure multiplier is independent of all structural parameters except the policy-determined

Figure 7.2 A Money-Financed Increase in Government Spending

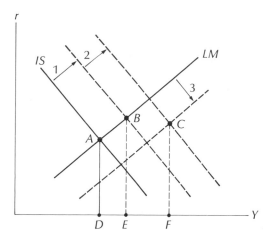

tax rate. The reader can verify that $1/k > F_G$—that is, that an increase in spending has a full-equilibrium effect on aggregate demand that is larger than the impact-period effect.

The graphic summary of this case is shown in Figure 7.2. The increase in government spending, shown as shift 1, moves the observation point from its initial position, point A, to point B. This is the impact-period result (distance $DE = F_G \, dG$). But as time passes beyond the impact period, the resulting budget deficit implies that $\dot{M}$ is positive, and with time, the money supply increases. Thus, shift 2 (due to the liquid asset effect on consumption) and shift 3 (due to the increase in M, which raises money supply more than money demand, since $L_A < 1$) occur, and the observation point becomes C. Shifts 2 and 3 continue until output is high enough to raise tax revenue sufficiently to balance the budget (and thereby let $\dot{M}$ tend to zero). At full equilibrium, at a point such as C, distance DF equals $(1/k) \, dG$.

A word of caution on the application of this model is in order. If we had no misgivings about the long-run version of this system, the $dY/dG = 1/k$ result would be exciting for analysts who favor active policy-making. We have, after all, derived more than the sign of the multiplier; we have seen that its magnitude depends only on a policy-determined parameter. In other words, this model can yield *quantitative* policy results without our having to estimate any behavior parameters for the private sector. Remember, however, that any long-run analysis involving fixed prices is a dubious one. Our purpose in including this model is primarily to demonstrate the way the stability condition changes with the mode of government deficit financing. Also, this analysis is a stepping stone for the more complete model discussed in later sections of this chapter.

Case (2): Bond-Financed Deficits

When the deficit is bond-financed—that is, when the government bond stock is the residually determined policy variable—the compact form of the model is

$$Y = F(G, k, M, B);$$

$$G + B = k(Y + B) + \left(\frac{1}{r}\right)\dot{B}.$$

For the impact period the endogenous variables are Y and $\dot{B}$, and the level of B is interpreted as the historically given stock of bonds. $\dot{B}$ is the rate at which bonds are about to be issued. As already discussed, this two-equation system is recursive at the point in time when a shock such as an increase in government spending occurs, so the impact effect on national output can be determined by using the first equation only. Thus, the impact-period multiplier is again F_G.

The other result we derive at this stage is the stability condition relevant under bond financing. This condition is $d\dot{B}/dB < 0$; to derive the expression for $d\dot{B}/dB$, we take the total differential of the model, setting the exogenous variable changes equal to zero ($dG = dk = dM = 0$):

$$dY = F_B \, dB;$$

$$dB = k(dY + dB) + \left(\frac{1}{r}\right)d\dot{B} - (\bar{\dot{B}}/\bar{r}^2)dr.$$

The bars above the variables indicate full-equilibrium values. Given that this linear approximation involves taking tangents evaluated at full-equilibrium values, the dr term can be dropped. The full-equilibrium value of its coefficient, $\bar{\dot{B}}$, is zero. Eliminating dY by substitution gives $d\dot{B}/dB = r[(1 - k) - kF_B]$. Thus, stability requires that $F_B > (1 - k)/k$.

Thus far, our examination of this model leads to two possible conclusions: either $F_B < (1 - k)/k$, so bond financing by the government involves instability and should, therefore, be avoided; or $F_B > (1 - k)/k$, so bond financing involves stability. In the latter case, we can derive the long-run effects of fiscal policy, and thus the model permits us to evaluate Friedman's claim that bond-financed fiscal expansion must eventually involve a one-for-one crowding out of pre-existing private demand.

The second possibility makes it worthwhile to examine the long-run version of the model:

$$Y = F(G, k, M, B);$$

$$G + B = k(Y + B).$$

The endogenous variables are now Y and B. We set $\dot{B}$ equal to zero to define full equilibrium and now interpret B as the level of bonds that results after the budget deficit returns to zero. Taking the total differential of this system—that is, setting $dk = dM = 0$—and eliminating dB by substitution, we get

$$\frac{dY}{dG} = \frac{F_B - (1 - k)F_G}{kF_B - (1 - k)}.$$

At first glance, the sign of this long-run multiplier appears to be ambiguous. However, we can use the correspondence principle here. To be at all relevant, the long-run multiplier must involve the presumption of stability—that is, that $F_B > (1 - k)/k$. This condition is sufficient to insure that the denominator of the multiplier is positive. And, since we have already noted that $1/k$ exceeds F_G (that is, that the long-run output multiplier exceeds the short-run multiplier under money financing), the stability condition is sufficient to make the numerator of the multiplier positive as well. Further, we can show that under bond financing, $dY/dG > 1/k$ (the full-equilibrium result under money financing). The proof is by contradiction: assume

$$\frac{F_B - (1 - k)F_G}{kF_B - (1 - k)} < 1/k.$$

This assumption implies $F_G > 1/k$, which we have already shown to be impossible.

Thus, we come to the following general conclusion. Bond financing may involve instability; if it does not, fiscal policy is more expansionary under bond financing than it is under money financing. Thus, Friedman's contention that the long-run fiscal policy multiplier is zero under bond financing is logically impossible, in a model that has no aggregate supply constraints. This is the main theoretical point derived by Blinder and Solow (1973).

As before, however, we must stress that the applicability of the long-run result is compromised by the fact that the long run has been defined in a rather awkward way—as an interval long enough for asset accumulation identities to work themselves out fully but not long enough for wages and prices to adjust at all. Because of this limitation, we emphasize that the significant message emerging from this analysis is that dynamic convergence is a serious issue when a budget deficit is bond financed. We shall find that this concern about the viability of bond-financed deficits is strengthened when we consider variable prices later in this chapter.

Blinder and Solow end their 1973 paper with a conjecture about the empirical likelihood of instability. Unfortunately, this discussion is marred by the fact that their interpretation of the expression for F_B involves a small error. When corrected, their empirical guesses concerning the parameters lead to the conclusion of instability, the interpretation that the two analysts stress in their later paper (1976). The generality of this conclusion is emphasized by Christ (1979) as well.

An appreciation for this likelihood of instability with bond-financed budget deficits can be had by referring to Figure 7.3. The economy starts at point A,

Figure 7.3 A Bond-Financed Increase in Government Spending

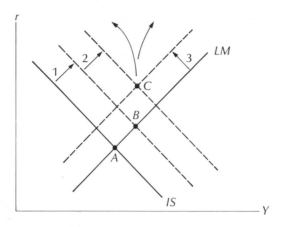

and then there is a once-and-for-all increase in the level of government spending. The effect during the impact period is shown by shift 1; B is the new observation point. But at point B, bonds must be issued to cover the budget deficit, so once time has passed, private agents will have an increased bond stock. This increased holdings of bonds has two results: liquid asset and interest income effects raise consumption, leading to shift 2, and the attempt by agents to try to transform some of the extra bonds into money, leading to an increase in money demand, which is shift 3. Shifts 2 and 3 continue until output increases enough to raise tax revenue sufficiently to balance the budget. Thus, we trace the observation point through a series of points such as C. The arrows in the figure show the possible time paths. Point C is to the left of point B if additional bonds lead to a contraction in aggregate demand—that is, if $F_B < 0$. Point C is to the right of point B if higher bond holdings stimulate aggregate demand—that is, if $F_B > 0$. Thus, the diagram shows that $F_B > 0$ is a necessary but not sufficient condition for stability. The necessary *and* sufficient condition, $F_B > (1 - k)/k$, is a stronger requirement.

The reasoning behind this requirement follows from consideration of both the direct and the indirect effects of bond issue on the budget deficit. The deficit is defined as

$$(\overset{\uparrow}{G} + B) - k(\overset{\uparrow}{Y} + B).$$

When government spending is increased, output increases, so tax revenue increases to some extent. But as long as investment is not sensitive to output levels ($I_Y = 0$), taxes cannot increase enough to avoid a deficit. If the government finances this deficit by money issue, it is not adding to its future financing requirements by issuing promises to pay interest in the future. The increased money supply further increases output, so eventually the tax base must increase enough to balance the budget (see the arrows over the components of the deficit above). In contrast, covering the deficit with bond issue directly affects future financing requirements; because of the interest that must be paid, future deficits go up by $(1 - k)$ times the current increase in bonds. This direct effect may be offset by the indirect effect on factor incomes, Y: more bonds may raise Y (by amount F_B times the increase in bonds), and the higher Y means more tax revenue for the government (by amount k times the increase in income, which equals $F_B\, dB$). Notice, however, that the economy avoids instability only if the indirect effect is large enough to dominate the destabilizing direct effect, a net outcome that many economists think is unlikely.

If bond financing of deficits does lead to macroeconomic instability, one must question the wisdom of the policymakers in many Western countries during the 1980s who have combined tight monetary policy with easy fiscal policy. Large bond-financed deficits have resulted and persist. But before we relate actual experience to the macro theory of bond-financed deficits, we must consider how this theory has been extended to a setting involving flexible prices.

7.4 FINANCING BUDGET DEFICITS: AGGREGATE SUPPLY CONSIDERATIONS

Does the possibility of macroeconomic instability under bond-financed deficits threaten Milton Friedman's suggestions for macro policy? There is no problem with Friedman's original proposal for a stable fiscal and monetary framework (1948). At that time he called for the complete phasing out of government bonds. He also argued that the rates of government spending and taxation should be set at values consistent with long-run allocation and equity objectives, and that temporary budget deficits and surpluses (which occur over the business cycle) should be entirely money financed. By 1959, however, Friedman had changed his mind. He no longer believed that politicians would apply fiscal policy in a responsible manner; rather, he decided, they would refuse to run budget surpluses in the boom years, and he feared that chronic inflation would result. So he began to call for an exogenous rate of monetary growth. Such a monetarist central bank policy involves bond-financed budget deficits. Thus, the advisability of such a policy (which was widely applied in the early 1980s) is definitely threatened by the result that bond financing could lead to macroeconomic instability —if that possibility remains in a flexible-price setting. We now show that this possibility should be considered a very likely outcome since all studies extending the Blinder/Solow analysis lead to this strong conclusion.

First, since $F_B = 0$ is a sufficient condition for bond financing to bring instability, consider the ways in which it can be imposed on the model. If $F_B = 0$ because of Ricardian equivalence, the stock of bonds must go to infinity, but since this phenomenon has no impact on agents' decisions, no other macro variables follow unstable paths. But even a slight departure from Ricardian equivalence makes F_B small but nonzero, so general instability results.

A second way in which F_B can equal zero is by adjusting the model to allow for variable prices. If we add a standard expectations-augmented Phillips curve, such as $\dot{P}/P = f(Y - \bar{Y})/\bar{Y} + \dot{M}/M$, and take the natural output rate, $\bar{Y}$, as exogenous, the stock of government bonds cannot have any effect on output in full equilibrium. This specification puts a constraint on tax revenue so it cannot grow indefinitely, as does the bond stock.

Scarth (1979) shows that instability continues to hold if we consider a policy of endogenous government expenditure, whereby direct spending on goods is reduced to make room in the budget for interest payments on the debt. In the same paper, it is stressed that bond financing also leads to definite instability in models of a small, open economy. It is also shown in Scarth (1980) that even if the price level is taken to be a jump variable that can be chosen with the intention of making unstable outcomes nonoperative, bond financing remains unstable. The reason is simple; the model has two unstable characteristic roots: one from the assumption of perfect foresight concerning inflationary expectations, and the other from the government budget constraint combined with an exogenous natural rate of output. Even though the price level is taken to be a jump variable, the stock of bonds cannot jump. The quantity of bonds adjusts only *through* time according to the accumulation identity (that is, the financing constraint). With two unstable characteristic roots and only one jump variable in the model, stability cannot obtain.

The one extension to the Blinder/Solow analysis that has been interpreted as increasing the likelihood of convergence under bond financing is to allow for positive economic growth. Let us follow that logic through. With variable prices, the government financing constraint is modified to

$$G + \frac{B}{P}(1 - k) - kY = \frac{1}{P}\dot{M} + \frac{1}{iP}\dot{B}. \tag{7.8}$$

If we divide equation 7.8 through by $\bar{Y}$, the natural rate of output, and define $g = G/\bar{Y}$, $b = B/P\bar{Y}$, $m = M/P\bar{Y}$, and $y = Y/\bar{Y}$, the financing constraint becomes

$$g + b(1 - k) - ky = (1/P\bar{Y})\dot{M} + (1/iP\bar{Y})\dot{B}.$$

Taking the time derivatives of the definitions of b and m, we have

$$(1/P\bar{Y})\dot{M} = \dot{m} + m(\pi + n);$$

$$(1/P\bar{Y})\dot{B} = \dot{b} + b(\pi + n);$$

where π and n stand for the inflation and the real growth rates—$\dot{P}/P$ and $\dot{\bar{Y}}/\bar{Y}$.

When these relationships are substituted into the budget constraint, the result is

$$\dot{m} + \dot{b} = i[g - ky - m(\pi + n)] + [i(1 - k) - \pi - n]b. \tag{7.9}$$

At full equilibrium, all liquid assets should grow at the underlying growth rate, n. Thus, in a growing economy, some money is issued even when deficits are bond financed, and we define bond financing by setting $\dot{m} = 0$.

Equation 7.9 is sufficient for assessing the stability of the debt/GNP ratio if it is legitimate to ignore fluctuations in the output gap, the interest rate, and the inflation rate through time. This is because equation 7.9 is a simple, first-order differential equation in one variable, b, if y, i, and π are constant. A slightly more general interpretation is possible if Ricardian equivalence is assumed. In that case, variations in y, i, and π can occur through time, but since they do not depend on b in any way, we can evaluate the convergence of b through time as if the other three variables were constant. With either interpretation, convergence to a constant debt/GNP occurs only if $db/db < 0$; given equation 7.9, this condition means that real growth rate must exceed the after-tax real interest rate, $n > i(1 - k) - \pi$. This condition is necessary for convergence, but, as we shall see later, it is not sufficient unless strict Ricardian equivalence holds.

Is it appealing to assume that the real growth rate exceeds the after-tax real interest rate? McCallum (1984) analyzes a model involving agents with infinite lives and money that enters the utility function; his conclusion is that the conditions of optimizing behavior preclude the growth rate's exceeding the interest rate. Burbidge (1984) reaches the same conclusion with an overlapping-generations model. The logic of this result follows from the fact that in full equilibrium, the marginal product of capital equals the real after-tax interest rate (as long as we ignore depreciation). If the growth rate exceeds capital's marginal product, society has sacrificed too much and overaccumulated capital; in such a situation, the return on capital is an amount of future consumption that is less than the amount that can be had by just allowing for ongoing growth, and the current generation of consumers can gain (and no other generation of consumers will lose) by consuming some of the nation's capital stock. Equilibrium involves exhausting such opportunities until the marginal product of capital is driven upward.

Even without formal microeconomic analyses, it is not appealing to assume that the growth rate exceeds the interest rate. If such a proposition were taken as true by people who carry out cost-benefit studies, they would calculate the present value of many of the component costs and benefits as infinity! To see this point, suppose that some cost or benefit item is estimated at x percent of GNP. The present value of this item is then $\int_t^\infty xe^{(n-R)t}$, where R is the after-tax real interest rate. Clearly, if $n > R$, this present value is infinite. To avoid such a situation in cost-benefit studies, analysts always assume $R > n$. If these analysts (or those who rely on their work) are to be internally consistent, they must assume that $R > n$ when considering stabilization policy issues (not just when considering allocation issues). Thus, internal consistency requires that they conclude against macroeconomic stability when bond-financed deficits are involved.

7.5 THE DESIRABILITY
OF BOND-FINANCED DEFICITS

Since macroeconomic policy in the 1980s has involved heavy reliance on the bond financing of very large budget deficits, it is clear that policymakers do not feel constrained by the microeconomic analyses and cost-benefit study considerations just discussed. For further comment on this issue then, it is useful to separate two issues: the feasibility and the desirability of bond-financed deficits. By the question of feasibility, we mean whether macroeconomic convergence can occur—that is, whether the bonds/output ratio converges to a steady-state value. By the question of desirability, we mean whether the deviations of actual output from full information output are smaller with bond-financed deficits than with money-financed deficits. The strategy in this section is to presume feasibility, even without the involvement of Ricardian equivalence, and to focus on the question of desirability.

A linear discrete-time version of the government budget constraint is required to facilitate a standard rational expectations analysis. We can obtain the linear approximation of equation 7.9 by using the Taylor series expansion. With full equilibrium values denoted by bars above variables, this approximation has the form $xy \simeq \bar{x}\bar{y} + \bar{x}(y - \bar{y}) + \bar{y}(x - \bar{x})$. Applying this technique to equation 7.9 and taking g and k as constant, we obtain the linear approximation

$$\dot{i}m + \dot{b} = \bar{i}[g - ky - (n + \bar{\pi})m - (\bar{m} + \bar{b})\pi] + (n\bar{b}/\bar{i})i \qquad (7.10)$$
$$+ [\bar{i}(1 - k) - \bar{\pi} - n]b.$$

Notice that irrelevant constant terms have been dropped here.

The discrete-time versions of equation 7.10 are now written for the two extreme assumptions about deficit financing: pure money financing ($\dot{b} = 0$), as proposed by Friedman in 1948, and pure bond financing ($\dot{m} = 0$), as advocated by Friedman in 1959.

$$m_t = (1 - n - \bar{\pi})m_{t-1} + g - ky_{t-1} - (\bar{m} + \bar{b})(p_t - p_{t-1}) + ai_{t-1}; \qquad (7.11)$$

$$b_t = \bar{i}(g - ky_{t-1}) - \bar{i}(\bar{m} + \bar{b})(p_t - p_{t-1}) + a\bar{i}i_{t-1} \qquad (7.12)$$
$$+ [1 + \bar{i}(1 - k) - \pi - n]b_{t-1}.$$

Lower case p stands for the logarithm of the price level, and $a = n\bar{b}/(\bar{i})^2$. Again, irrelevant constant terms are dropped.

The remainder of a conventional rational expectations macro model can be specified as follows:

$$y_t = \alpha m_t + \beta b_t + \gamma g - \delta k + \psi E_{t-1}(p_{t+1} - p_t) + u_t; \qquad (7.13)$$

$$\bar{y}_t = 1 + v_t; \qquad (7.14)$$

$$p_t - p_{t-1} = E_{t-1}(\bar{p}_t) - \bar{p}_{t-1} + \theta(y_{t-1} - \bar{y}_{t-1}). \qquad (7.15)$$

The new symbols are as follows: $\bar{p}_t$ is the value of the log of price that makes output equal its capacity value (that is, $y_t = \bar{y}_t$); $\bar{y}_t$ is capacity, defined as the value of output that would occur if there were no expectational errors; $E_{t-1}(p_{t+1})$ is the value for p_{t+1} that is expected as of period $t-1$; and u_t and v_t are stochastic shocks with zero means, constant variances, and no serial or cross correlation.

Equation 7.13 is a linear version of the standard expectations-augmented *IS–LM* system with the nominal interest rate substituted out. The u_t term is an aggregate demand shock, and the standard sign assumptions apply (all parameters are positive except β, which is ambiguous). Equation 7.14 specifies that capacity output differs from the natural rate by a stochastic term, v_t, which represents aggregate supply shocks. Finally, equation 7.15 is McCallum's (1980) sticky price aggregate supply function, which we discussed in earlier chapters. This relationship makes the price level predetermined at a point in time, but preserves the natural rate properties of the model in the longer run.

To solve the model, we substitute either equation 7.11 or 7.12 into 7.13 to eliminate m_t or b_t and solve the result for p_t. In the case of money-financed deficits, we have

$$
\begin{aligned}
p_t = [\alpha(1 - n - \bar{\pi})m_{t-1} &+ (\alpha + \gamma)g - \delta k + \beta b_t + a\alpha i_{t-1} \\
&+ \alpha(\bar{m} + \bar{b})p_{t-1} + \psi E_{t-1}(p_{t+1}) + u_t - \alpha k y_{t-1} \\
&- y_t]/[\alpha(\bar{m} + \bar{b}) + \psi];
\end{aligned}
\tag{7.16}
$$

$$
\begin{aligned}
\bar{p}_t = [\alpha(1 - n - \bar{\pi})m_{t-1} &+ (\alpha + \gamma)g - \delta k + \beta b_t + a\alpha i_{t-1} \\
&+ \alpha(\bar{m} + \bar{b})p_{t-1} + \psi E_{t-1}(p_{t+1}) + u_t - \alpha k y_{t-1} \\
&- \bar{y}_t]/[\alpha(\bar{m} + \bar{b}) + \psi].
\end{aligned}
\tag{7.17}
$$

Using equations 7.16 and 7.17 to obtain expressions for $p_t - E_{t-1}(\bar{p}_t)$ and $p_{t-1} - \bar{p}_{t-1}$, and substituting these expressions and the definition $\hat{y}_t = y_t - \bar{y}_t$ into equation 7.15, we have

$$
\hat{y}_t = (1 - \theta\phi)\hat{y}_{t-1} + u_t - v_t,
\tag{7.18}
$$

where $\phi = \alpha(\bar{m} + \bar{b}) + \psi$ in the case of money-financed deficits, and $\phi = \beta\bar{i}(\bar{m} + \bar{b}) + \psi$ in the case of bond-financed deficits.

Following McCallum (1980), we define stabilization policy losses in terms of deviations of actual output from full-information (capacity) output. Specifically, we investigate which financing regime minimizes the asymptotic variance of output deviations, so stabilization policy losses are given by

$$
\sigma_{\hat{y}}^2 = (\sigma_u^2 + \sigma_v^2)/[1 - (1 - \theta\phi)^2],
\tag{7.19}
$$

provided $|\theta\phi| < 1$, or

$$
0 < \theta\phi < 2.
\tag{7.20}
$$

The analysis shows that having the growth rate larger than the after-tax real interest rate is not a sufficient condition for the bonds/output ratio, b, to remain finite under bond financing. Inspection of equation 7.12 shows that this condition is helpful, but it also shows that output, inflation, and the interest rate must not continue to move systematically, and condition 7.20 is required to preclude their doing so. Notice, furthermore, that θ and ϕ are independent of n. Thus, the relative magnitude of the growth rate and the interest rate is irrelevant for deciding the desirability of money or bond financing as measured in equation 7.19, and (as just mentioned) it is not even sufficient to determine the feasibility of bond financing.

The analysis indicates that the relative desirability of the two methods of deficit financing cannot be decided without recourse to some quantitative assumptions. Certainly, $\sigma_{\tilde{y}}^2$ is lower under money financing if $\alpha > \beta \bar{i}$. We can get some feel for whether this condition is met by considering the standard *IS–LM* aggregate demand model in two special cases. First, assume that Ricardian equivalence holds; then $\beta = 0$, and money financing is definitely preferred. Second, consider the case in which Ricardian equivalence does not hold and in which current income effects are quantitatively much more important than wealth effects. In this case, bonds have an effect on aggregate demand that is exactly the same as that of any standard transfer payment; it is simply the government expenditure multiplier scaled down by the factor $(1 - k)$ times the marginal propensity to consume, MPC. Hence, the condition for preferring money-financed deficits is

$$\begin{matrix} \text{money multiplier} & & \text{government expenditure} & & \\ \text{on aggregate} & > & \text{multiplier on} & [\bar{i} \text{ MPC} (1 - k)]. & (7.21) \\ \text{demand} & & \text{aggregate demand} & & \end{matrix}$$

Most monetarists consider the money multiplier on aggregate demand to be greater than the government expenditure multiplier. In any event, all the terms within the square brackets in equation 7.21 are fractions. There is no controversy about the following values: $\bar{i} = 0.03$, MPC $= 0.8$, $k = 0.4$. Thus, analysts who believe bond-financed deficits are desirable must expect the government expenditure multiplier to be 69 times larger than the money multiplier. Surely few economists would push this proposition.

The intuition here runs as follows. The more quickly budget deficits resulting from shocks are closed, the less output deviations persist. Deficits are closed quickly if the money or bond issue has a larger short-run effect on output. (For this reason, a large money multiplier on aggregate demand—a high value of α—keeps the asymptotic variance of output deviations low under money financing.) Since the money price of bonds $(1/\bar{i})$ is so much higher than the price of money (unity), the number of bonds needed to cover any given budget deficit is much smaller than the amount of money that must be issued for the same purpose. Thus, for the deficit to be closed quickly, the bond multiplier on aggregate demand would have to be much larger than the money multiplier. This argument is simply not plausible; bonds do not have a multiplier effect on aggregate demand that is so much larger than the effect of money. Thus, even if bond-financed deficits are feasible, they are not desirable. Scarth (1987a) considers several variations of this model, establishing the generality of this stricture against inordinate reliance on bond-financed deficits.

Throughout this chapter, we have limited discussion to the polar cases of financing deficits purely with money and purely with bonds; as a result, we have not provided any definition of how much reliance on bond financing is inordinate. To pursue this application issue further would take us beyond the scope of this text, but perhaps one observation is worthwhile. During the past 30 years in Canada, the proportion of federal government financing requirements met by bond issue has never averaged less than 75 percent. The widely acknowledged crises in macro policy-making have occurred only during periods when the proportion exceeded 94 percent. These two facts suggest that macroeconomic instability does not emerge until the reliance on bond financing is quite heavy. It is noteworthy, however, that the Canadian government has exceeded this 94 percent mark throughout the 1980s.

7.6 CONCLUSIONS

This chapter has had two purposes: to demonstrate the methodology used for analyzing the intrinsic dynamics of a model, and to examine alternative methods of financing government deficits.

First we explained how macroeconomic analysis must be altered to allow for intrinsic dynamics—the dynamics that are an integral part of a model because they stem from the accumulation *identities* that relate certain stock and flow variables. Our analysis has only scratched the surface of this overall issue. To pursue it further, the reader must study models whose primary focus is longer-run growth issues, rather than shorter-run stabilization questions.

The second theme of this chapter flowed from the first: as an example of the implications of intrinsic dynamics, we looked at constraints on the financing of government budget deficits. This focus was motivated by the record levels of deficits that have occurred in the 1980s. Influential economists have used the presumption that pure bond financing is infeasible to offer an explanation of why the disinflation policy of the early 1980s took so long to work. Sargent and Wallace (1981) note that if the fiscal deficit is exogenously set and if bond financing can be used only temporarily, a reduction in money issue today must mean an increased reliance on money issue in the future. They show that, therefore, rational agents would not necessarily expect the inflation rate to fall along with the current money-growth rate. By explaining the presumption that bond financing is infeasible as a long-run alternative, this chapter has facilitated an understanding of this important policy debate.

The ultimate issue is which policy variables—the fiscal or the monetary instruments—should be set residually. Macroeconomic policy in many countries in the 1980s has involved imposing monetary policy as a constraint on fiscal decisions, an approach that has led to extreme reliance on bond-financed deficits and a dramatic increase in debt/GNP ratios. The analysis of this chapter indicates that it might well be more appropriate for monetary policy to be determined residually, as Friedman originally proposed in 1948. As long as fiscal parameters are set so that the budget deficit averages zero, this arrangement would control the longer-run growth in the money supply and, therefore, the underlying inflation rate. It would also have the advantage of avoiding the instabilities associated with inordinate reliance on bond financing. But these benefits can be had only if the fiscal policy record is consistent and credible. Friedman gave up expecting this in 1959, and he switched to supporting an exogenous monetary policy, even for the short run. Most central banks have adopted his later view. Yet the analysis of this chapter suggests that this exogenous monetary policy involves a decrease in the built-in stability properties of the macroeconomy. This outcome is the legacy of the fiscal policies of earlier periods that produced deficits even during the boom phase of business cycles.

CHAPTER 8

AN INTRODUCTION TO OPEN-ECONOMY MACROECONOMICS

8.1 INTRODUCTION

The last 20 years have seen an increased international interdependence, as controls on capital flows between countries have been much reduced. Also, since the early 1970s, many countries have permitted much more flexibility in their exchange rates. These developments have raised several issues: how does the exchange-rate regime affect the efficacy of domestic monetary and fiscal policies undertaken by small, open economies? why have exchange rates been so volatile, and why do they appear to diverge, for significant periods of time, from the fundamental determinant of exchange rates (differences in inflation rates across countries)? can expansionary policies in one group of countries lead to contractionary effects on their trading partners? In response to questions such as these, many analysts have contributed to the rapid development of open-economy macro models. The purpose of this chapter and the next is to survey some of these developments.

We shall start in this chapter by explaining the model that forms the basis of all this work—the Mundell (1963)/Fleming (1962) model; it is an open-economy version of the standard fixed-price *IS–LM* system. Then, in Chapter 9, we shall consider several extensions of this basic framework: particularly, rationally formed exchange-rate expectations, variable goods prices, the macroeconomic effects of changes in the world price of primary commodities, and stock/flow issues.

8.2 THE STANDARD MUNDELL/FLEMING MODEL

The standard model is a simplification of the system defined by the following equations. (It is convenient to explain this more detailed structure here and then to introduce the simplifying assumptions. After the simplest model is analyzed, we shall reintroduce, in stages, a number of the complicating features in Chapter 9.)

$$Y = C(Y^d) + I(r) + G + X(EP^x/P^d) - \frac{EP^m}{P^d} \cdot IM\left(Y^d, \frac{EP^m}{P^d}\right); \qquad (8.1)$$

$$Y^d = P^d Y/P; \qquad (8.2)$$

$$P = \gamma P^d + (1 - \gamma)EP^m; \qquad (8.3)$$

$$P \cdot L(Y, r) = D + R; \qquad (8.4)$$

$$\dot{R} = P^d\left[X\left(\frac{EP^x}{P^d}\right) - \frac{EP^m}{P^d} \cdot IM\left(Y^d, \frac{EP^m}{P^d}\right)\right] + K\left(r - r^f - \frac{\dot{E}}{E}\right); \qquad (8.5)$$

$$Y = F(N); \qquad (8.6)$$

$$\overline{W} = P^d \cdot F_N(N). \qquad (8.7)$$

Equation 8.1 is the demand-equals-supply condition for the domestically produced good, whose price is P^d. The good is either bought by domestic households, firms, or government, or it is exported, X, to foreigners. Since C, I, and G stand for total spending by these groups (on both the domestically produced good and on imports), imports, IM, must be subtracted to avoid overstating demand for the domestically produced good. But, since imports and the domestically produced good are different commodities, this subtraction must be accomplished in domestic good units. That is why imports are multiplied by their world price, P^m, yielding their measure in units of foreign exchange. The exchange rate, E, is the domestic currency price of one unit of foreign currency, so $EP^m IM$ measures imports in domestic currency units. Finally, by dividing by P^d, imports are measured in the same physical units as the domestically produced good. The imports are assumed to be final goods or services.

Exchange-rate changes involve both substitution and income effects. The substitution effects are involved by assuming $X_E = \partial X/\partial(EP^x/P^d) > 0$ and $IM_E = \partial IM/\partial(EP^m/P^d) < 0$. If the good that the domestic economy exports is indistinguishable from the goods available elsewhere, the foreign demand function for the domestic product is infinitely elastic: $X_E \rightarrow \infty$. In this case, what is known as purchasing power parity would obtain: $P^d = EP^x$. We shall not focus on this special case, however, since purchasing power parity is observed only in longer-run, average terms.

The income effects of exchange-rate changes are specified in equations 8.2 and 8.3. The basis for calculating the agents' real income is, of course, the total value of real production, Y. The nominal value of this income is $P^d Y$; to get the real spending value of this amount, we divide by the average price of the goods purchased by domestic residents, P. This price index is defined in equation 8.3, where γ and $1 - \gamma$ are the average propensities to spend on the domestically produced good and the imported good, respectively. In a closed economy, $\gamma = 1$, so $Y^d = Y$ when taxes are ignored. This is not true for an open economy. This income effect of the exchange rate is usually referred to as the Laursen/Metzler effect.

Equation 8.4 is the LM curve. It is standard, except that the central bank balance sheet is used to define the money supply. The central bank has two assets: D, the quantity of government bonds it holds, and R, the official stock of foreign exchange reserves (measured in domestic currency units). Whenever the bank purchases these assets, its liabilities, which consist of the stock of high-powered money (the monetary base), increase in a one-for-one fashion. (As in our discussion of intrinsic dynamics in Chapter 7, no private banking system is considered here, so the monetary base and the money supply are the same variable.)

Equation 8.5 introduces some intrinsic dynamics into the system. It states that the change in the official holdings of foreign exchange reserves must equal the excess of the sources over the uses of foreign exchange that flow into and out of the economy during each market period. This change in reserve holdings is the balance of payments; we measure it in domestic currency units, and we denote it by $\dot{R}$. Foreign exchange is used for imports; it is earned through selling goods, $X - IM$, or financial assets to the rest of the world. Net exports constitute the current account of the balance of payments. K stands for the inflow of foreign exchange that follows from the net sales of financial assets to foreigners. This net capital inflow constitutes the capital account in the balance of payments. It is assumed that the net capital inflow depends positively on the expected yield differential between domestic and foreign bonds. From a domestic resident's point of view, the yield on a domestic bond is r, and the yield on a foreign bond is $r^f + \dot{E}/E$. When domestic residents hold foreign bonds, they receive the direct interest payment, as well as a capital gain if the foreign currency appreciates during the holding period. We assume that the interest rates can be observed at each instant so there is no need for agents to forecast them. We shall ignore the exchange-rate effect until section 9.2, where we shall assume rational expectations—or at least perfect foresight. That is why the actual (not the expected) percentage change in the exchange rate has been included in the capital inflow function, for this introduction to the topic.

In a sense, both equation 8.4 and the net capital inflow function must be satisfied for the domestic bond market to be clearing. To appreciate this point, assume that domestic residents hold only domestic money and bonds and that foreigners hold their money, their bonds, and our (domestic) bonds. Although a stock/flow misspecification is involved here (we shall correct it in the next chapter), the K function must be interpreted as specifying the foreigners' demand for domestic bonds. Thus, equation 8.4 *and* the satisfaction of the K function imply that the domestic bond market is clearing.

Analysts often assume that the domestic economy is small vis-à-vis the world bond market—that perfect capital mobility exists. This situation can be specified in one of two ways: deriving the general multipliers expressions and then letting $K_r = \partial K / \partial(r - r^f - \dot{E}/E)$ approach infinity, or assuming perfect capital mobility from the outset by setting $r = r^f + \dot{E}/E$, and dropping equation 8.5 from the analysis (since that equation is essentially overridden by the assumption of completely passive behavior on the part of foreign bond holders).

Equations 8.6 and 8.7 are the production function and the labor market-clearing condition. The form used here is generally referred to as a Keynesian specification of the labor market since it has employment determined by the intersection of the labor demand curve and the given money-wage line, $\bar{W}$. Note that only the price of the domestically produced good is of interest to firms in calculating the marginal revenue product of labor.

The endogenous variables are Y, Y^d, P, P^d, N, and r plus E if the exchange rate is flexible or R and $\dot{R}$ if the exchange rate is fixed. Under fixed exchange rates, the model contains intrinsic dynamics. In the short run, the stock of reserves, R, is predetermined by previous history, and the balance of payments, $\dot{R}$, is endogenous. The long run is defined by the condition that endogenous variables stay constant, so $\dot{R} = 0$ by definition. In this case, R (reinterpreted to denote the final equilibrium value of reserves) is endogenous.

Rather than work with this fairly complicated system from the outset, we shall now list the standard simplifying assumptions (which were used, at least implicitly, by Mundell and Fleming). With fixed coefficient technology, $F_{NN} = 0$. This assumption and equation 8.7 imply that P^d is constant and can be set at unity. Also, to eliminate the Laursen/Metzler effect, we assume $\gamma = P^x = P^m = 1$, so the domestic consumer price index, P, also equals unity and $Y^d = Y$. This means that there are horizontal marginal cost curves both at home and abroad. The model is still not entirely a fixed-price one, however, as long as the exchange rate is flexible. Also, this second assumption is clearly a misspecification, since γ cannot really equal one unless imports do not exist. Despite this embarrassment, we shall follow the convention of accepting this simplification, so that we can explain the standard results. The final simplification is to ignore speculation in the foreign exchange market—that is, to drop the $\dot{E}/E$ term in equation 8.5.

The resulting simpler model can be written as

$$Y = C(Y) + I(r) + G + X(E) - E \cdot IM(Y, E); \tag{8.8}$$

$$L(Y, r) = D + R; \tag{8.9}$$

$$\dot{R} = X(E) - E \cdot IM(Y, E) + K(r - r^f). \tag{8.10}$$

After taking the total differential of equations 8.8 through 8.10 and arranging them in matrix form, we have

$$
\begin{bmatrix}
1 - C_Y + E \cdot IM_Y & -I_r & 0 \\
L_Y & L_r & 0 \\
-E \cdot IM_Y & K_r & -1
\end{bmatrix}
\begin{bmatrix}
dY \\
dr \\
d\dot{R}
\end{bmatrix}
=
\begin{bmatrix}
1 & 0 & 0 & A & 0 \\
0 & 1 & 1 & 0 & 0 \\
0 & 0 & 0 & -A & K_r
\end{bmatrix}
\begin{bmatrix}
dG \\
dD \\
dR \\
dE \\
dr^f
\end{bmatrix}
, \tag{8.11}
$$

where $A = X_E - E \cdot IM_E - IM \gtrless 0$. The sign of expression A is considered in section 8.5.

We shall now consider three cases: the impact period in a fixed-exchange-rate regime; full equilibrium under fixed exchange rates; and flexible exchange rates. With no intervention in the foreign exchange market by the central bank under flexible exchange rates, there are no intrinsic dynamics and so there is no distinction between the impact period and full equilibrium.

8.3 FIXED EXCHANGE RATES: THE IMPACT PERIOD

Our first analysis of the simplified model is of the impact period under a regime of fixed exchange rates. $Y, r,$ and $\dot{R}$ are the endogenous variables. The matrices of equation 8.11 apply.

Except for the $E \cdot IM_Y$ term, the fiscal and monetary policy multipliers, dY/dG and dY/dD, that follow are exactly the same as those for a closed economy, so they are not presented. The stability condition can be derived by evaluating $d\dot{R}/dR$ from the matrices, using Cramer's rule:

$$\frac{d\dot{R}}{dR} = \frac{K_r(1 - C_Y + E \cdot IM_Y) - I_r E \cdot IM_Y}{L_r(1 - C_Y + E \cdot IM_Y) + I_r L_Y} < 0.$$

Since $d\dot{R}/dR < 0$, the model is necessarily stable; it is, therefore, sensible to derive full-equilibrium multipliers. It also is noteworthy that $d\dot{R}/dR \rightarrow -\infty$ as $K_r \rightarrow \infty$, so the time path for the reserve stock becomes the solid step function shown in Figure 8.1, instead of the curve showing asymptotic approach to full equilibrium (which obtains when the law of one price does *not* hold in the world bond market). This time path means that the adjustment to the long run takes place immediately in the special case that is usually referred to as perfect capital mobility.

Figure 8.1 The Time Path of Foreign Exchange Reserves with Varying Degrees of Capital Mobility

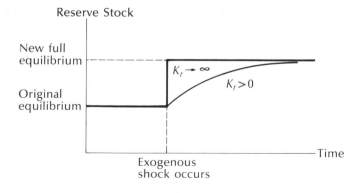

Many analysts regard the assumption of perfect capital mobility as an excellent approximation for small, open economies, and Boothe et al. (1986) verify that this common practice is quite appropriate for Canada. As a result, we emphasize the perfect capital mobility case here and so regard the full equilibrium effects as results that are fully relevant for *short-run* stabilization policy questions.

8.4 FIXED EXCHANGE RATES: FULL EQUILIBRIUM

Full equilibrium obtains when the balance of payments, $\dot{R}$, is zero and thus the *LM* curve is not shifting. The endogenous variables are $Y, r,$ and R.

To derive the full-equilibrium multipliers, we must transpose the $d\dot{R}$ and dR columns in the matrices in equation 8.11 and then use Cramer's rule again. The results are

$$\frac{dY}{dG} = \frac{K_r}{K_r(1 - C_Y + E \cdot IM_Y) - I_r E \cdot IM_Y} > 0;$$

$$\frac{dY}{dD} = 0;$$

$$\frac{dR}{dD} = -1.$$

By dividing the top and bottom of the fiscal policy multiplier by K_r and then letting $K_r \to \infty$, we see that dY/dG approaches $1/(1 - C_Y + E \cdot IM_Y)$. We conclude that there is a set of assumptions under which simplistic fiscal multipliers (which depend only on direct marginal propensities to respond) apply, and under which monetary policy does not apply. That is, the results for this economy are the same as those that apply to a closed economy in a liquidity trap. Thus, we see that there is a set of more plausible circumstances (a small, open economy under a fixed exchange-rate regime) in which there are no crowding-out effects from changes in interest rates. It is reassuring that most policy analysts who think in these terms also favor fixed exchange rates (so that a case can be made for the internal consistency of their views).

It is left for the reader to derive this case's other multipliers, such as the effects on the domestic economy of a devaluation or an increase in foreign interest rates. The reader can verify that $dY/dE > 0$, so a devaluation of the domestic currency stimulates aggregate demand, and that $dY/dr^f < 0$, so an increase in foreign interest rates causes a recession.

To many analysts, this prediction concerning foreign interest rate increases seems consistent with the experience of the early 1980s, when the United States dramatically increased its interest rate levels and other countries also had recessions. It must be emphasized, however, that a model of a small, open economy precludes questions about rest-of-the-world developments from being well posed. For example, if foreign interest rates go up because of a monetary contraction in the rest of the world, the domestic economy will face *both* higher world interest rates *and* a reduction in exports (following from the decreased level of income in the rest of the world). Conversely, if foreign interest rates go up because of a fiscal expansion in the rest of the world, the domestic economy will face both the rise in world interest rates and an expansion in exports. Yet the dY/dr^f multiplier in our model ignores these direct shifts in the *IS* curve. To gain a more complete analysis of shocks that occur in the rest of the world, economists analyze two-country models. (See Argy and Salop 1983 for a representative example.)

8.5 FLEXIBLE EXCHANGE RATES

In our third case, a regime of flexible interest rates obtains. Since the central bank is now not intervening in the foreign exchange market, it makes no asset trades, and we need not distinguish between impact-period and full-equilibrium results.

By transposition, we arrange the matrices of equation 8.11 so that the left-hand matrix has columns in dY, dr, and dE (the three endogenous variables under flexible exchange rates). The monetary and fiscal policy multipliers are

$$\frac{dY}{dG} = \frac{L_r}{L_r(1 - C_Y) + I_r L_Y - K_r L_Y} > 0$$

and

$$\frac{dY}{dD} = \frac{I_r - K_r}{L_r(1 - C_Y) + I_r L_Y - K_r L_Y} > 0.$$

Since both these derivations involve a canceling off of expression A (which was defined earlier as $X_E - E \cdot IM_E - IM \gtreqless 0$), they involve the presumption that A does not equal zero, a presumption we consider later in this section. In the case of perfect capital mobility, $K_r \to \infty$, these multipliers become $dY/dG \to 0$ and $dY/dD \to 1/L_Y$. Thus, there is a set of assumptions under which the simplistic quantity theory of money applies and fiscal policy does not matter. That is, it is as if the *LM* curve is vertical. It is reassuring that economists who discuss policy in these terms favor flexible exchange rates, since we have just established that unless $L_r = 0$, floating exchange rates are required to establish the plausibility of these monetarist views.

Again, it is left for the reader to derive other multipliers, such as the effects of increases in foreign interest rates. Under a regime of floating exchange rates, the result of a hike in foreign interest rates is $dY/dr^f > 0$, so foreign interest rate hikes cause a boom in the domestic economy. The reasoning is that the temporarily higher foreign interest rate attracts funds away from the domestic economy. The decreased demand for the domestic currency causes it to depreciate, stimulating net exports (by making domestic exports cheaper for foreigners to buy and imports more expensive for domestic residents to buy). Many analysts react to this particular result by arguing that it is inconsistent with what they observed in the early 1980s. When the United States raised its interest rates dramatically, other countries of the Organisation for Economic Co-operation and Development (OECD) suffered a recession, not a boom, despite allowing considerable flexibility in exchange rates.

The fact that our basic model predicts a recession following an increase in foreign interest rates only in the case of fixed exchange rates suggests to some analysts that a modification in the model is required to make its predictions for a regime of floating exchange rates consistent with the stylized facts. The modification usually proposed is to incorporate flexible goods prices—that is, to allow supply-side effects from the currency depreciation. (We shall consider these cost-increasing effects in the next chapter.) It should be pointed out again, however, that questions concerning foreign shocks are not well posed with models of a *small*, open economy because the interdependencies within the rest of the world are left unspecified.

Let us now consider dynamic convergence under a regime of flexible exchange rates. Since we have not specified any intrinsic dynamics in the floating-exchange-rate version of the model, we must make some sort of out-of-equilibrium assumptions to perform a stability analysis. (Of course, we could have assumed lack of market clearing in the fixed-exchange-rate case too. However, in that case we followed convention, ignoring the possibility of sluggish market adjustment, to keep the dynamic analysis as simple as possible—that is, involving only one differential equation.)

The set of sluggish market-adjustment assumptions that is common for analyzing convergence under flexible exchange rates is

$$\dot{Y} = a(C + I + G + X - E \cdot IM - Y) \qquad a > 0;$$

$$\dot{E} = b(X - E \cdot IM + K) \qquad b < 0.$$

These equations state that output increases whenever aggregate demand exceeds aggregate supply, and that the value of the domestic currency rises (E falls) whenever there is an excess supply of foreign exchange (a balance of payments surplus). The full-equilibrium version of the model (equations 8.8 and 8.10) involves the assumptions that the adjustment parameters a and b are infinitely large. We can substitute in the functions for consumption, investment, exports, imports, and net capital inflows and use the *LM* relationship (equation 8.9) to eliminate the interest rate. We are then left with two differential equations for output and the exchange rate. The standard stability requirements—that the determinant be positive and the trace negative—hold if and only if expression A (which equals $X_E - E \cdot IM_E - IM$) exceeds zero. Hence the presumption of stability insures that $A \neq 0$.

Many writers on international finance (in contrast to general macroeconomists) discuss the stability of the foreign exchange market as if it were one market in isolation; that is, they assume our $\dot{E}$ equation but take Y and r as constants. Their result is that stability requires the Marshall/Lerner condition: starting from balanced trade, the sum of the export and import elasticities must exceed unity.

Our $A > 0$ is the same condition. To see this identity, define the export and import elasticities as

$$\eta_{XE} = \frac{\partial X/X}{\partial E/E} = X_E\left(\frac{E}{X}\right);$$

$$\eta_{IM \cdot E} = \frac{-\partial IM/IM}{\partial E/E} = -IM_E\left(\frac{E}{IM}\right).$$

Using these definitions to eliminate X_E and IM_E in the equation that defines A, we have

$$A = IM\left[\eta_{XE}\left(\frac{X}{E \cdot IM}\right) + \eta_{IM \cdot E} - 1\right].$$

8.6 GRAPHIC SUMMARY FOR THE SMALL, OPEN ECONOMY

We shall close this chapter by providing a graphic interpretation of the monetary and fiscal policy multipliers, in the case of perfect capital mobility. The fiscal policy effects are shown in Figure 8.2. The economy starts at point A in both panels of the diagram. With an increase in government spending the *IS* curve shifts to the right, so there is pressure to move to point B in the *IS–LM* diagram. But this move would involve a domestic interest rate that exceeds the foreign interest rate. What precludes this situation is an inflow of funds as foreigners acquire domestic bonds. To do this, foreigners must supply more foreign currency to the foreign exchange market, so the supply curve in the right-hand diagram shifts out. If the exchange rate is floating, E falls to the value given by point

Figure 8.2 Fiscal Policy with Perfect Capital Mobility

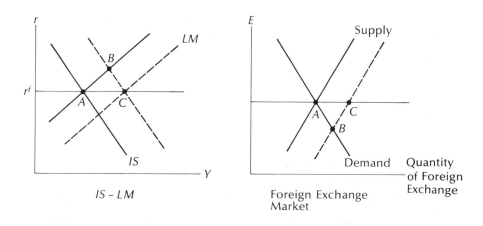

B. The appreciation of the domestic currency means that net exports are reduced, so the *IS* curve shifts back to its original position, and $dY/dG = 0$. If the exchange rate is fixed, the domestic central bank must purchase the otherwise unwanted foreign currency that is coming in (amount *AC* in the right-hand diagram) and pay for it by issuing domestic currency. Thus, the *LM* curve shifts to the right, and the increase in output is given by distance *AC* in the left-hand diagram.

Figure 8.3 Monetary Policy with Perfect Capital Mobility

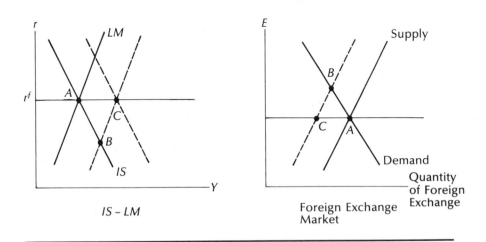

IS – LM

Foreign Exchange Market

Monetary policy effects are shown in Figure 8.3. Again, the economy starts at point *A* in both panels. With an increase in the money supply (a higher *D*), the *LM* curve shifts to the right, so there is pressure to move to point *B* in the *IS–LM* diagram. But that shift would involve a domestic interest rate less than the foreign rate; this tendency causes a capital outflow, so the supply curve for foreign exchange shifts to the left. If the exchange rate is floating, *E* increases to point *B*. This depreciation of the domestic currency stimulates net exports, so the *IS* curve shifts to the right and the economy moves to point *C* in the left-hand diagram. If the exchange rate is fixed, however, the domestic central bank must supply the otherwise unavailable foreign exchange (amount *CA* in the right-hand diagram) and receive previously circulating domestic money in payment. As a result, the *LM* curve shifts back to the left, and the economy is unable to move from point *A* in the *IS–LM* diagram.

8.7 CONCLUSIONS

When the Mundell/Fleming model is applied to a *small*, open economy, we have seen that monetary policy works through exchange rates, not interest rates, and that the crowding-out effect of fiscal policy works through exchange rates, not interest rates. Most analysts conclude that these predictions have been solidly confirmed by experience. For example, Scarth (1979) shows that fiscal policy failed to affect aggregate demand significantly under floating exchange rates during the 1958–62 battle between the Canadian government and the Bank of Canada (which involved easy fiscal and tight monetary policy). Another example noted by Scarth concerns the way monetary policy was tried but was quickly nullified during 1969–70, when the Bank of Canada tried to have a more contractionary policy than the United States, under fixed-exchange-rate regimes.

The prediction concerning the irrelevance of fiscal policy for aggregate demand under floating exchange rates can be generalized to say that any foreign shock that shifts the domestic *IS* curve in a similar way (such as increases in P^x and P^m or foreign tariff changes) has no effect on aggregate demand. However, this "insulation" property of floating exchange rates does not keep domestic price and output from being affected when the analysis involves temporary exchange-rate overshooting or supply-side effects of exchange rates. It is to these extensions of the standard open-economy model that we shall turn in the next chapter.

CHAPTER 9

THE OPEN ECONOMY: RECENT CONTRIBUTIONS

9.1 INTRODUCTION

The purpose of this chapter is to extend our analysis of a small, open economy to allow for several important phenomena. It is obvious to anyone who pays attention to the daily news about exchange rates that participants in the foreign exchange market allow their expectations of exchange-rate changes to affect their actions significantly. Thus, we cannot leave our discussion of open-economy stabilization policy with the assumption of static expectations (as we did in Chapter 8). To correct this deficiency, we shall consider rationally formed exchange-rate expectations.

The second extension that is considered in this chapter is variable prices. We shall elaborate the aggregate supply side of the model by considering imports as intermediate products. This change makes the exchange rate a shift variable for the aggregate supply curve; it also facilitates an analysis of changes in the world price of primary commodities.

The third extension involves correcting a misspecification in the Mundell/ Fleming model: the treatment of stocks and flows in the balance of payments. This correction is important not only to improve the logical consistency of the model but also to facilitate a discussion of problems of international indebtedness.

For pedagogic convenience, we shall consider each of these extensions in turn, rather than simultaneously.

9.2 EXCHANGE-RATE EXPECTATIONS

There has been increased flexibility in exchange rates during the last 15 years, and one of the surprises of this experience is that exchange rates have been more volatile than most analysts expected. Dornbusch (1976) shows that overshooting in the exchange rate can easily occur in a model in which exchange rates adjust more quickly than goods prices. Product prices that are sluggish and cannot adjust as much in the short run as they do in the long run can force more adjustment for the exchange rate in the short run than is required in the long run.

Dornbusch's analysis is based on closed-economy models involving over-shooting that were constructed by Tucker (1966) and Laidler (1968). These earlier studies involve a fixed-price *IS–LM* model with either partial adjustment or the permanent-income hypothesis. (For example, with consumption depending on permanent income, current consumption and income do not adjust as much within a short period as they do in full equilibrium. This forces the interest rate to overshoot its long-run response.) Dornbusch extends the perfect capital mobility version of the Mundell/Fleming flexible-exchange-rate model to allow for exchange-rate expectations and interprets the resulting overshooting as explaining exchange-rate volatility. Dornbusch's model is defined by the following equations (all the variables except the interest rates are measured in logarithms):

$$y = a + b(e + p^f - p) - hr; \tag{9.1}$$

$$m - p = ky - gr; \tag{9.2}$$

$$r = r^f + \dot{e}; \tag{9.3}$$

$$\dot{p} = f(y - \bar{y}). \tag{9.4}$$

Equation 9.1 defines a standard *IS* relation: aggregate demand depends positively on the terms of trade and negatively on the interest rate. Equations 9.2 and 9.4 are standard *LM* and Phillips curve relationships. Since Dornbusch assumes that the money growth rate is zero, we do not need a steady-state inflation term in the Phillips curve; also, for simplicity, we do not distinguish between the nominal and the real interest rate. (Buiter and Miller 1981 show that these limitations do not affect the analysis at all.) Equation 9.3 is the interest parity condition, which states that arbitrage by risk-neutral agents keeps the domestic interest rate equal to the foreign rate plus any expected capital gain that can be had by holding wealth in an asset denominated in the foreign currency. Since the model includes no error terms, the assumption of rational expectations is synonymous with the assumption of perfect foresight. As a result, the anticipated capital gain term is set equal to the actual appreciation of the foreign currency.

There are five endogenous variables to be determined by the four equations: $y, r, \dot{p}, e$, and $\dot{e}$ are determined on the basis of given values for $m, p^f, r^f, a, \bar{y}$, and the preexisting level of p. The price level is predetermined at any point in time, but the exchange rate can jump at any instant. The exchange rate is an asset price that is determined in an auction market; there is no reason for its changes to be pinned down by long-term contracts or some historically given accumulation identity. Since both the level and the rate of change of the exchange rate are endogenous, the model is underdetermined. However, we shall see that all possible solutions except one involve instability, so the initial jump in the exchange rate can be assumed to be that required to insure that this one solution is the operative one.

To explain this determination of the exchange rate fully, we formally consider the dynamics of the system. Equations 9.1 and 9.2 are used to solve for y and r as functions of e and p and the exogenous variables. These expressions are then substituted into equations 9.3 and 9.4 to give

$$\dot{e} = [bk(e + p^f) + (1 - bk)p - m + ka]/(hk + g) - r^f; \tag{9.5}$$

$$\dot{p} = [bg(e + p^f) - (h + gb)p + hm + ga]f/(hk + g) - f\bar{y}. \tag{9.6}$$

To analyze the model graphically, we use equations 9.5 and 9.6 to derive the properties of the $\dot{p} = 0$ and $\dot{e} = 0$ loci. As a representative shock, we consider an increase in r^f, the foreign interest rate. Since r^f enters only equation 9.5, only the $\dot{e} = 0$ locus shifts when the foreign interest rate changes. From equation 9.5 we derive the slope of the $\dot{e} = 0$ locus: $de/dp = 1 - 1/bk$. This locus may be either positively or negatively sloped. Still using equation 9.5, we have $de/dr^f = (hk + g)/bk > 0$, so, in a diagram with the exchange rate on the vertical axis, the $\dot{e} = 0$ locus shifts up with increases in r^f. Also from equation 9.5, $d\dot{e}/de = bk/(hk + g) > 0$, so whenever the observation point in Figure 9.1 is above the $\dot{e} = 0$ locus, the exchange rate must be rising, and whenever the observation point is below the $\dot{e} = 0$ locus, the exchange rate must be falling. These forces pushing the observation point away from full equilibrium represent an unstable characteristic root in the dynamic system.

Now consider the $\dot{p} = 0$ locus. We derive its slope from equation 9.6: $de/dp = 1 + h/bg$. This locus is always positively sloped, and by comparing this slope expression to that given for the $\dot{e} = 0$ locus in the previous paragraph, we know that if the $\dot{e} = 0$ locus is also positively sloped, the $\dot{p} = 0$ locus must be steeper. Also from equation 9.6, we have $d\dot{p}/dp = -f(h + gb)/(hk + g) < 0$, which implies that when the observation point in Figure 9.1 is to the right of the $\dot{p} = 0$ locus, the price level is falling, and when the observation point is to the left of the $\dot{p} = 0$ locus, the price level is rising. These forces pushing the observation point toward full equilibrium represent a stable characteristic root in the dynamic system.

Since one of the two characteristic roots is unstable and since one of the variables (the exchange rate) is free to jump at a point in time, the initial value of that variable can be set at just what is required to preclude the unstable root from operating. In graphic terms this setting constitutes placing the system on the saddle path shown in Figure 9.1.

Full equilibrium in this model exists when all endogenous variables are constant, which requires that $\dot{e} = \dot{p} = 0$. Thus, full equilibrium is determined by the intersection of the $\dot{e} = 0$ and $\dot{p} = 0$ loci. Consider what happens if the economy starts out at some arbitrary price level different from that which occurs at the full equilibrium point A in either panel of Figure 9.1. Will the economy converge to point A? In general, if an arbitrary starting value for the exchange rate is also chosen, the arrows of motion indicate that the system is unstable, so that point A will not be reached. However, if the initial value of the exchange rate is assumed to be on the saddle path (line SS in each panel of the figure), convergence

Figure 9.1 Derivation of the Saddle Path

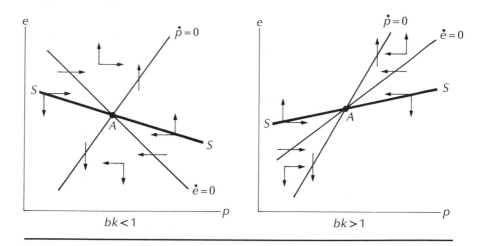

does occur. The standard procedure is to assume that instability does not occur in practice, so the additional restriction that makes the model determinate is that the initial value of the exchange rate jumps to insure that the economy is on the saddle path.

To illustrate the properties of the model, let us examine an increase in the foreign interest rate. We noted earlier that raising r^f shifts the $\dot{e} = 0$ locus up (as shown by the dashed lines in both panels of Figure 9.2). The initial equilibrium is point A. With the higher foreign interest rate, the new full equilibrium is point B, but the economy can move there only gradually, since the price level is not a jump variable. The exchange rate can jump, however, and to avoid instability

Figure 9.2 The Effect of an Increase in Foreign Interest Rates

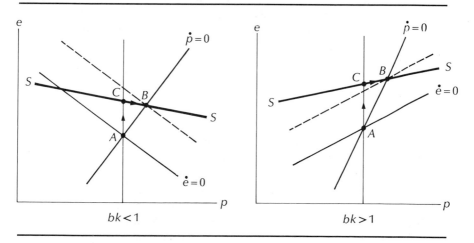

it must jump so that the economy moves to point C instantaneously. Then the economy moves gradually from point C to B. Since an overshoot in the exchange rate is possible, this model can explain the "excess" variability in the exchange rate. Since overshoots in the exchange rate cause overshoots in the level of output, this model has also been used to defend an interventionist policy that limits exchange-rate flexibility to some degree.

Like the simple Mundell/Fleming system, this basic version of the overshooting model does not involve supply-side effects of the exchange rate. As a result, the increase in foreign interest rates causes a temporary boom, not a recession. Buiter and Miller (1981; 1982) extend the overshooting model to allow for these supply-side effects and for nonzero interest rate expectations as well. Their results are similar to Dornbusch's.

Others, such as Buiter and Purvis (1983), have used this framework to consider the effects of domestic resource discoveries. In this case, the domestic currency appreciates, and the overshoot is particularly damaging to the nonresource sector (that is, to manufacturing) since the exchange-rate change reduces the export of manufactures. This spillover effect is thought to explain such things as the 20 percent decline experienced by the United Kingdom's manufacturing sector in the decade following the discovery of North Sea oil. Since this problem was first discussed with reference to the Dutch discovery of natural gas, it is often referred to as the "Dutch disease."

9.3 SUPPLY-SIDE EFFECTS OF EXCHANGE RATES

Two of the biggest macroeconomic shocks to occur in the last 15 years were the dramatic changes in the world prices of primary commodities and in the level of US interest rates. What are the effects of these external events (or of any shock in the terms of trade) on a small, open economy? To answer questions concerning raw materials prices, we must modify the structure of the model so that imports are intermediate products. This modification permits exchange-rate changes to affect the position of the aggregate supply curve. A similar modification of the basic model also allows a fuller analysis of foreign interest rate increases; any resulting depreciation in the domestic currency can have stagflationary effects since it raises the cost curves of domestic firms.

Supply-side effects of exchange rates can be inserted by dropping one of the simplifying assumption used in Chapter 8—that $\gamma = 1$ in equation 8.3. With $\gamma < 1$, this equation, $P = \gamma P^d + (1 - \gamma)EP^m$, implies that a depreciation of the domestic currency raises the cost of living directly. Thus, even if the aggregate supply curve is horizontal (as we assumed in Chapter 8), its position shifts up as a result of the depreciation in the domestic currency. Other things being equal, this effect causes higher prices and lower output. The overall effect on output is ambiguous, however, since this contractionary effect on aggregate supply competes with the standard expansionary effect of domestic currency depreciation on aggregate demand (through the balance of trade, as in the Mundell/Fleming model).

Another way of appreciating these competing effects is to consider the *IS–LM* diagram. In the basic Mundell/Fleming framework, the exchange rate is a shift variable for *IS* but not for *LM*. However, if the cost of living is directly increased by a depreciation in the domestic currency and if it is the general cost of living that deflates the nominal money supply to define real balances in the *LM* curve, the exchange rate becomes a direct shift variable for the *LM* curve. With the exchange rate and the level of output in both the *IS* and the *LM* relationships, more general multiplier effects emerge. For example, the reader can verify that $dY/dr^f \gtreqless 0$ and $dY/dG > 0$ given flexible exchange rates and perfect capital mobility. Fiscal policy now "matters" under floating exchange rates. The reason is that the appreciation in the domestic currency (which follows the temporary pressure for a higher domestic interest rate) decreases the cost of imports and, therefore, the cost of living. Since the general price level is a shift variable for the *LM* curve, this schedule moves to the right when the *IS* curve does. The intersection remains on the world interest rate line, but at a higher level of domestic output.

The other way of introducing the supply-side effects of exchange rates is by allowing for intermediate imports, as we now explain.

If imports are primary commodities (say, raw materials such as oil), it is reasonable to assume that they must be combined with domestic value-added, y, in fixed proportions. Hence,

$$Y = \min(y, IM).$$

We assume a standard neoclassical production function for the value-added operation, and for simplicity we ignore physical capital: $y = F(N)$. Further, we assume that firms hire no inputs that they do not use, and that units are defined so that one unit of domestic value-added and one unit of imports are needed to produce one unit of total product, Y. The resulting production relationships are $Y = y = IM = F(N)$, and, since all imports are intermediate products, $P^d = P$ (that is, the price of the domestically produced good and the general cost of living are the same). To derive the revised labor demand function, we assume that firms maximize profits, $PY - WN - EP^m IM = PF(N) - WN - EP^m F(N)$, by setting the derivative with respect to employment, N, equal to zero. The result is equation 9.11. The full revised model is defined by the following five equations:

$$Y = C(Y^d) + I(r^f) + G + X\left(\frac{EP^x}{P}\right); \tag{9.7}$$

$$Y^d = \left(1 - \frac{EP^m}{P}\right)Y; \tag{9.8}$$

$$\frac{M}{P} = L(Y, r^f); \tag{9.9}$$

$$Y = F(N); \tag{9.10}$$

$$\bar{W} = (P - EP^m)F_N. \tag{9.11}$$

National income, Y^d, is less than domestic product, Y, since part of domestic product (or total sales) must be paid to foreigners for the intermediate input. Similarly, domestic firms only receive a fraction $(1 - EP^m/P)$ of the marginal physical product of labor, so that is what is equated to the real wage for profit maximization. In specifying the model, we assume perfect capital mobility from the outset and return to the assumption of static exchange-rate expectations (by setting $r = r^f$). With the interest rate made exogenous in this way, the equation for the sources and uses of foreign exchange can be dropped, since it simply determines the net capital inflow as a residual. The five-equation system determines Y, Y^d, N, P, and either E or M.

To simplify the multiplier expressions and to come as close as possible to the same simplifying assumptions we used in the basic Mundell/Fleming model, we assume rigid money wages, a constant marginal product of labor, and an initial value of one for the nominal prices. Under these conditions, equation 9.11 can be replaced by

$$dP = dE + EdP^m. \tag{9.11a}$$

Thus, the aggregate supply curve is horizontal, but it shifts up one-for-one with a depreciation of the domestic currency.

The multipliers can be derived by writing the model in compact form as follows. Substitute equation 9.8 into equation 9.7 to eliminate Y^d; take the total differential of the result and equation 9.9; use equation 9.11a to eliminate dE; arrange the result in matrix form and set the initial values of P^x, P^m, and P equal to unity to obtain

$$
\begin{bmatrix}
1 - C_{Yd}(1 - E) & -(1 - E)(X_E - C_{Yd}Y) \\
L_Y & M
\end{bmatrix}
\begin{bmatrix}
dY \\
dP
\end{bmatrix}
=
$$

$$
\begin{bmatrix}
1 & 0 & I_r & EX_E & -EX_E \\
0 & 1 & -L_r & 0 & 0
\end{bmatrix}
\begin{bmatrix}
dG \\
dM \\
dr^f \\
dP^x \\
dP^m
\end{bmatrix}. \tag{9.12}
$$

(Equation 9.10 has not been used, since it just determines employment residually.)

The basic determinant of this system is the determinant of the matrix on the left-hand side of equation 9.12: $\Delta = M[1 - C_{Yd}(1 - E) + L_Y(1 - E)(X_E - C_{Yd}Y)]$. Given the usual assumptions, the sign of Δ is ambiguous, but a sufficient condition for Δ to be positive is $(X_E - C_{Yd}Y) > 0$. The standard method of removing this basic ambiguity in a flexible-exchange-rate model is to assume the Marshall/Lerner condition: that the trade balance (exports minus imports) is increased by a depreciation in the domestic currency; that is, that the partial derivative of $X(EP^x/P) - EP^mY/P$ with respect to E is positive. This partial derivative is $X_E - Y$

when evaluated with initial price values of unity. The Marshall/Lerner assumption that $X_E - Y$ is positive is sufficient to sign the basic determinant ($\Delta > 0$) since $X_E - C_{yd}Y > 0$ is a weaker condition than the Marshall/Lerner condition as long as the marginal propensity to consume is a fraction.

The reader can now readily verify the various policy effects we now discuss. (To perform this verification, use Cramer's rule with equations 9.12.) First, consider fiscal policy, which involved complete crowding out in the simple Mundell/Fleming model that did not have supply-side effects of exchange rates. In the intermediate-imports model, we have $dY/dG > 0$ and $dP/dG < 0$. The increase in government spending raises output and lowers the price level under flexible exchange rates since the temporary upward pressure on the domestic interest rate (from *IS* shifting to the right) causes an appreciation of the domestic currency. This lowers business costs and so causes the aggregate supply curve to move down.

Another real shock is an increase in foreign interest rates. In the intermediate-imports model, the results are $dP/dr^f > 0$ and $dY/dr^f \gtrless 0$. The higher foreign yield causes a depreciation of the domestic currency (as funds leave the domestic economy), and this has both a demand and a supply effect. Net exports are stimulated so the aggregate demand curve shifts up. But the depreciation in domestic currency also raises the cost of intermediate imports and so shifts the horizontal aggregate supply curve upward. With both the demand and the supply curve shifting up, the price level must increase, but the effect on output is ambiguous. The same basic results hold when the marginal product of labor is allowed to vary; the only modification is that the aggregate supply curve is positively sloped. It is clear, then, that this model is certainly capable of explaining the 1970s events that followed the increase in the world price of oil.

The final real disturbance that we discuss is an increase in the world price of the intermediate input, P^m. The results are $dP/dP^m > 0$ and $dY/dP^m < 0$. Firms' costs are increased by this disturbance so the aggregate supply curve shifts up. This is why these stagflationary effects are logically plausible.

A number of authors (for example, Argy and Salop 1983) examine two-country models with supply-side effects of exchange rates. In these analyses, neither country is "small" since both have an impact on the one "world" rate of interest that prevails in both countries. There is also direct interdependence in the goods markets since one country's net exports are the other country's net imports.

One interesting result from these studies concerns "beggar-my-neighbor" effects that occur when one of the countries raises government expenditure. If that country has fixed nominal wages and the second country has fixed *real* wages, there must be stagflation in the second country. This occurs since the first country's policy involves a shift to the right of its *IS* curve and so results in its interest rate's being temporarily higher. This rise attracts foreign funds and so appreciates the first country's currency. But an appreciation of its currency is a depreciation of the second country's currency. This depreciation raises the cost of intermediate imports in the second country so the aggregate supply curve there shifts to the left. This effect is particularly dramatic if there is real wage rigidity in the second country. With money wages tied to increases in goods prices, the labor component of firms' costs in the second country increases as well. In this situation, it turns out that the contractionary effect of the currency depreciation in the second country on its aggregate supply curve *must* dominate the stimulating effect of this depreciation on its aggregate demand curve (and a recession must follow).

When expansion in one country leads to recession in another country, it is said that the policy has "beggar-my-neighbor" effects. It is often thought that nominal wage rigidity characterizes the United States, while real wage rigidity characterizes European countries (see Branson and Rotemberg 1980 and Sachs 1980). Also, for less-developed countries, the labor market is often modeled as involving real wage rigidity (at the subsistence level). Thus, these two-country models of the supply-side effects of exchange rates have been used as a vehicle for stressing the hardships that expansionary policies in the United States can have on both its OECD partners and the less-developed countries.

9.4 STOCKS VERSUS FLOWS IN THE BALANCE OF PAYMENTS

All the models discussed so far in this and the previous chapter on the open economy involve foreigners' standing ready to buy or sell large quantities of domestic bonds, but the definitions of domestic disposable income and the accumulation identity for foreign exchange take no account of the domestic economy's ever paying foreigners any interest. This is one aspect of the stock/flow misspecification mentioned in Chapter 8 when the Mundell/Fleming model was introduced. The other aspect is the inconsistency between standard portfolio theory (which is embodied in the *LM* curve) and the net capital inflow equation. If foreigners have stock demand functions for money and bonds that are the same as domestic residents', their desired holding of the domestic economy's bonds should depend on the *level* of the yield differential (that is, on $r - r^f$, if we return once again to static exchange-rate expectations). The net capital inflow is the rate at which the foreigner *changes* his holdings of bonds (per unit time) as he closes the gap between desired and actual holdings. Thus, if the level of holdings depends on $r - r^f$, the time change in the holdings should depend on $\dot{r} - \dot{r}^f$. The standard open model ignores this difference. The model defined by the following list of equations corrects the problem:

$$Y = C(Y^d, A) + I(r) + G + X(E) - E \cdot IM(Y^d, E, A); \tag{9.13}$$

$$Y^d = Y - B^f; \tag{9.14}$$

$$A = M - B^f/r; \tag{9.15}$$

$$M = L(Y, r, A); \tag{9.16}$$

$$\dot{M} = X(E) - E \cdot IM(Y^d, E, A) - B^f + (1/r)\dot{B}^f; \tag{9.17}$$

$$B^f/rE = F(r - r^f, Y^f, A^f). \tag{9.18}$$

In defining this system, we return to the treatment of imports as final products and ignore direct exchange-rate effects on the cost of living (that is, we set γ, the weight in the consumer price index, equal to unity). We assume fixed prices but allow for the intrinsic dynamics that must exist when financial claims exist between domestic and foreign residents.

A stands for the net liquid assets of domestic residents. For simplicity, we assume no government bonds, so net liquid assets equal the money stock minus the market value of the privately issued bonds that have been purchased by foreigners. B^f stands for the number of these domestically issued bonds held by foreigners; since each bond is a promise to pay the holder one unit of domestic currency per period forever, B^f also stands for the interest payment obligations to foreigners. These interest payments are accounted for in the definition of the disposable income of domestic residents (equation 9.14) and in the balance of payments (equation 9.17). To the extent that foreigners already hold domestically issued debt, interest payments must be made to foreigners; this is a *use* of foreign exchange, and it is indicated by the $-B^f$ term in equation 9.17. To the extent that foreigners buy more domestic bonds during this period, foreign exchange *flows in* to the domestic economy (in an amount equal to $(1/r)\dot{B}^f$). Perfect capital mobility can be imposed by making the foreigners' demand function for domestic bonds infinitely elastic (that is, by setting F_r to infinity in equation 9.18).

This model is probably the simplest one that can be specified to make explicit both the stock and the flow aspects of foreign borrowing in a context that is interesting for considering stabilization policy. Early work on these stock/flow interactions was simpler in that agents held only foreign currencies (not bonds), so there were no interest payments. In this case, the yield differential is simply the expected exchange-rate change. But this simplification meant that the early models could not be used to examine such things as the time path for the ratio of foreign debt service payments to national income (a highly topical issue in the 1980s). As well, these models often involved other bold simplifications (such as a purchasing power parity condition at each point in time, instead of an *IS* relationship, and an exogenous level of national output). This literature was known as the "monetary approach" to the balance of payments and exchange-rate determination. Important references are Kouri (1976), Branson (1972), and Boyer (1975).

Rodriguez (1979) gives a full analysis of a model very similar to the system we defined above. Without any formal analysis, however, it should be clear immediately that the long-run results in this framework must differ from those in the standard model. Since we are abstracting from underlying growth, the balance on the capital account, $\dot{B}^f$, must be zero in full equilibrium. Hence, the lasting implication of a net capital inflow (for example, $\dot{B}^f > 0$ during the adjustment period following an increase in domestic government spending) is a higher level of B^f. This is a higher need for foreign exchange, not a higher source of foreign exchange. This difference fundamentally changes the results. For example, in a situation of flexible exchange rates ($\dot{M} = 0$) and perfect capital mobility, $dY/dG > 0$, since in the long run, net exports must rise to balance the higher debt service obligations to foreigners. (That is, the full-equilibrium version of equation 9.17 is $X - E \cdot IM - B^f = 0$ under floating exchange rates, and if B^f rises, so must net exports.) Thus, even without supply-side effects of the exchange rate or exchange-rate expectations, the perfect insulation from *IS* shocks (which was a property of the perfect capital mobility, flexible-exchange-rate version of the original Mundell/Fleming model) is lost.

It is a straightforward matter to verify this result formally. First, perfect capital mobility can be assumed from the outset by replacing equation 9.18 by $r = r^f$. Equations 9.14 and 9.15 can be used to substitute Y^d and B^f out of the other relationships, and the time derivative of equation 9.15 can be used to replace the $\dot{M} - (\dot{B}^f/r^f)$ terms in equation 9.17 by $\dot{A}$. Then, once the total differential is taken, the compact form of the system is

$$
\begin{bmatrix} (1 - C_{Yd}) & -1 \\ L_Y & 0 \end{bmatrix} \begin{bmatrix} dY \\ d\dot{A} \end{bmatrix} = \begin{bmatrix} -r^f(1 - C_{Yd} - C_A/r^f) & 1 \\ -L_A & 0 \end{bmatrix} \begin{bmatrix} dA \\ dG \end{bmatrix}
\tag{9.19}
$$

as long as the changes in the other exogenous variables are set to zero.

Equations 9.19 are set up to calculate impact effects by using Cramer's rule. The immediate effect on output of an increase in government spending is zero $(dY/dG = 0)$, for the usual Mundell/Fleming reasons, since the intrinsic stock/flow dynamics cannot come into effect at an instant in time. But the rise in government expenditure does make international indebtedness start to grow $(d\dot{A}/dG = -1)$. To derive the condition for convergence to a new full equilibrium, we calculate $d\dot{A}/dA$ from equations 9.19. The result is $d\dot{A}/dA = -\theta/L_Y$, where $\theta = L_A(1 - C_{Yd}) - r^f L_Y(1 - C_{Yd} - C_A/r^f)$. Stability requires that θ be positive, and this condition is not guaranteed. If, for example, the liquid asset effects on consumption and money demand are small (that is, if C_A and L_A approach zero), θ must be negative, and convergence to full equilibrium will not occur. As a result, international indebtedness will get ever larger. The 1980s have seen interest in the stability conditions for models like this one, given the widespread concern that several countries are involved in a vicious circle of growing debt that they may not be able to honor.

If we assume that the stability condition holds, we can derive the full-equilibrium multipliers by transposing the $d\dot{A}$ and dA columns in equations 9.19 and then using Cramer's rule again. The results are $dY/dG = L_A/\theta$, which is positive given stability, and $dA/dG = -L_Y/\theta$, which is negative given stability. These results verify the verbal discussion given earlier.

9.5   CONCLUSIONS

This chapter has been necessarily rather taxonomic since we have traced through the implications of several different branches of the open-economy literature: exchange-rate overshooting that follows from forward-looking expectations; supply-side effects of exchange rates; and international indebtedness effects. Space limitations preclude our combining several of these features in one model, but some analysts (for example, Buiter and Miller 1982) have made significant progress in this endeavor. Rather than restricting attention to the polar cases of purely fixed or purely floating exchange rates, authors (for example, Turnovsky 1983) often focus on the optimal degree of official intervention in the foreign exchange market. The reader can develop some familiarity with this optimal-intervention literature by answering question 4 on page 195 at the end of this book.

Despite our space limitations, we hope that this survey of the branches of open-economy macroeconomics will enable the reader to benefit from the rapidly growing literature on the international interdependence of stabilization policies.

THEORIES OF STICKY WAGES AND UNEMPLOYMENT

10.1 INTRODUCTION

In the first five chapters of this book, we stressed that the hypothesis of sticky wages (or prices) is one of the critical assumptions separating Keynesian and New Classical analyses, no matter which model of expectation formation is involved. These chapters examined the implications of sticky wages and prices but did not provide any detailed analysis of why agents choose to have sticky wages in the first place. (In Chapter 1, we noted that the rate at which wages are adjusted through time depends on nonlinear adjustment costs; however, we did not provide any detailed labor market analysis explaining the *source* of these adjustment costs.)

One purpose of this chapter is to provide a survey of several theories that have been advanced as explanations for sticky wages: risk-sharing, the efficiency wage hypothesis, unions, and adjustment costs. Each of these theories offers a reason why decentralized agents do not find it in their interest to have the labor market operate like an auction (a situation that would guarantee constant employment since the effects of all random shocks would be absorbed in continuous fluctuations in the wage rate).

It is important that we have some specific rationale for sticky wages, because without a clear explanation we are unable even to define terms such as voluntary and involuntary unemployment. If this distinction cannot be made, we are without a firm foundation for advocating any government policy that tries either to increase the degree of wage flexibility or to manipulate aggregate demand to make up for the lack of wage flexibility.

The second purpose of this chapter is to introduce the reader to some models that do not involve a unique equilibrium level for unemployment. Some of these models do not involve any assumption about sticky wages. Instead of focusing on the difficulties involved in getting to ''the'' full equilibrium (and on how policy can affect this process), these models highlight the fact that policy can shift the economy from one full equilibrium to another that is Pareto-superior. As a result, the role of policy is not simply one of affecting the built-in stability properties about a given equilibrium. For examples of this approach, we shall consider models involving search theory, the implications of overhead labor costs, linked demand curves (due to informational asymmetries), and hysteresis in unemployment. Most of these models involve a trading externality, an incomplete markets problem, or a free-rider problem, and these are the basis for government policy's having a role in full equilibrium. Models such as these combine the rigor of the New Classicals with an analysis of market failure that provides the basis for Keynesian policy prescriptions.

10.2 RISK-SHARING AND IMPLICIT CONTRACTS

Business cycles involve increases and decreases in the demand for labor. If households are risk-averse, they want to insulate their real income from these disturbances. An employment contract that specified that the real wage would stay constant and that guaranteed full employment would satisfy this requirement. If households had no option other than labor earnings (that is, if their reservation wage were zero), firms would be able to lower their wage costs enough to absorb all the business-cycle risk for their workers. On the other hand, if households' reservation wage is positive, firms may be unable to lower the wage rate enough to make it profitable for them to guarantee full employment. As a result, layoffs can occur even if workers and firms have a contractual arrangement, explicit or implicit, that involves prespecified wage rates to shift business-cycle risk from workers to firms. We now examine a specific model of this sort, to see if it can provide a microeconomic rationale for Keynesian macroeconomics.

Figure 10.1 Diminishing Marginal Utility and Risk Aversion

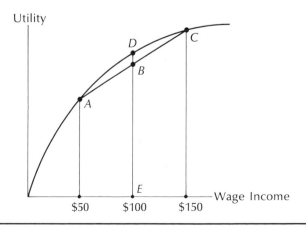

Risk-aversion on the part of workers is automatically involved through the assumption of diminishing marginal utility of income. This means workers will reject a "fair bet." For example, they will refuse to pay $100 for the fifty-fifty chance of receiving either $50 or $150, since the utility received from $100 without uncertainty (shown by distance ED in Figure 10.1) is greater than that received from a $100 expected value with uncertainty (distance EB). Firms maximize expected profits, rather than the expected utility of profits, since they are risk-neutral. (The assumption that entrepreneurs are less risk-averse than workers is appealing on two counts. First, people choose to be entrepreneurs for this very reason; second, entrepreneurs typically own more physical capital than workers and so can diversify risk better.)

In the simplest version of contract theory, there is no labor supply decision; households either work a fixed amount of time or are unemployed. L_1 represents the amount of leisure available when households are working and L_2 the amount available when they are unemployed ($L_2 > L_1$); w denotes the real wage (the nominal wage divided by the general price index); and R stands for the real value of the monetary equivalent of the extra leisure that is obtained when a worker is unemployed. With this notation, the utility associated with being employed is $U(w, L_1)$, and the utility obtained when unemployed is $U(O, L_2) = U(R, L_1)$. Defining the monetary equivalent of leisure has two advantages. First, we can now proceed with a utility function that has only one argument; the two possible utility levels are $U(w)$ and $U(R)$. Second, we have a parameter, R, that can stand for the level of unemployment insurance benefits, so changes in this policy variable can be analyzed.

Our discussion of contracts now follows Sargent (1979) closely. The uncertainty involved in the model takes the form of a stochastic element in the price of the good that the firm produces. We let p represent the price of the firm's product defined in real terms—that is, as relative to the general price index. For this relative price, we consider two values, p_1 in a high-demand period and p_2 in a low-demand period, and each of these outcomes occurs with a probability of 0.5. The firm and the workers must agree explicitly or implicitly to a contract that specifies the level of wages to be paid in each of the high- and low-demand periods and the amount of employment, N, to be offered in each period. N_1 is defined as full employment. It is assumed that the contract has no provision for the firm to pay the workers if they are not employed—that is, severance payments are not part of the model.

To solve for the parameters of the contract, which we can list as w_1, N_1, w_2, and N_2, firms maximize expected profits subject to three constraints. One constraint is the production function, $Y = F(N)$. Another is that goods cannot be stored. The third is the fact that the firm's offer to the workers must be at least as appealing as their other option. This other option is defined as a utility level, $\bar{U}$. A full general equilibrium analysis solves for $\bar{U}$, while a partial equilibrium analysis, which is presented here, can just take this level as given (and the constraint can be specified as an equality).

To maximize expected profits, the firm differentiates

$$0.5[p_1 F(N_1) - w_1 N_1 + p_2 F(N_2) - w_2 N_2] + \lambda(U - \bar{U})$$

with respect to N_1, N_2, w_1, and w_2 and sets these derivatives equal to zero. λ is a Lagrange multiplier, and the expected utility of the workers, U, is defined as

$$0.5\left[U(w_1) + \frac{N_2}{N_1}U(w_2) + \left(\frac{N_1 - N_2}{N_1}\right)U(R) \right].$$

N_2/N_1 and $(N_1 - N_2)/N_1$ are the probabilities of being employed and unemployed in the low-demand period. These probabilities are involved because any layoffs that occur in that period are assumed to be allocated to the workers on a random basis.

Once λ is eliminated from the two first-order conditions that follow from differentiating with respect to w_1 and w_2, the result is

$$U'(w_1) = U'(w_2).$$

Since $U'' < 0$, this condition can be satisfied only when w_1 and w_2 are equal, so these agents respond to the uncertainty by arranging in advance for rigid wages.

It is worth noting that this theory predicts *real* wage rigidity, not the nominal wage rigidity that is the standard assumption involved in Keynesian macro models. This distinction is not particularly important if there is no correlation between the changing product price of the firm that is being considered and the general cost of living. However, if we want this theory to apply in the aggregate, with the high- and low-demand periods interpreted as the phases of the business cycle, all industries have higher prices at the same time. In this case it is clear that the model predicts real, not nominal, wage rigidity.

The remaining issue is whether the unemployment that occurs within this model should be interpreted as voluntary or involuntary. The implications for layoffs can be seen without formally deriving the derivatives with respect to N_1 and N_2. Instead, we can simply compare two rigid-wage contracts: one with layoffs—denoted by $\bar{w}, N_1, \bar{w}$, and N_2—and one without layoffs—denoted by $\hat{w}, N_1, \hat{w}$, and N_1). To compare these contracts, we consider the case in which they involve the same wage bill, so $2\hat{w}N_1 = \bar{w}(N_1 + N_2)$, initially assuming that the extra leisure obtained during a layoff yields no utility or unemployment insurance payment, so $R = 0$. With these assumptions, the layoffs contract and the no-layoffs contract give households the same income, and, of course, they bear no risk with the second, so they prefer it. To see that the firms have the same preference, we simply calculate the difference between the profits received with the two contracts:

$$0.5[p_1 F(N_1) - \hat{w}N_1 + p_2 F(N_1) - \hat{w}N_1] - 0.5[p_1 F(N_1) - \bar{w}N_1$$
$$+ p_2 F(N_2) - \bar{w}N_2].$$

This expression simplifies to $0.5p_2[F(N_1) - F(N_2)]$, since $2\hat{w}N_1 = \bar{w}(N_1 + N_2)$.

Figure 10.2 Implicit Contracts

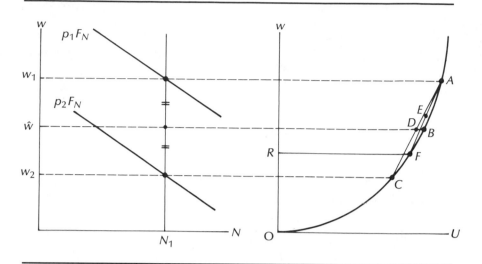

Since $N_1 > N_2$, the expression is positive, so firms also prefer the no-layoffs contract.

The logic behind this result is made clear in Figure 10.2, which shows the labor market in the left-hand panel and the worker's utility of wage income schedule in the right-hand panel. If the labor market operates as an auction market (through the classical assumption of complete wage flexibility), the wage jumps between w_1 and w_2 as the high-demand and low-demand periods occur. The individual then bounces between points A and C on his utility function, and the average (expected) utility level is given by point D. But a higher utility level (given by point B) can be obtained if that same average wage is received without any uncertainty. Thus, with a reservation wage, R, of zero, agents prefer a fixed wage, $\hat{w}$, and full employment. But with the reservation wage given by distance OR in the figure, an agent can choose to risk being laid off in the low-demand period. This permits him to bounce between points A and F, getting the average utility given by the midpoint on line AF, which is point E. Since point E can be to the right of point B, the agent can *choose* to risk layoffs, to obtain higher utility.

Our interest in this model stemmed from the fact that we are looking for an explicit microeconomic rationale for macroeconomic models that involve sticky money wages and unemployment that is involuntary in some sense. Thus far, the analysis is not consistent with these phenomena. The model leads to rigid real wages and layoffs only if $R > 0$,—that is, if households get some utility from being laid off. In this case they will voluntarily accept some chance of being unemployed in return for a higher average wage while employed. This is not a prediction of involuntary unemployment. It is true that once individuals are unemployed, they will say yes to the question "Would you rather be employed at the current wage?" But this is the wrong question. The relevant issue is the ex ante question: "Would you be willing to enter the same risky situation again next period?" Since the answer to this question is yes, the unemployment has to be viewed as voluntary, and the model provides no underpinnings for government reduction of unemployment.

It is worth emphasizing, however, that this no-role-for-government conclusion hinges on the original assumption that side payments to the unemployed are not possible (on some unspecified grounds) and that the authorities have no special ability to alleviate this constraint. This assumption precludes the workers' and firms' reaching the fully efficient solution, in which firms—the risk-neutral party—bear all the risks.

The unemployment that emerges in implicit-contract models can be interpreted as involuntary in more complicated versions. (For a survey, see Stiglitz 1986.) Perhaps the most common extension involves asymmetric information—that is, workers' and firms' having different sets of information. But the simple model illustrates that without a clearly identified reason for market failure (such as imperfect information), the implicit-contract model contains no formal microeconomic rationale for stabilization policy.

10.3 THE EFFICIENCY-WAGE HYPOTHESIS

Rather than extend the implicit-contract model to allow for market failure, we shall move on to an alternative theory of the labor market that stresses variations in labor's productivity, instead of risk-sharing. The unemployment that occurs in this model can be regarded as involuntary since it follows from a market failure. Markets fail because of adverse selection and moral hazard problems. In its simplest terms, this model is based on the proposition that a happy worker is a good worker. It is assumed that workers are inspired to put forth extra effort on the job only if their real wage is high, an assumption that, in essence, makes the real wage a direct argument in the production function. It is also assumed that firms are unable to distinguish between workers who are putting forth real effort on the job and those who are shirking. Thus, firms cannot be sure they are employing the workers who are not shirking.

The workers face a trade-off. The more they relax on the job (shirk), the lower the marginal product of labor, so the lower firms' overall demand for workers and the greater the chance of unemployment for an individual worker. The threat of unemployment serves as a mechanism that limits shirking at the individual level. It is not rational for firms to try to insure themselves *fully* against shirking by raising the real wage. If they do so, the resulting increase in labor productivity so increases the demand for labor that the unemployment rate falls. With a reduced chance of being laid off, workers have an increased incentive to shirk. This is the moral hazard aspect of the model: as the firm pays more "insurance", the likelihood of the "crime" goes up. It is for these reasons that we cannot expect decentralized agents to choose the optimal level of "insurance." As a result, unemployment will not settle at its optimal value. So this model supports government involvement to reduce unemployment.

The efficiency-wage model can be explained more fully as follows. Firms maximize profits, $F(E) - wN$, where N is the quantity of labor hired and E is the amount of effective work actually received, subject to the constraint $E = b(w)N$. The constraint stipulates that effective labor effort received is proportional to the size of the firm's work force, but that factor of proportionality, b, is positively related to the real wage. Thus, both F' and b' are positive.

The nonshirking constraint follows from three assumptions. First, workers will shirk if the wage they receive is less than some critical value. Second, this critical value depends directly on the probability of reemployment in case of layoff; the lower that probability, the lower the critical wage value. Third, the probability of being rehired depends inversely on the unemployment rate. Since the demand for labor depends inversely on the wage rate (making unemployment rise with the wage rate), workers shirk less at higher wage rates. This argument holds even if all workers are identical.

The implications of this model are illustrated in Figure 10.3, which depicts three relationships. One is the labor supply curve, which, for simplicity, we assume is perfectly inelastic. The second curve is the labor demand function. In the usual case, in which variations in work effort are ignored and the wage is flexible, the intersection of these two lines (at point A) gives the outcome: no unemployment. But with variations in work effort allowed for, b becomes less than one. By affecting the productivity of labor, this change modifies the position and slope of the labor demand function, but the curve remains negatively sloped. More important, the third curve in Figure 10.3 becomes relevant. This is the

Figure 10.3 The Labor Market with Work Effort Depending on Wages

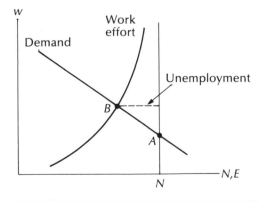

nonshirking constraint, and it can be interpreted as the relevant supply of work effort schedule; since it is to the left of the supply of persons line, equilibrium now occurs at a point such as B, and there *is* unemployment. The unemployed want jobs at the going real wage, but the firm cannot afford to hire these individuals because it knows that the lower real wage that must accompany an increase in hiring will induce more shirking and so reduce profits. (Again, it must be emphasized that monitoring individual work effort is assumed to be impossible on technical grounds.)

Formally, the firm chooses both the level of employment and the real wage by setting the derivatives of $F[b(w)N] - wN$ with respect to N and w equal to zero. The results are $F'b = w$ and $F'b' = 1$, which imply $wb'(w)/b(w) = 1$. As long as $b'' \neq 0$, the total differential of this condition implies that real wages must be constant. Thus, the efficiency-wage model predicts both a nonoptimal level of unemployment and rigid real (not nominal) wages.

Our specific discussion of this model has involved the assumption of homogeneous workers, but perhaps a nonmathematical interpretation of a version involving heterogeneous workers would be helpful. When the demand for labor falls, it does not pay the firm to cut wages because it then stands to lose only its best workers, who would voluntarily look elsewhere. By cutting employment and assigning the layoffs randomly, the firm can insure that only some of the lost workers are ''good'' workers (those who shirk less).

In a sense, the efficiency-wage model involves an incomplete markets problem, since there is only one price, w, yet the adjustment in w is trying to clear two ''markets'' (the market for workers and the market for effort). In more elaborate efficiency-wage models, the analysis considers workers who post a bond, providing an additional price. Stiglitz (1986) gives a fuller treatment of both this model and the implicit-contracts model. He concludes that the efficiency-wage model involves involuntary unemployment, as does the simple version presented above (so we have limited our attention to the simple case).

Stiglitz (1984) shows how the general notion behind this efficiency-wage model (that the demanders of an item judge its quality by price) can explain procyclical movements in the real wage, as well as involuntary unemployment. Katz (1986) provides an extensive survey of the efficiency-wage literature.

10.4   UNIONS IN THE LABOR MARKET

We continue our exploration of labor market arrangements that can lead to sticky wages by considering theories of union behavior. The literature focuses on two different models, which are referred to as the noncooperative and cooperative theories of union/firm interaction. Our purpose is to explain each so that we can evaluate whether the existence of unions is sufficient to justify the hypothesis of sticky wages in macroeconomic analyses.

Figure 10.4 Models of Union/Firm Interaction

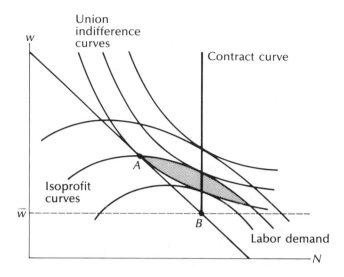

The noncooperative model involves firms' maximizing profits defined by $F(N) - wN$, where, as before, w is the real wage. This is achieved when the familiar condition $F' = w$ holds. This labor demand function is shown in Figure 10.4 as the locus of all points that are at the apex of an isoprofit curve. The slope of the isoprofit lines can be derived by setting the total differential of the definition of profits equal to zero. Thus, the slope of the isoprofit lines is $dw/dN = [F'(N) - w]/N$, which is positive for low levels of N and negative for high levels of N (when the marginal product is low).

Unions are assumed to maximize the income of a representative member of the group. This can be defined as $w(N/L) + \bar{w}(L - N)/L$, where N and L denote employment and size of union membership respectively, w is the wage paid to union members if they are employed, $\bar{w}$ is the wage they receive if they are unemployed (which could be interpreted as unemployment insurance), and N/L is the probability that a union member will be employed. The slope of the union's indifference curves is derived by setting the total differential of the expected income definition to zero. The result is $dw/dN = -(w - \bar{w})/N$, which is negative since the union wage cannot be less than the individual's reservation wage.

The union achieves the highest indifference curve by picking the wage that corresponds to the point at which the labor demand curve is tangent to an indifference curve (point A in Figure 10.4). Once wages are set, firms are free to choose employment. But since the union has taken the firm's reaction into account, its members know that point A will be chosen. We can derive whether this model predicts real wage rigidity by including a shift variable for the marginal product of labor, γ, which can represent changes in tax rates or any exogenous variable that affects the demand for labor. Comparative static predictions are then calculated by taking the total differential of the labor demand curve and the equal slopes condition:

$$\gamma F'(N) = w;$$

$$\gamma[NF''(N) + F'(N)] = \bar{w}.$$

The employment and real wage effects are:

$$\frac{dN}{d\gamma} = \frac{-\bar{w}}{\gamma(2F'' + NF''')} > 0;$$

$$\frac{dw}{d\gamma} = \frac{-\bar{w}F'' + w(2F'' + NF''')}{\gamma(2F'' + NF''')} \gtrless 0.$$

The denominator of these multipliers must be negative, since this is required by the second-order conditions of the union's maximization problem. We conclude that the model embodies employment multipliers that are entirely standard, but, in general, the model does not predict real (or nominal) wage rigidity.

Our purpose in examining this model was to see whether the existence of unions in labor markets leads to wage ridigity and involuntary variations in employment. Since the model contains no explicit explanation of why individuals deal with the firm exclusively through the union (are they forced to? did they choose to?), it is not possible to say whether employment decreases in the model constitute involuntary unemployment. As noted, wage ridigity is not a general property of the model either, but wages in it can be invariant to changes in γ. For an example of this outcome, the reader can verify that $dw/d\gamma = 0$ when the production function is Cobb/Douglas. However, it must be appreciated that this result occurs because points A and B in Figure 10.4 coincide in the Cobb/Douglas case. Unions maximize income by moving down the labor demand curve as far as possible; this limit is reached when $w = \bar{w}$. In the Cobb/Douglas case, the labor supply curve is effectively the horizontal $\bar{w}$ line in Figure 10.4, and the wage achieved through the union is just equal to the reservation wage.

Let us now investigate whether wage rigidity occurs in the cooperative model of union/firm interaction. The outcome in the previous model is inefficient since there are many wage/employment outcomes—all the points within the shaded, lense-shaped region in Figure 10.4—that can make *both* the firm and the union better off than they are at point A. The cooperative model assumes that the two parties reach an agreement and settle at one of the Pareto-efficient points that lie along the contract curve. Completing the model now requires some additional assumption that defines how the two parties divide the gains from trade. The additional assumption that is most common (see McDonald and Solow 1981) is that the two bargainers reach a Nash equilibrium. Without specifying some rule of this sort, we cannot derive any predictions about how the wage level responds to shifts in the position of the labor demand function.

Employment effects can, however, be derived without any such specification. The equation of the contract curve is had by equating the slope expressions for the isoprofit and the indifference curves. With the shift variable for labor's marginal product inserted as before, this equal slopes condition is $(\gamma F' - w)/$

$N = -(w - \bar{w})/N$, or $\gamma F' = \bar{w}$. The contract curve is vertical since w does not enter this equation. From this equation of the contract curve, we see that we can determine the effects on employment of changes in γ and $\bar{w}$ without having to specify the bargaining model that is required for the model to yield any real wage predictions. Thus, this cooperative union model does not support the hypothesis of real wage rigidity, but we can derive the employment effects that follow from this theory if we impose real wage rigidity in a macroeconomic context. For macroeconomic employment effects, it is *as if* real wages were fixed.

A Summing Up

Space limitations preclude our surveying more models that explore the micro-economic rationale for the two macroeconomic assumptions that characterize the Keynesian approach: wage rigidity and involuntary unemployment. (The reader is referred to Solow 1979; Stiglitz 1986; and Mitchell 1986.) But before closing this section, we shall summarize our findings.

The basic implicit-contract model of risk-sharing predicts voluntary unemployment and rigid real—not nominal—wages. The union models make no clear predictions concerning either unemployment or wage rigidity. The noncooperative model does show employment that is less than what would occur if the union wage equaled the reservation wage, but this level of employment is the one chosen by the union members. In general, neither union model supports rigid real or nominal wages. Of the theories surveyed, only the efficiency-wage model predicts rigid real wages and a level of unemployment that is above the optimum. But even this model does not support the sticky *nominal* wage assumption that is so common in macroeconomic work.

10.5 ADJUSTMENT COSTS

Some of the labor market models that were surveyed in the three previous sections provide support for the hypothesis of *real* wage rigidity, but the fundamental problem for business-cycle theory is to explain why purely nominal shocks have real effects. The Keynesian approach to this question relies on *nominal* wage and/or price rigidity. Must we therefore conclude that we have no alternative but to stick with the theory of adjustment costs for nominal wages that is based on negotiation costs (as presented in Chapter 1)? There is nothing obviously unappealing about that proposition, but some analysts argue that the other theories of wage rigidity can apply to *nominal* wages, after all. When wages are set, the thought process or bargaining is about the *real* wage (as the theories surveyed in the previous three sections indicated). But the item that is actually set as a result of these decisions is the money wage. It is set at the level intended to deliver the desired real wage, given inflationary expectations. Given this interpretation, we can argue that the theories apply to money wage-setting, although an additional assumption regarding indexation is required. We would expect agents to set the money wage with a full indexing clause so there would be no need to incur errors in inflationary expectations. But given that catch-up provisions can roughly replace ex ante indexing formulae, and given that households and firms want to tie wages to different price indexes, the costs of full indexation are probably not worth the benefit. McCallum (1986) stresses this point.

Quite apart from the preceding argument, many analysts are uneasy about applying an adjustment-cost model to explain sticky *goods* prices. In that context, negotiation costs are far from obvious for many commodities, and it does not seem compelling to rest all sticky-price macroeconomics on items that seem rather trivial (such as the costs of printing new prices in catalogs and the costs of informing sales staff about price changes). The response that one can make to the charge that adjustment costs for many nominal prices cannot be that important is simply to demonstrate that even explicitly small price-change costs can lead to large welfare losses. Akerlof and Yellen (1985) and Mankiw (1985) provide analysis to support this view.

Let us examine a brief summary of Mankiw's argument. He considers a monopolist who must set his nominal price before the relevant period but can change that price later (during the period) at a "small" cost. A situation in which the price has been set at too high a value is illustrated in Figure 10.5. When the firm set its price, it did not guess the then-future position of its demand curve perfectly. As it enters the period analyzed in Figure 10.5, it has already posted a price equal to *OP*, but the appropriate price is *OE*. The firm must now decide whether making the change is worthwhile. Since the firm's private profits

Figure 10.5 The Different Effects of Price Changes on Total Welfare versus the Firm's Profits

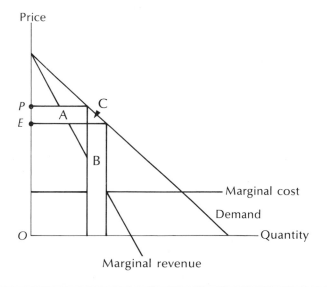

equal the area between the price line and the marginal cost line, the firm will lower its price only if area B exceeds area A by more than the adjustment cost. Even if the adjustment cost is fairly small, areas A and B may be so similar that the price will remain sticky. But the diagram shows that even if no adjustment is appropriate from the individual firm's point of view, total welfare is decreased by an amount equal to area B plus area C. It is obviously quite possible for this sum to be dramatically larger than the difference between areas B and A. Mankiw gives numerical illustrations and concludes that the social gains from price adjustment far exceed the private gains for any plausible demand function. This analysis illustrates that Keynesians do not have to assume ''large'' nominal price-adjustment costs to sustain their simultaneous claims that:

1. Prices may be sticky.
2. The welfare losses that follow from sticky prices may be large (at least if general equilibrium expectational effects—such as those stressed in Chapter 4—are ignored).
3. Government policy may be justified since individual firms consider only the private benefits of price flexibility.

10.6 MULTIPLE EQUILIBRIA

Through much of this book, we have assumed that the economy has just one full equilibrium (the natural rate of output). We have restricted our investigation of the role for government to questions of how alternative policy rules affect the speed with which the economy approaches that full equilibrium or how these rules affect the asymptotic variance of variables about their full-equilibrium values. Thus, our analysis has followed Tobin's (1975) suggestion that classical models be accepted as descriptions of *the* long-run outcomes but Keynesian models be recognized as very helpful descriptions of the adjustment paths. Now, however, we wish to consider some work that embodies a rejection of this conventional view that Keynesians concede the long run to the Classicals.

We have already encountered one body of literature in which the long-run equilibrium *itself* is affected by policy: the literature on the average opinion problem in rational expectations. In section 6.3, the model economy had at least two equilibria fully consistent with rational expectations—one corresponding to each possible view of what all agents expect all the others to take as the going market price. Our purpose here is to indicate that the multiple equilibria issue is more general than we have seen so far, and that some of the other examples in the literature stem from a more familiar microeconomic basis.

Diamond (1984) and Howitt (1985) examine *search theories*, which analyze how households and firms interact to evaluate whether the individual is hired (or wants to be hired). A key feature of these models is the presence of a trading externality. The probability of obtaining a positive match between workers and jobs depends on the amount of resources firms devote to recruitment. But much of the benefit of increasing the information flow emerges as a general social benefit—a lower equilibrium level of frictional unemployment. There is no direct link between this general benefit and the individual decision process of any particular firm. It is rational for the individual firm to think that if it increases expenditures on the hiring and searching process, the overall level of frictional unemployment will be unaffected. In any event, the firm is unable to appropriate any general benefits that occur. Since the private return to recruitment expenses from the firm's point of view is less than the social return, the economy reaches an equilibrium that is Pareto-inefficient.

The trading externality means that there is nonprice interaction between agents, and that the problems that ensue cannot be eliminated by price flexibility. As Howitt (1986b, 636) has summarized it, "if everyone believes that markets will be inactive they will anticipate a high cost of transacting; this will discourage them from undertaking transactions, and the initial beliefs will be self-fulfilling."

The idea here is that there is more than one equilibrium, each involving rational expectations for all agents, and, in principle at least, government involvement to switch the economy to a Pareto-superior full equilibrium is justified. What Diamond and Howitt do is to provide modern standards of analytical rigor to defend the very early summary of Keynesian economics—that the economy could remain stuck *indefinitely* with a suboptimal amount of unemployment.

Salop's (1979) model of the labor market involves *overhead costs associated with labor*. A firm's labor costs depend not only on how many hours each employee works but also on how many employees are on the payroll. There is an incomplete markets problem, since there is just one price (the wage rate) available to try to clear two markets (the market in workers and the market in hours per worker). This problem could be solved by assuming that decentralized agents rely on an additional price that might emerge. It would have to be a membership fee (which could be positive or negative). This fee would be collected by a firm, and paying it would give individuals the right to be regarded as officially part of that firm's labor force. But because the fee would necessarily be independent of the number of hours any individual actually worked, a firm could simply collect fees and hire no hours. This free-rider problem means that the institution of a Pareto-optimal membership fee cannot be expected to emerge from a decentralized free market. Thus, Salop's model has at least two equilibrium levels of unemployment: the one reached by private agents struggling with the free-rider problem and the Pareto-superior one that requires government policy.

Woglom (1982) and Rowe (1987) have also constructed models involving multiple equilibria. The key feature in these models is that competitive firms face kinked demand curves. The reason for the kink is not the traditional oligopoly consideration based on rivals' reactions (a theory that is more or less discredited). Instead, the kink is based on Stiglitz's (1979) assumption of *asymmetries* in the *dissemination of information* to customers. Customers learn immediately about any price change at the firm with which they have been trading, but they learn only slowly of other price changes. The kink causes a discontinuity in the firms' marginal revenue schedule, which leads to a range of aggregate equilibria that all involve agents' having rational expectations. Individual firms face a free-rider problem when adjusting prices, but monetary policy does not face this problem.

Blanchard and Kiyotaki (1986) have built a model of monopolistic competition that has an aggregate demand externality. Other papers on multiple equilibria include Diamond (1987) and Woodford (1987). All of these analyses show that the microeconomic rationale for Keynesian propositions concerning full macro-economic equilibrium can be as thorough as that provided by the New Classicals for their models.

The most general notion of multiple equilibria is found in models that involve *hysteresis*. This term is used in the physical sciences for any process in which the full equilibrium value of a variable cannot be defined without reference to the path that the variable actually followed in the preceeding time periods. Tobin (1972) suggested that the unemployment rate seems to behave in this way.

Recently more attention has been paid to this issue. Time-series studies (Nelson and Plosser 1982; Campbell and Mankiw 1986; and Hall 1986) suggest that output and employment do not revert to stable trends following disturbances. These studies suggest that a simple random walk (with some drift) is a reasonable approximation to the actual stochastic properties of real GNP data from the United States. As a result of this observation and similar findings regarding the time paths of unemployment rates in Europe, Blanchard and Summers (1986; 1987) have developed models of the labor market that predict hysteresis in the unemployment rate.

The simplest model of unemployment that Blanchard and Summers present is based on the idea that the more senior members of a union (the "insiders") are the ones who make the decisions on wages. These workers are assumed to give no weight to the preferences of members who are now unemployed; the insiders' power stems from median-voter considerations. The wage is set equal to the value that makes the firm want to hire just the number of workers who were employed in the previous period. Thus, the expected employment in time t, denoted as $E(N_t)$, equals the last period's employment, N_{t-1}. An expression for expected employment can be had by specifying a labor demand function. Blanchard and Summers assume a simple aggregate demand function for goods, $Y_t = c(M_t - P_t)$, and constant returns to scale in production; thus, if units are chosen so that labor's marginal product is unity, $Y_t = N_t$ and $P_t = W_t$ (where Y stands for output, M for money supply, P for price, and W for the wage rate). The implied labor demand function is $N_t = c(M_t - W_t)$. If the expectations operator is taken through this relationship and the resulting equation is subtracted from the original, we have $E(N_t) = N_t - c[M_t - E(M_t)]$, since wages are set so that $W_t = E(W_t)$. Replacing expected employment by N_{t-1}, the time path for employment becomes

$$N_t = N_{t-1} + c[M_t - E(M_t)].$$

Thus, this model is consistent with the random-walk observation. Unexpected changes in aggregate demand affect employment, and there is nothing to pull the level of employment back to any particular equilibrium (because the preferences of laid-off workers no longer matter for wage-setting).

Blanchard and Summers consider several variations of this and other models to test the robustness of the hysteresis prediction. Some of these extensions allow the "outsiders" to exert some pressure on wage-setting. Blanchard and Summers have certainly succeeded in placing the issue of hysteresis on the priority list of important macroeconomic research topics.

10.7   CONCLUSIONS

This chapter has had two goals. The early sections examined implicit-contract, efficiency-wage, standard-union and adjustment-cost models, primarily with a view to finding a microeconomic rationale for wage rigidity. This was necessary so that we could assess the viability of macroeconomic policies intended to change adjustments toward a given full equilibrium. On the other hand, the studies on search theory with trading externalities, overhead labor costs, demand curves kinked by informational asymmetries, and hysteresis (which were discussed in the last section) were not intended to explain wage rigidity. Instead, they were meant to show how Pareto improvements are possible even if the entire focus of the analysis is on full equilibrium.

The chapter cannot have a tidy conclusion since the analyses indicate that the existing microeconomic rationale for *nominal* wage and/or price rigidities is incomplete. Further, only some of the models yield support for the interpretation that unemployment is involuntary. Nevertheless, our survey does indicate major progress toward clarifying the theoretical underpinnings of macroeconomic policy. Analysts are now identifying clear sources of market failure on which to base the case for government intervention. This means that the principles that underlie normative analysis in macroeconomics are becoming consistent with the principles that underlie microeconomic policy analysis.

CHAPTER 11

CURRENT
CONTROVERSIES

11.1 INTRODUCTION

A primary focus throughout this text has been the question: can—and, indirectly, should—policy be used to stabilize employment? Considerations of space have restricted our attention almost exclusively to theoretical issues, but our study would be incomplete without a brief look at some of the evidence that bears on this question. One purpose of this chapter is to provide this survey.

To introduce the discussion, the next section focuses on a particular, but very conventional policy issue: does a steeper income tax function give the economy more built-in stability? This question is legitimate since it poses stabilization policy as an ongoing rule, rather than as a one-time, discretionary event. We shall discuss how this issue is approached both with and without the Lucas critique being respected. Not only does this discussion facilitate a review of earlier material in the context of a specific policy example, but it also exposes the important issues that require empirical support.

These issues are the ones for which we shall consider empirical evidence in the remainder of the chapter. We shall examine particular empirical projects (for example, estimating an individual structural equation such as the consumption function) to explain how the hypothesis of rational expectations affects empirical work. We shall also discuss the empirical success, as complete models, of the three major competing business-cycle theories. The chapter will close with some assessment of the controversy generated by the competition among these theories—that is, between the work of the New Classicals and the work of the New Keynesians.

11.2   STABILIZATION POLICY

A standard analysis of the built-in stabilizer question can be accomplished with the following model (which we have already considered at various stages in the text):

$$y = \phi g + \theta(m - p) + \psi \dot{p}; \tag{11.1}$$

$$\dot{p} = f(y - \bar{y}) + \dot{m}. \tag{11.2}$$

Equation 11.1 is an aggregate demand function that involves rational expectations (specifically, perfect foresight) for price inflation and for which the parameters have the standard *IS–LM* interpretation:

$$\theta = I_r M / \Delta PY,$$

$$\psi = -I_r L_i / \Delta Y,$$

$$\Delta = L_i[1 - C_{yd}(1 - k)] + I_r L_Y,$$

which is fully explained in section 4.4 above. Equation 11.2 is an aggregate supply function (an expectations-augmented Phillips curve) that was derived in section 1.4. There we saw that parameter f has the following relationship with the underlying structural coefficients:

$$f = 1/(\psi + \theta/a), \tag{11.3}$$

where a is a technology parameter that depends on the cost of adjusting wages relative to the cost of having wages at a value other than that which would make employment equal its natural value. Partial-adjustment parameter a does not depend on the tax rate, k, but the slope of the short-run Phillips curve, f, does since both ψ and θ depend on the steepness of the tax function.

This dependence of f on the underlying parameters of the system can be used to keep the analysis of tax policy free of the Lucas critique, at least as far as the aggregate supply side of the model is concerned. Thus, we shall consider the implications of a higher tax rate (a higher k) both with and without using equation 11.3 to show how the traditional macroeconomic analysis of stabilization policy (which preceded the Lucas critique) differs from more modern analysis (which respects the Lucas critique). But first we shall review and thus emphasize some of the key assumptions underlying *both* analyses.

The income tax rate would not affect disposable income or consumption at all if households were not liquidity-constrained to some degree. In section 1.3 we saw that for Ricardian equivalence to be avoided in this way, we must assume that households incur some transactions or adjustment costs. Further, the *IS–LM* interpretation of equation 11.1 involves the assumption that the monetary and real sectors are connected via a firm's investment function and that it involves nonlinear adjustment costs for capital (see section 1.2). Finally, on the aggregate supply side, to keep the short-run Phillips curve from being vertical (so that y

does not always equal $\bar{y}$), we must assume adjustment costs for nominal wage- or price-setting (see section 1.4). Thus, whether our stabilization policy analysis is traditional or modern, for it to be relevant at all, we must have some confidence that *adjustment costs* are important for the consumption, investment, and wage- and price-setting decisions. That is why we shall discuss some of the empirical work on these three issues in the later sections of this chapter. The evidence is consistent with the notion that these adjustment costs are important. Thus, while the maintained hypotheses that underlie both our traditional and our modern stabilization policy analyses do not seem to be rejected, we must appreciate that the ultimate reason for the adjustment costs for wages—be it risk-sharing, efficiency-wage considerations, or simply the costs of rewriting price lists (often referred to as menu costs)—is not yet well understood, as we stressed in Chapter 10.

One convenient way to analyze whether a steeper tax function involves more or less built-in stability is to consider a drop in autonomous expenditure, g, which causes a temporary recession. Does a higher tax rate reduce the size of the temporary recession? Does it make that recession disappear at a faster rate? If the answer to both these questions is yes, we might call the tax system a built-in stabilizer.

We derived in section 4.4 that the impact-period multiplier and the equation that defines adjustment speed for the macro model specified above are:

$$dy/dg = \phi/(1 - \psi f); \tag{11.4}$$

$$\dot{y} = -s(y - \bar{y}) = \left(\frac{-f\theta}{1 - \psi f}\right)(y - \bar{y}). \tag{11.5}$$

These results were given as equations 4.15 and 4.16, except that the summary parameter s has now been introduced. Recall that $1 - \psi f$ was assumed to be positive given the presumption of stability.

In a traditional analysis of built-in stabilizers—in which the steepness of the short-run Phillips curve is taken as a deep or fundamental parameter that is unaffected by k (in other words, $df/dk = 0$)—we find $d(dy/dg)/dk < 0$ and $ds/dk < 0$. These results mean that a steeper tax function involves a trade-off: the initial temporary output deviation that follows a drop in aggregate demand is made smaller by a steeper tax function, but that output deviation is eliminated at a slower rate. Thus, even ignoring the incomplete microeconomic underpinnings of a traditional macroeconomic analysis, we conclude that it provides only mixed support for the notion that the tax system acts as a built-in stabilizer.

A modern analysis of stabilization policies tries to avoid the Lucas critique by rederiving how the structural equations are affected by the change in policy. In our example this means allowing the slope of the short-run Phillips curve to be affected by the steeper tax function (that is, no longer ignoring equation 11.3). From this relationship and the definitions of θ and ψ, it is immediately clear that $df/dk > 0$. Since the traditional analysis of built-in stability ignores this impli- cation of its standard microeconomic underpinnings, it limits the tax rate to having effects only on aggregate demand. The modern analysis, by going back to first principles and by taking the adjustment-cost parameter, a, not f, as independent of the tax rate, allows k to have a direct aggregate supply-side effect as well. Since the higher tax rate makes the short-run Phillips curve steeper, we may expect this additional effect to increase the speed with which output deviations are eliminated, compared to what we found in the traditional analysis. Indeed, substituting the expression for f into that for the adjustment-speed parameter, we find that $s = 1/[(1/a) - 1 + (\theta/\psi)]$. Since the ratio θ/ψ is independent of k, a higher tax rate does not slow adjustment. Further, $d(dy/dg)/dk$ is still less than zero, even with equation 11.3 involved. Thus, the modern analysis gives unambiguous support to interpreting the higher tax rate as a built-in stabilizer.

That a steeper tax function gives the economy an increased degree of built-in stability is usually thought to be a proposition that follows from a Keynesian view of stabilization policy. It is, therefore, interesting that the strongest support for this proposition comes from the version of the analysis that most thoroughly involves the analytical methods pioneered and advocated by New Classicals. In the introduction to this book, we stressed that a useful synthesis of Keynesian and New Classical elements could be (and is in the process of being) constructed. Our analysis of built-in stabilizers provides a specific example to substantiate that general claim.

The reader is encouraged to explore other proposals that have been made to increase the built-in stability properties of the economy. For example, Gray (1976) examines wage indexation within a stochastic but static aggregate demand and supply model. Since indexation limits changes in the real wage, it makes the aggregate supply schedule steeper, thus decreasing the effects on employment of demand shocks, but increasing those of supply-side shocks. More recently, Weitzman (1985; 1986) advocates profit-sharing. His analysis involves a static, inverted-L-shaped aggregate supply function. The adoption of profit-sharing lowers this schedule's horizontal section. Thus, leftward shifts in the aggregate demand curve are more apt to cause decreases in the price level than decreases in output and employment. Blinder (1986a) integrates the issues of wage indexation and profit-sharing to some degree. Assuming that the demand curve for a firm's product is downward sloping, he explains how an indexation scheme in which wages are linked to the firm's own selling price must make marginal labor cost less than the money wage (which is the critical feature of Weitzman's profit-sharing proposal).

Much research needs to be done before we can support the proposition that tax incentives be used to stimulate the adoption of compensation schemes that make marginal labor cost less than the wage. For one thing, these indexing and profit-sharing proposals need to be examined within a *dynamic* framework that allows for the simultaneous interaction of inflation and output gaps. (For a preliminary analysis of this sort that parallels and extends the discussion of income tax rates above, see Scarth 1987b.) More fundamentally, we must extend our theory of contracts. Indexing schemes like Blinder's were used many years ago in some industries in both the United States and the United Kingdom, but those involved subsequently dispensed with such compensation arrangements; we do not yet fully understand why.

This brief review of stabilization policy proposals has served two purposes. First, it has illustrated how the Lucas critique can be respected in the analysis of Keynesian policies and how this modern analysis can strengthen support for these proposals. The more widely this point is appreciated, the more quickly the recent revolution in macroeconomics can lead to a constructive synthesis of old and new ideas. Second, our review of the standard framework for stabilization policy analysis has clarified what are perhaps the most important questions that need to be investigated empirically: are adjustment costs important in consumption decisions? in investment decisions? in wage-setting decisions? It is to these empirical issues that we now turn.

The issue as to whether wages and prices are sticky or not is often tested by considering the general predictions of entire models. For example, analysts compare the properties of various New Classical models (for example, those using the "monetary misperceptions" theory and those using the "real business cycle" theory) with more traditional sticky-price systems that are favored by Keynesians. We shall review those comparisons in section 11.4 below. But first we shall consider empirical work done at the level of particular structural relationships, rather than the general properties of a full model.

11.3 EMPIRICAL CONSIDERATIONS FOR PARTICULAR STRUCTURAL RELATIONSHIPS

In this section we consider whether the theories of the consumption function, the investment function, and the wage-setting relationship that were discussed in Chapter 1 and used in Chapters 2 through 9 are consistent with the data. As we discuss each structural relationship in turn, no attempt is made to provide a survey of all the relevant empirical studies. Rather, our intention is to stress the general findings and to explain how the hypothesis of rational expectations affects a particular empirical project.

Consumption

Many empirical studies of the consumption function have focused on Friedman's (1957) permanent income theory of consumption. Friedman's hypothesis was that current consumption is proportional to broadly defined wealth, which is equal to the present value of the individual's entire future disposable income stream:

$$C_t = \beta \sum_{j=0}^{\infty} Y_{t+j}[1/(1 + r)^j].$$

Friedman defined permanent or long-run average disposable income, Y^P, as the yield on broadly defined wealth. It is that amount of "interest income" that the individual could consume every period forever, without reducing his "principal value." Thus, the conceptual definition of permanent disposable income is

$$Y_t^P = r \sum_{j=0}^{\infty} Y_{t+j}[1/(1 + r)^j],$$

and the consumption function can be reexpressed as

$$C_t = hY_t^P,$$

where $h = \beta/r$.

Friedman's analysis was, in fact, a very early precursor of the Lucas critique. The model involves a very strong stricture against countercyclical income tax changes. Let us assume that Ricardian equivalence does not hold, so the tax system does affect disposable income. If taxes are changed in a permanent fashion, all the terms in the present value summation are affected, so current consumption is affected as well. But if taxes are changed on a temporary basis (for example, if they are cut during recessions and increased during booms), the present value summation is not affected. Notice that the two policies could involve the same tax change in the first period, but the household's reactions would be very different. Friedman's analysis shows that before tax policy effects can be properly simulated, the analyst must go back to first principles so that he can derive the full household response to different ongoing policy *rules*. (This example is stressed in Lucas 1976.)

Although Friedman stressed that his analysis of the policy issue was based on the fact that households are forward-looking, he actually defined permanent income as a backward-looking variable for estimation purposes in a time-series context. He assumed that long-run average disposable income estimates can be had by assuming adaptive expectations:

$$Y_t^P - Y_{t-1}^P = \lambda(Y_t - Y_{t-1}^P).$$

With this definition, the unobserved theoretical construct, Y^P, is eliminated from the consumption function:

$$C_t = h\lambda[Y_t + (1 - \lambda)Y_{t-1} + (1 - \lambda)^2 Y_{t-2} + \ldots].$$

The final estimating equation is then derived by multiplying the lagged version of the last equation by $1 - \lambda$ and then subtracting the result from the original equation. This manipulation is known as a Koyck transformation. The final result is

$$C_t = h\lambda Y_t + (1 - \lambda)C_{t-1}.$$

This formulation appeared to be consistent with the data, and the consensus developed that this model could explain a series of observations that had pre-viously been thought to be inconsistent (when interpreted in terms of a theory of consumption that was totally liquidity based).

Today, with the hypothesis of rational expectations prominent, a number of researchers have returned to Friedman's theory, replacing the adaptive expec-tations formula with a rational forecast of long-run average income. But rational expectations cannot be implemented without specification of the process that actually generates income through time. For illustration, we assume that this process is given by

$$Y_t = \gamma Y_{t-1} + u_t.$$

This equation can be used to get expressions for $E_t(Y_{t+1}) = \gamma Y_t$, $E_t(Y_{t+2}) = \gamma^2 Y_t$, and so on, which are then substituted into

$$C_t = hrE_t[Y_t + Y_{t+1}/(1 + r) + Y_{t+2}/(1 + r)^2 + \ldots] + v_t$$

to yield the reduced-form equation for consumption:

$$C_t = \left(\frac{hr\gamma}{1 - \gamma/(1 + r)} \right) Y_{t-1} + v_t.$$

Both u and v are error terms. Under the permanent-income hypothesis with no current liquidity constraints, h should equal unity, and the value for the long-run average real interest rate, r, should be a number in the 0.025 range. If these two values are imposed, the estimated consumption equation yields one value for γ, and the estimated income equation yields another. The two equations should be estimated by a systems method to allow for cross-equation restrictions of this sort, so that only one estimate for γ is obtained. The appropriateness of this restriction can be tested.

By comparing the rational and adaptive versions of the permanent-income hypothesis, we see that parameter γ has replaced λ. But since λ was a free parameter (one that the computer can choose so as to maximize the fit of one regression) and since γ is not free, given the cross-equation restriction that is involved in estimation of two equations simultaneously, the rational expectations version of the hypothesis is easier to reject. Thus, it is not surprising that it has been rejected when analysts (Sargent 1978; Flavin 1981) formally compared the restricted and unrestricted versions of the regressions.

Hall (1978) has suggested an alternative method of testing the joint hypotheses of permanent income and rational expectations. The original household problem is to maximize discounted utility,

$$\sum_{t=0}^{\infty} \left(\frac{1}{1 + \rho} \right)^t U(C_t),$$

where ρ is the rate of time preference, subject to the budget constraint $C_t = L + rA_t - (A_{t+1} - A_t)$. L is constant labor income, A is accumulated assets, and

r is the interest rate earned on those assets. When C_t is eliminated by substitution into the utility function and the derivative with respect to A_t is set to zero, we have

$$U'(C_{t-1}) = \left(\frac{1+r}{1+\rho}\right)U'(C_t).$$

Assume a log-linear utility function, $U = \ln C$, so that $U' = 1/C$, and the first-order condition simplifies to

$$C_t = \left(\frac{1+r}{1+\rho}\right)C_{t-1}.$$

According to the last equation, the theory says that if one runs a regression making consumption a function of its own lagged value and *anything* else dated at $t-1$—such as Y_{t-1}—the other variable(s) should not be significant. However, Y at some lag often does seem to be significant; thus, researchers speak of consumption being "too sensitive" to income, and the joint hypotheses of rational expectations and permanent income are rejected.

It should be noted, however, that this rejection does not mean that we should ignore the permanent-income hypothesis' implications for the distinction between temporary and permanent income-tax changes. That policy discussion really hinged on the fairly general idea that households care about their long-run average income; it did not depend on households' making the optimal forecast of what they could consume forever.

The strict version of the permanent-income hypothesis may fail because households are liquidity-constrained, to at least some degree, in the way we discussed when considering Ricardian equivalence in section 7.2. In that discussion, we stressed that without liquidity constraints, disposable income should be income minus what the government spends $(Y-G)$, rather than income minus what the government calls taxes $(Y-T)$. Thus, it would have been more natural for those who have tested the strict version of the permanent-income hypothesis to have used the $(Y-G)$ series instead of the $(Y-T)$. Other empirical studies directly geared to testing Ricardian equivalence (for example, Kormendi 1983) have examined these alternative measures of disposable income without directly testing the strict version of the permanent-income hypothesis. It is odd that all of this has not been tested in an integrated way, and it is also surprising, given the results referred to in the previous paragraph, that the hypothesis of Ricardian equivalence is difficult to reject categorically. Seater (1985) summarizes much of the evidence; it is so mixed that it does not seem to have changed anyone's priors regarding Ricardian equivalence.

Before closing this discussion on consumption, let us return to the general issue of empirical work involving rational expectations. In almost all empirical applications, the cross-equation restrictions seem to be rejected by the data. This has led some empirical researchers to move away from relying on any particular theoretical base and to estimate unstructured vector autoregressions (VARs). To learn how these studies can and cannot be used, and to see their relationship to the Lucas critique of generating counterfactuals for policy analysis, see Taylor (1981), Sargent (1984), and Blinder (1984). (All these articles are nontechnical, and Blinder's discussion is particularly entertaining.)

Investment

In section 1.2, we derived the standard investment function. If the nonlinear adjustment costs for capital are specified as proportional to the size of the firm's capital (that is, as bI^2/K instead of bI^2), the two versions of the investment function are

$$\frac{I}{K} = \frac{1}{2b}\left(\frac{F_K}{r + \delta} - 1\right) \tag{11.6}$$

and

$$\frac{I}{K} = \frac{1}{2b}(q - 1), \tag{11.7}$$

where q is Tobin's stock market evaluation ratio and all the other notation is as defined earlier. Bailey and Scarth (1980) show that the derivation of version 11.6 requires the assumption of static expectations but no particular assumption regarding returns to scale in the production process. They also show that the derivation of version 11.7 requires the assumption of constant returns to scale but no particular assumption regarding expectations. Since most researchers feel that imposing the assumption that firms have static expectations when making forward-looking decisions is far more unappealing than imposing the assumption of constant returns to scale, version 11.7 has formed the basis of many empirical studies in recent years.

For empirical work, the two pertinent aspects of the Lucas critique are: (1) that researchers should estimate only deep parameters representing taste or technology; and (2) that analysts should impose only functional forms that are invariant to the time paths of the exogenous variables. Since parameter b is a production function parameter and since no expectations assumption was required to derive equation 11.7, only that version of the investment theory can withstand both aspects of the Lucas critique. Unfortunately, the empirical success of version 11.7 has been qualified, no doubt partly because of the fact that the theory requires the user to have data on firms' marginal q but the stock market gives information on average q. But simultaneity should be less of an issue for version 11.7 than for version 11.6 since a firm cannot choose the price at which the stock market values its equities—at least not in the same direct way that it can choose its level of output while deciding investment expenditures.

To put the recent work on investment functions in some historical perspective, let us briefly examine how the empirical implementation of version 11.6 has proceeded. With a Cobb/Douglas form for the basic production function, version 11.6 becomes equation 11.8, and the full set of equations describing the firm is:

$$I = (\alpha/2b)[Y/(r + \delta)] - K/2b; \tag{11.8}$$

$$Y = K^\alpha N^{1-\alpha};$$

$$(1 - \alpha)Y/N = W/P;$$

$$I = \dot{K} + \delta K.$$

The investment function is simply one of these four structural equations following from the standard theory of the firm. Even if one ignores the supply side of the investment goods market and Lucas critique considerations, both I and Y are chosen simultaneously. Thus, one must either use some two-stage estimation method or estimate the reduced form for investment,

$$\frac{I}{K} = \frac{1}{2b}\left(\frac{\alpha[W/P(1 - \alpha)]^{(\alpha - 1)/\alpha}}{r + \delta} - 1 \right).$$

Taking the latter approach and using the approximation that $\ln(x - 1) \approx \ln x$, the appropriate regression equation is

$$\ln I - \ln K + \ln(r + \delta)$$

$$= \left[\ln\alpha - \ln 2b - \left(\frac{\alpha - 1}{\alpha} \right)\ln(1 - \alpha) \right] + \left(\frac{\alpha - 1}{\alpha} \right)\ln(W/P).$$

The square-bracketed term in this regression (the constant) permits an estimate of the adjustment-cost parameter b, since α can be independently derived from the estimated coefficient on $\ln(W/P)$. But if we derived the reduced form for labor demand from this same set of four structural equations, we would see that an *additional* estimate for α (and, therefore, for b) was forthcoming. So proper estimation requires running the entire set of reduced forms with the cross-equation overidentifying restrictions imposed. These restrictions have nothing to do with rational expectations or the Lucas critique; they simply follow from the basic theory of the firm. While equation 11.8 fits the data adequately when it is run without recognizing the simultaneity issue, Brechling (1975) shows that the fit breaks down completely when simultaneity is addressed.

More recently, empirical researchers working on factor demands have had somewhat more success using a framework of cost minimization, rather than profit maximization (probably because the former does not involve imposing any misspecification concerning the structure of the product market). Nevertheless, parameter estimates remain discouragingly imprecise (see, for example, Mahmud et al. 1987).

Aggregate Supply and Phillips Curves

Disagreements concerning alternative specifications of aggregate supply are at the core of the controversy between New Classical and New Keynesian theories of the business cycle. We shall consider the empirical success of these full models in the next section. Here we shall restrict our attention to single-equation studies that have been used to estimate the natural unemployment rate (or at least the nonaccelerating inflation rate of unemployment), since this concept is so fundamental in the models we examined in earlier chapters.

Keynesians (such as Blanchard et al. 1986) estimate the natural rate of unemployment by fitting an expectations-augmented Phillips curve, such as

$$p_t - p_{t-1} = c_0 - c_1 u_t + c_2[E_{t-1}(p_t) - p_{t-1}] + c_3 z_t, \tag{11.9}$$

where u stands for the unemployment rate and z for a set of variables that measure demographic or structural influences. Since estimates for parameter c_2 are almost always insignificantly different from unity, a time path for the natural unemployment rate can be calculated by using the estimated coefficients in the following formula:

$$u_t^N = \frac{c_0 + c_3 z_t}{c_1}.$$

The result is a time series that is significantly lower than the actual unemployment time series.

When New Classicals (such as Sargent 1973) estimate trade-offs between the unemployment rate and inflation, they make unemployment the dependent variable and investigate how price level or money-supply surprises affect it. The results of choosing this alternative normalization (dependent variable) are dramatic. When Keynesians estimate expectations-augmented Phillips curves, the coefficient on the unemployment rate is small, so the data are deemed consistent with a very flat short-run Phillips curve. But when New Classicals estimate the effect of price surprises on the unemployment rate, they too get very small coefficients, so the data are deemed consistent with a very steep short-run Phillips curve. It is not appealing to find both groups confirming their priors when the only difference in the empirical work is which variable is on the left-hand side during estimation.

This disparity in results is also refected in estimates of the natural unemployment rate. Lilien (1982)—although not intending to represent the New Classicals—estimates the natural rate by running a regression of the form

$$u_t = d_0 + d_1[m_t - E_{t-1}(m_t)] + d_2 z_t \tag{11.10}$$

and calculates the natural rate series as

$$u_t^N = d_0 + d_2 z_t.$$

It turns out that this series is almost indistinguishable from the actual unemployment rate.

It is most disconcerting to have such widely different estimates for the steepness of the short-run aggregate supply curve and for the natural unemployment rate. After all, the surprise supply function and the expectations-augmented Phillips curve can be viewed as alternative normalizations of the same relationship. The problem is one of simultaneity: inflation and unemployment are jointly determined. What is called for is an estimation method that copes with simultaneity and is invariant to normalization, and this means maximum-likelihood techniques. Using such techniques, Taylor (1979a) obtains estimates of the slope of the short-run Phillips curve that are of the same order as previous Keynesian estimates.

A second reason for using maximum-likelihood techniques follows from the basic fact that a *complete system* must be specified before the concept of rational expectations can be defined operationally. As a result, the analyst must always use some systems method of estimation. Although instrumental variables methods have been used (for example, by McCallum 1976), maximum-likelihood techniques are particularly appealing, since with these techniques the full set of cross equations can be considered. Thus, to exploit the rational expectations consistency restrictions fully and to avoid arbitrary normalizations, the maximum-likelihood estimation method should be used.

11.4 ALTERNATIVE THEORIES OF BUSINESS CYCLES

Three distinct approaches to modeling business cycles have been prevalent in recent years. One is called the monetary misperceptions theory since the key feature is that full information on nominal variables, such as the money supply or the overall price index, is available to agents only after a lag. Thus, suppliers have difficulty distinguishing overall nominal shocks from changes in their own relative prices, and this is why monetary disturbances have real effects.

A second approach is called real business-cycle theory. Explaining business cycles as the result of random shifts in technology, it involves households' deliberately varying their labor supply across time so that they work more in the periods during which real wages are expected to be high. Accumulation identities (such as that relating investment to the capital stock) are used as "propagation mechanisms" that allow random shocks to have persistent effects. This approach is essentially supply-side economics: money has no real effects; fiscal policy matters only through incentive effects; and aggregate fluctuations are caused entirely by supply (not demand) shocks.

The third approach involves nominal rigidities—the assumption of sticky wages and/or prices.

Let us now discuss some of the empirical issues that must be considered for us to establish a preference for any one of these approaches.

Monetary Misperceptions

As McCallum (1986, 397) notes, there has been a "recent downturn in popularity of the ... theory of cyclical fluctuations induced by monetary misperceptions." The problem that confronts this theory is that agents have access to preliminary estimates of the money supply that are accurate and unbiased estimates of the actual money supply figures (which themselves are available with very little lag). Therefore, if no serious misperception occurs, this theory cannot predict business cycles (see Grossman 1983).

Ten years ago, the initial evidence for this theory seemed supportive. Barro (1977) and others presented regressions in which real variables, such as the unemployment rate, were functions of both the anticipated and the unanticipated money supply; only the unanticipated series was statistically significant. Data for the unanticipated money supply were first constructed by running a regression with the money supply as a function of government spending and several other variables intended to capture the influences of the government budget constraint or monetary policy reactions. The residuals from this regression were taken as observations on the unanticipated money supply. It was soon pointed out, however, that this auxiliary money supply equation did not fit well, so one could credibly claim that the residuals might contain a noticeable element of anticipated money. This problem became particularly apparent when both quarterly and annual versions of the tests were presented. If agents actually acquired new information within one quarter, much of what was called unanticipated in the annual studies was really anticipated. Later work by Fischer (1980b), Gordon (1982), Mishkin (1983), and Pesaran (1982) showed conclusively that anticipated money does matter. Since only the nominal rigidities theory can predict that anticipated nominal shocks have real effects, the evidence intended to back the monetary misperceptions theory ended up supporting the Keynesian approach to business cycles instead.

Some analysts have interpreted the United States' contractionary monetary policy of the early 1980s as a test of the monetary misperceptions theory. Surely, they argue, the contractionary policy could not be assumed to be unanticipated for very long; how then could the biggest recession since the 1930s have followed a monetary policy that had been largely anticipated? In response, the New Classicals usually note that given the unprecedented levels of the U.S. government budget deficit in the early 1980s, the announced contractionary monetary policy was not credible—agents expected it to be reversed. But Laidler (1986) notes that this response means that the New Classicals are saving their model by relying on a free parameter: their model does not specify how the credibility of policy is determined or revised.

Real Business-Cycle Theory

Much of the support for real business-cycle models stems from the simulation studies of Kydland and Prescott (1982) and Prescott (1986). Kydland and Prescott took a fairly standard aggregative growth model and added a stochastic element to allow for changes in productivity. They selected numerical values for the parameters, taking care to insure that the estimates used did *not* come from time series regressions run by researchers studying business cycles. Stochastic simulations with this model produced time series for output, employment, consumption, and investment that appeared to be rather close approximations to the actual U.S. time series. These simulations have attracted a good deal of attention because many have felt that the wage elasticity of labor supply is simply not large enough for business cycles to be explained by shifts of a labor demand curve up and down a given labor supply function. Real business-cycle theorists stress that simple competitive equilibrium models are the easiest to use, since most of the profession's accumulated knowledge involves analyzing competitive equilibrium; they argue that macroeconomists should not reject this accumulated expertise unless the equilibrium business-cycle theory is clearly rejected. The Kydland/Prescott results suggest that rejecting models of this sort is much harder than all analysts (including Prescott and Lucas) thought it would be.

But the impact of the Kydland/Prescott simulations is difficult to appreciate since Adelman and Adelman (1959) performed similar simulation experiments intended to show that a standard Keynesian model (with a very few, imposed numerical parameter values) can mimic the real data too. Since *both* groups established that their model *can* explain significant parts of business-cycle data (and therefore should be taken seriously), how can any one of them argue that its preferred approach should have priority in the profession's research agenda (for this reason alone)?

In addition to this general issue, several aspects of the Kydland/Prescott simulations give critics cause for concern. Altug (1985) shows that they do not mimic the real data accurately enough to avoid rejection of the model when formal hypothesis tests are conducted. This reason in itself is not, however, sufficient for ignoring the simulations, since they can best be regarded as quantitative theoretical exercises, which are illustrative.

A more serious problem with the simulations is that it is impossible to observe technology shocks directly, and Kydland and Prescott chose the variance for these shocks so that the model's GNP variability would be consistent with the actual economy. This basis for choice is unfortunate because it is the one exception to the commendable rule followed by Kydland and Prescott: that the parameters be chosen with reference to data on long-run growth or data contained in micro cross-sections. It is important to calibrate a model with empirical evidence that is not directly related to the phenomenon under study (in this case, aggregate business-cycle time series). Recently, Prescott (1986) reports on calculations that measure technical change in terms of production function residuals. But according to the growth accounting literature (for example, Dennison 1962), the use of unadjusted capital and labor inputs leads to severe overestimation of the effects of technical change. This finding means that the methods of the real business-cycle analysts are still overstating the likely real effects of technology shocks.

In their original simulations, Kydland and Prescott ran afoul of a basic problem that virtually all economists expected; given what conventional wisdom says about the size of the wage elasticity of labor supply, they could not get the generated data to display enough variation in hours worked without producing dramatically counterfactual time paths for real wages. For their 1982 paper, Kydland and Prescott avoided this problem by changing the representative agent's utility function so that utility at each point in time depends on consumption at that point and on a weighted average of current *and past* levels of leisure. This specification is quite unconventional and does little to impress anyone who is not sympathetic to real business-cycle analysis in the first place.

More recently, Prescott (1986) draws on work by Rogerson (1984) involving labor indivisibilities. Standard models assume a convex relationship between the amount of time each agent spends not pursuing leisure and his labor supply (a relationship like *OF* in Figure 11.1). Rogerson suggests that a relationship such as *OACE* is more plausible since it has a nonconvex region (*OAC*) to reflect the fact that time is lost in such things as commuting to work. The simplest function that captures this nonconvexity is the stepped function *OBCD*, which is appropriate if the amounts of time allowed for work and for commuting to work are both fixed. It turns out that with nonconvexities, what is involved in a competitive economy is a complicated labor contract that can include lotteries to decide which individuals work in low-demand periods. This means that the primary margin of adjustment for hours of work is the number of persons, not the hours per worker. With this modification, Prescott's simulations can predict variations in the unemployment rate and a large wage elasticity of labor supply at the aggregate level, while remaining consistent with the small estimates for this

Figure 11.1 An Individual's Time and Labor Supply

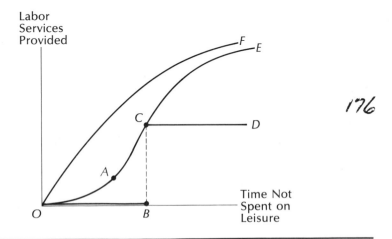

parameter that are found with micro data (by, for example, Altonji 1982 and Mankiw et al. 1985).

Despite this clever device for getting around the wage elasticity of labor supply issue, a number of economists regard the intertemporal substitution model as outrageous. In its simplest terms, it suggests that the Great Depression of the 1930s was the result of agents' anticipating World War II and deciding to withhold their labor services for a decade until that high labor-demand period arrived. Stiglitz (1986) remarks that even if workers took such a prolonged voluntary holiday during the 1930s, how can the same strategic behavior be posited for the machines that were also unemployed?

Several other particular points have also been raised by those who are critical of real business-cycle theory. For example, they say, when employment falls, it is layoffs, not quits, that rise, and consumption falls (instead of rising as it should do if leisure and consumption are complements). Also, most of the unemployed are in the long-term category, a situation that does not seem consistent with random separations. Finally, they point out, during the 1970–85 period in Europe, employment did not rise, although total factor productivity there increased more than twice as much as it did in the United States, where employment rose.

Given these problems, why does real business-cycle theory continue to appeal to some of the best young minds of the profession? Blinder (1987) attributes the attraction to "Lucas's keen intellect and profound influence," but it also comes from the theory's firm basis in microeconomic principles and its ability to match significant features of business cycles.

Perhaps another appeal of this approach is that its simplicity admits straightforward normative (not just positive) analysis. Since the theory is so explicitly grounded in a competitive framework with optimizing agents who encounter no market failure problems, the output and employment calculations are not just "fairly realistic"; they can be viewed as *optimal* responses to the exogenous technology shocks that hit a particular economy. Using this interpretation, economists have a basis for calculating the welfare gains from stabilization policy. For example, by considering a plausible utility function, Lucas (1985, 19) notes that "eliminating aggregate consumption variability entirely would ... be the equivalent in utility terms of an increase in average consumption of something like one or two tenths of a percentage point." He then concludes that the marginal social product of additional advances in business-cycle theory is very small.

Now it is understandable that New Classicals would like to have their own back-of-the-envelope calculation to use as rebuttal to the Keynesian quip: "It takes a heap of Harberger triangles to fill an Okun's gap" (Tobin 1977, 468). This comment was meant to justify the microeconomic losses that would accompany policies such as temporary wage/price controls, since these measures were thought to be necessary to remove the fear of inflation as an obstacle to reducing the underutilization of resources. The remark can be justifiably criticized if Keynesians cannot make clear the source of market failure (at the micro level) that leads to that general underutilization; if they cannot, the Okun's gap is simply not commensurable with the Harberger triangles. But similarly, unless the New Classicals can be confident that market failures such as those well identified by New Keynesians (for example, thin market trading externalities and incomplete market problems) do not exist, there is no justification for calculating the gains of stabilization policy from a model that does not admit these problems.*

Nominal Rigidities

The sticky-wage and/or sticky-price theory of the business cycle can explain the main stylized facts adequately (see McCallum 1980; 1982). Monetary shocks have real effects since at least some agents are locked into contracts for nominal wages or prices. Accumulation identities and/or adjustment costs force these disturbances to have lasting effects (so that output and employment time series display persistence). Some versions of this class of models (such as those involving sticky money wages and flexible goods prices, which we have discussed in this text) do involve a counterfactual prediction—that the real wage must vary countercyclically. But as McCallum (1980; 1982) shows, if prices are also sticky (an assumption we have often made in earlier chapters), a slight variation in the underlying theory of wage adjustment can eliminate that prediction concerning the real wage.

When the nominal rigidities model is tested in a way that places it directly against a competitor, it seems to pass the tests. For example, Poterba et al. (1986) note that with complete wage and price flexibility, the incidence of a tax does not depend on whether it is levied on producers or consumers. Their test of alternative business-cycle models exploits the fact that this equivalence does not hold if there are nominal rigidities. Their tests show that real variables were affected when the direct/indirect tax mix was changed in the United States and in the United Kingdom, and that this finding is consistent only with the nominal rigidities approach.

Mankiw (1987) provides an informal test of the adjustment-cost theory that has been used to explain nominal rigidities. One implication of the so-called menu-cost approach is that aggregate demand should have smaller real effects in high-inflation economies. (The reason is that the more frequent are price changes, the faster an aggregate demand shock can be incorporated into prices —since those prices were going to be changed anyway.) Mankiw tested this theory against Lucas's signal extraction model (which involves agents' trying to infer relative prices from observed nominal prices) by running a cross-section

---

* McCallum (1986) and Blinder (1987) also discuss Lucas's welfare calculations, and the exchange between Summers (1986) and Prescott (1986) on real business cycles is recommended reading.

regression involving many countries. Real output was made a function of lagged real output (to capture inertia), the change in nominal output (to capture the effects of aggregate demand changes), and the variance of nominal output (following Lucas 1972, to capture the signal extraction behavior). The results showed that the variance term was not significant, but the change in nominal output was, and the size of the coefficient on the latter term fell as the level of inflation rose (just as the menu-cost theory implies).

Using data from seven countries of the Organisation for Economic Co-operation and Development, Helliwell (1986) has performed extensive tests in which the New Classical and Keynesian theories are nested within a generalized adjustment-cost model that involves producers' choosing the utilization rate for all employed inputs. The restrictions that define the New Classical model are rejected for all seven countries. The restrictions that define the Keynesian model are sometimes accepted and sometimes not for Japan, Italy, West Germany, and the United Kingdom. The formal statistical tests reject both particular theories in favor of the encompassing model for Canada, the United States, and France. But for these seven countries taken as a whole, there is not decisive evidence that the Keynesian model requires generalization to three factors (all involving adjustment costs) to be consistent with the data.

The nominal rigidities approach has gained acceptance not only from statistical tests, such as those described above, but also from the simple fact that numerous contracts fixed in nominal terms for significant periods do exist. The main drawback to this approach is that tractability problems have severely limited attempts to provide a full microeconomic rationale for the macro model. The majority view of the profession seems to be that while this deficiency must be worked at, we can live with it for the present. For example, McCallum writes:

> It is better, according to this view, to use a poorly understood but empirically substantiated price-adjustment relation than to pretend—counterfactually—that all nominal adjustments take place promptly. ... It is hard to keep from having considerable sympathy with this view. But the logic of the "Lucas Critique" is inescapable. One possible way out of this dilemma ... is to proceed with models incorporating price-adjustment equations that can be rationalized by subsidiary arguments even though those arguments cannot clearly find expression in terms of the model's explicit taste and technology representation. (1987, 128)

The latter part of McCallum's remarks seem an apt description of the quadratic cost-minimization that we used for wage- or price-setters in section 1.4.*

---

* McCallum's remarks could also be taken as support for Taylor's model of overlapping wage contracts. We have chosen to give heavier emphasis to the partial-adjustment derivation described in section 1.4 (rather than Taylor's specific model) throughout this text for the following reason. In Taylor's model, the only way output persistence can occur in the face of demand disturbances is if those shocks are serially correlated.

Some Suggested Reading

On broad issues, such as comparing whole approaches to explaining business cycles, it is particularly important for students to avoid losing sight of the forest for the trees. The best insurance against this problem is to read carefully the survey articles and the interpretive position pieces written by leading macroeconomists. The reader can develop perspective by perusing the following: Akerlof and Yellen (1987), Blanchard (1987), Blinder (1986a; 1987), Fischer (1986), Howitt (1984; 1986a; 1986b), Klamer (1984), Laidler (1986), Lucas (1981; 1985), McCallum (1982; 1987), Phelps (1982), Purvis (1985), Sargent (1982; 1986, chapter 1), Solow (1979; 1986), and Tobin (1980).

11.5 CONCLUSIONS

As developments now stand, macroeconomists must choose between the following two general approaches to the subject:

1. The New Classical approach. It uses models involving general equilibrium and rational expectations with no market failures. These models usually have micro underpinnings that are well developed in the sense that the constrained maximization used as the underlying rationale consistently considers all parts of the model in a connected whole. (A particularly popular theoretic framework is the overlapping-generations model.)

   Because of the internal consistency and the explicit specification of tastes and technology, these models are free from the Lucas critique. However, they assume away any microeconomic rationale for stabilization policy and so cannot be used in debates on the merits of such policy any more than can the old-fashioned Keynesian models (which lack an explicit microeconomic basis). Also, as noted in the previous section, the New Classical models seem inconsistent with several empirical regularities.

2. The New Keynesian approach. These rational expectations models involve either sticky nominal wages/prices or well-defined reasons for market failure (such as an incomplete markets problem, an average opinion problem, or a thin market trading externality). Generally speaking these models are consistent with most of the empirical regularities, and since partial microeconomic underpinnings are often provided, the analyses can be free of the Lucas critique in important ways. But the lack of a complete microeconomic rationale for all aspects of the model (such as why there are nominal rigidities without indexing provisions) means that there is not yet a fully satisfactory basis for arguing that stabilization policy is necessarily good.

New Classicals tend to downplay the empirical limitations of their approach, on the grounds that it is no victory for Keynesian models to obtain better fits simply by allowing more of what they call free parameters. Keynesians tend to downplay the imperfect micro foundations of their approach, since they regard the methods for solving nonuniqueness problems as no less arbitrary, and since they do not see why the mere labelling of an assumption as a matter of taste or technology is not arbitrary in itself.

Nevertheless, despite the caustic rhetoric exchanged between these camps in the late 1970s, Lucas (1981) has acknowledged that there is little to separate the two methodologies if Keynesians are genuinely concerned about clarifying the microeconomic basis of their concepts of equilibrium within a framework of rational expectations. This genuine concern is clearly evident in the work of numerous New Keynesians (such as Neary and Stiglitz 1983, and those discussed in section 10.6). And other New Keynesians are adamant in their pleas for rationality in the policy activist debate. For example, Taylor (1986) emphasizes that we should evaluate only stabilization policies that can be stipulated as an ongoing rule. This increased tolerance between the two approaches is most encouraging.

The quality of our macroeconomic analysis is enhanced if there is a balance between the two criteria for judging models: internal consistency and consistency with observation.

AGGREGATION ISSUES

A.1 INTRODUCTION

The standard macro model involves representative agents who produce and use only two goods—consumption goods and capital equipment. In this appendix, we shall show that these two kinds of goods are not distinguished in a logically consistent manner within the conventional model. In section A.2, we shall investigate whether the standard stabilization-policy conclusions that follow from the model are affected when this misspecification regarding aggregation across goods is considered.

The very existence of an aggregate production function has been debated in what is often called the Cambridge controversy. We shall explain this dispute in section A.3.

Another limitation of conventional macroeconomics is that agents have only two tradable forms of wealth: money and a composite interest-earning paper asset that is referred to as either bonds or equities. In section A.4, we shall investigate whether standard macro theorems still hold when bonds and equities are not lumped together into one asset.

Finally, in section A.5, we shall consider aggregation across individuals (instead of across goods or assets). This aggregation issue may be as important as the Lucas critique.

A.2 AGGREGATION ACROSS GOODS

The standard macro model is inconsistent in that it involves two production functions. When aggregate demand and supply are defined, we have $Y = C + I$ and $Y = F(N, K)$, so the production function for goods available for consumption is

$$C = F(N, K) - I. \tag{A.1}$$

However, at the level of the individual firm—to which we refer to justify the aggregate investment function—the production function for consumer goods is

$$C = F(N, K) - I - bI^2, \tag{A.2}$$

where the bI^2 term captures the nonlinear adjustment costs.

Since we assume that all agents are the same, the macro model must contain equation A.2, not equation A.1, if it includes the standard investment function,

$$I = \frac{1}{2b}\left(\frac{F_K}{r + \delta} - 1\right),$$

which follows from equation A.2. Thus, if equation A.1 is replaced by equation A.2 in an otherwise standard macro model, we have a consistent two-good model. $F(N, K)$ can be interpreted as the gross output of consumer goods, which can be either consumed or installed (passed through an adjustment-cost process) to become investment or capital goods. According to equation A.2, the marginal rate of transformation between these two goods is not unity. Indeed, the total differential of equation A.2 implies that

$$\frac{dC}{dI} = -(1 + 2bI) = -q$$

when $dN = dK = 0$ (to specify given quantities of the factor inputs) and when we realize that $I = (1/2b)(q - 1)$. Thus, q, in addition to the interpretations given in Chapter 1, also represents the marginal cost of investment goods in terms of consumption goods. The standard macro model ignores this point. It assumes that q always equals one (by using equation A.1, not equation A.2), but at the same time it assumes that q differs from one (to establish the key linkage between the monetary and real sectors). The simplest respecification that allows both an independent investment function and a consistent disaggregation of consumer and investment goods is to replace equation A.1 with equation A.2.

One implication of this respecification is that the *IS* curve is much more likely to be positively sloped than in the standard models. In models involving equation A.1, the *IS* curve is positively sloped if $I_Y > 1 - C_Y$ (as noted in Chapter 2). With equation A.2, this condition is modified to $\bar{q}I_Y > 1 - C_Y$. The equilibrium value of the relative price, $\bar{q}$, must exceed one since, in full equilibrium, replacement investment is positive. (Indeed, the data suggest that $\bar{q}$ is approximately 1.25.) Once this point is acknowledged, Bailey and Scarth (1980) show that it may be difficult to avoid the conclusion that the *IS* curve is positively sloped in a logically consistent model.

Scarth (1984) shows that if the adjustment-cost process for installing capital is modified so that labor is involved, investment becomes a shift variable for the labor demand function. Thus, any "aggregate demand" policy that affects investment must shift the position of both aggregate demand and supply schedules. This effect makes the standard inconsistent treatment of goods aggregation more fundamental. The importance at the policy level can be easily appreciated.

For example, if a contractionary monetary policy decreases investment and this reduction shifts both aggregate demand and supply schedules to the left, it would not be surprising for the short-run outcome to be a significant drop in output and only a very modest reduction in the price level.

A number of macroeconomists have analyzed two-sector models that have two production functions, two labor demand functions, and so on, so separate consumption and investment goods sectors are fully defined. But as we have just explained, such a wholesale proliferation of parameters (with the accompanying ambiguities in virtually all multipliers) is not required to obtain explicit disaggregation. All that is needed is a logically consistent treatment of the adjustment costs for capital.

A.3   AGGREGATION ACROSS CAPITAL GOODS

For all the models examined in this text, we have assumed the existence of a well-behaved aggregate production function. A key property of this function is that the higher the relative price of labor (that is, the higher the wage/rental cost of capital ratio), the more capital intensive the production methods (that is, the higher the full equilibrium capital/labor ratio). This standard assumption is made particularly explicit in the basic theory of Neoclassical growth as described by Solow (1956), who is from the Massachusetts Institute of Technology, Cambridge, Massachusetts. But a group of economists from Cambridge, England, led by Joan Robinson (1970), questioned this assumption. This debate is often referred to as the Cambridge controversy.

The concern expressed by the economists of Cambridge, England was essentially about an aggregation issue. They noted the existence of a whole group of capital goods that differ according to how long it takes labor and other pieces of capital to produce them. The longer the production period for each piece of capital, the higher the interest costs (compared to the labor costs) as a proportion of the total production costs. This means that when the wage/rental cost of capital ratio changes in the economy, different techniques (that is, particular capital goods) become cost-minimizing. It turns out that "reswitching" is possible—a particular technique can be the least-cost one at both high and low interest rates but not at intermediate interest rates. This, in turn, implies that the Neoclassical assumption that the capital/labor ratio be inversely related to the wage/rental ratio is not logically necessary. Indeed, discontinuities and reversals are possible.

This work on reswitching is an example of a widespread problem in economics: microeconomic theory has macroeconomic implications only under rather restrictive assumptions. Most macroeconomists react to this proposition in a pragmatic way. If aggregate models seem consistent with the macroeconomic "facts", then, no matter how restrictive the aggregation requirements (needed to preclude such things as reswitching) seem, analysts conclude that not too much is lost by assuming that the economy operates as if these restrictions were appropriate.

A minority of economists remain unimpressed with this "positive" methodology. It certainly must be admitted that some of the mainstream "tests" of aggregate production theory (which is the example discussed in this section) have very low power (see, for example, Shaikh 1974). Nevertheless, the general implications of aggregative macro theory do seem helpful in explaining business cycles, which is no doubt why the majority of economists operate as if the reswitching controversy had not taken place. That is, they derive macroeconomic relationships from microeconomic analyses without any reference to aggregation issues.

A.4 AGGREGATION ACROSS TRADABLE ASSETS

Let us now investigate whether the standard fiscal and monetary policy conclusions depend on the assumption that all nonmonetary assets can be treated as perfect substitutes and lumped together as "equities" or "bonds". To do this, we distinguish equities, which are issued by firms to finance investment and yield r^e, from bonds, which yield r. The revised macro model is

$$Y = C(Y) + I(q - 1) + G; \tag{A.3}$$

$$q = F_K/r^e; \tag{A.4}$$

$$M = L(Y, r, r^e, A); \tag{A.5}$$

$$B = b(Y, r, r^e, A); \tag{A.6}$$

$$qK = V(Y, r, r^e, A); \tag{A.7}$$

$$A = M + B + qK. \tag{A.8}$$

Since we wish to focus on disaggregation within the *LM* sector, we avoid complications that follow from a positively sloped *IS* curve by interpreting F_K as the average or expected level, which is assumed to be constant. Thus, the exogenous variables are G, M, B, K, and F_K, and the endogenous variables are Y, q, r, r^e, and A. There are six equations in five unknowns, but only three of equations A.5 through A.8 are independent. To see this, substitute equation A.5, A.6, and A.7 into equation A.8, and take the total differential:

$$dA = (L_Y + b_Y + V_Y)dY + (L_r + b_r + V_r)dr \tag{A.9}$$
$$+ (L_{r^e} + b_{r^e} + V_{r^e})dr^e + (L_A + b_A + V_A)dA.$$

From A.9 we see that the following restrictions must hold:

$$L_Y + b_Y + V_Y = 0; \tag{A.10a}$$

$$L_r + b_r + V_r = 0; \tag{A.10b}$$

$$L_{r^e} + b_{r^e} + V_{r^e} = 0; \tag{A.10c}$$

$$L_A + b_A + V_A = 1. \tag{A.10d}$$

Given these conditions, we drop equation A.7 from the analysis. In addition, we assume that all assets are normal $(0 < L_A, b_A, V_A < 1)$ and that gross substitutability exists:

$b_r > 0;$ $L_r, V_r < 0;$

$V_{r^e} > 0;$ $L_{r^e}, b_{r^e} < 0;$

$L_Y > 0;$ $b_Y, V_Y < 0.$

Taking the total differential of equations A.3, A.4, A.5, A.6, and A.8, we have

$$
\begin{bmatrix} (1 - C_Y) & 0 & -a \\ L_Y & L_r & (L_{r^e} + fL_A) \\ b_Y & b_r & (b_{r^e} + fb_A) \end{bmatrix} \begin{bmatrix} dY \\ dr \\ dr^e \end{bmatrix} = \begin{bmatrix} 1 & 0 & 0 \\ 0 & (1 - L_A) & -L_A \\ 0 & -b_A & (1 - b_A) \end{bmatrix} \begin{bmatrix} dG \\ dM \\ dB \end{bmatrix}
$$

where $a = -I_q F_K/(r^e)^2 < 0$, $f = -F_K K/(r^e)^2 < 0$, and the basic determinant is

$$\Delta = L_r[(1 - C_Y)(b_{r^e} + fb_A) + ab_Y] - b_r[(1 - C_Y)(L_{r^e} + fL_A) + aL_Y].$$

At first glance, the sign of Δ appears indeterminant. However, the gross substitutability conditions imply that $L_Y > |b_Y|$ and $b_r > |L_r|$, so that $-b_r aL_Y > L_r ab_Y$ and $\Delta > 0$.

The signs of the standard fiscal and monetary multipliers are unaffected by the disaggregation across assets:

$$\frac{dY}{dG} = \frac{L_r(b_{r^e} + fL_A) - b_r(L_{r^e} + fL_A)}{\Delta} > 0; \tag{A.11}$$

$$\frac{dY}{dM} = \frac{-a[b_r(l - L_A) + b_A L_r]}{\Delta} > 0. \tag{A.12}$$

To sign the numerator in equation A.12, we must use equations A.10b and A.10d to eliminate b_r and $(1 - L_A)$. This monetary policy multiplier corresponds to a "helicopter drop" of new currency. An open-market purchase of bonds can be examined by setting $dB = -dM$ and deriving dY/dM. It is left for the reader to verify that this multiplier is also positive. Thus, even though monetary policy involves changes in the money and bond markets while firms' investment spending depends only on developments in the equities market, the assumption of gross substitutability is sufficient to sign the multiplier. (A fuller discussion of disaggregation within the financial sector is given in Tobin 1969.)

Two final results are worth noting: $dY/dG > 0$ even if $L_r \to 0$, and $dY/dM > 0$ even if $L_r \to -\infty$. Thus, even if one wishes to stress either the extreme Monetarist or the extreme Keynesian assumption regarding the demand for money function, *both* fiscal and monetary policy remain effective when there is more than one nonmonetary asset. Except in these extreme cases, however, we have seen that disaggregation across financial assets does not complicate standard macroeconomics as long as gross substitutability is assumed.

A.5   AGGREGATION ACROSS INDIVIDUALS

To respond to the Lucas critique, we must go behind demand and supply curves to focus on the primitive parameters of taste and technology. But if these parameters are to be estimated with aggregate data, the exercise implicitly involves the assumption that the aggregation restrictions are also primitive (that is, that the aggregator function is invariant to changes in the policy regime).

Geweke (1985) investigates this common assumption by considering simple models in which exact aggregation is always possible. He can then compare the order of magnitude of both the aggregation and the expectations issues. He finds that the aggregators depend on the policy regime to about the same extent as does expectation formation. Blinder (1986c) and Hendry (1987) have argued that the Lucas critique may have been overemphasized.

A.6   CONCLUSIONS

We have learned that the conditions required for consistent aggregation throughout the macro model are such that there is no logical reason why constrained maximization at the individual level should have any macroeconomic implications. Nevertheless, macroeconomists have proceeded with representative agent theory involving a minimum disaggregation for goods and assets for two reasons: (1) the resulting models seem broadly consistent with the stylized facts concerning aggregate data; and (2) there is no obvious alternative to micro theory that can be used as a basis for macroeconomic model building. But by proceeding in this way—as if aggregation were not an issue—while giving ever-greater weight to microeconomic underpinnings (in an attempt to solve the Lucas critique), macroeconomists and empirical researchers may be pushing the ''as if'' methodology too far.

QUESTIONS

CHAPTER 1

1. Intertemporal models of household or firm behavior have been increasingly relied on to specify several of the key structural equations in the macro model. Explain one of these theories, and make clear the macro policy complications that follow from this micro underpinning.

2. What is the Lucas critique? Illustrate it with reference to the Phillips curve.

3. Suppose the government subsidizes firms' investment spending by paying a fixed proportion of all investment purchases. To explain how this subsidy parameter enters the investment function, derive the investment function that follows from present value maximization with nonlinear adjustment costs.

4. Corporate tax laws allow firms to claim that capital depreciates faster than it actually does, but the tax system is not indexed. Summarize the Boadway (1980) analysis to explain how these features of the tax system affect the rental cost of capital and thus affect investment.

CHAPTER 2

1. What is the logic behind the correspondence principle? Explain any use you make of this principle in deriving the effect on the interest rate of an increase in the tax rate in the following model:

$$Y = C[(1 - k)Y] + I(Y, r) + G;$$

$$M/P = L[Y, r(1 - k)];$$

$$\dot{P}/P = H[(Y - \bar{Y})/\bar{Y}].$$

2. Each of the following propositions concerns a fixed-price model. State whether each is true or false, and explain your answer.

   a. A higher tax rate makes the *IS* curve steeper.

   b. Monetary and fiscal policies have no effect on national product if there are no adjustment costs for capital.

   c. The balanced-budget multiplier is unity if the central bank pegs the interest rate, but not if it pegs the money supply.

   d. The higher the interest sensitivity of money demand, the larger the effect of a tax rate change on investment.

3. Add inventories to the simple fixed-price macro model, and explain how its properties are affected.

4. Explain why you agree or disagree with this statement: the tax system is a built-in stabilizer in the following model:

$$Y_t = C_t + I_t + \bar{G};$$

$$C_t = c(1 - k)Y_t;$$

$$I_t = \bar{I} + vY_{t-1} + u_t.$$

Bars indicate exogenous variables; u_t is a disturbance term with mean zero, constant variance, and no serial correlation; t indicates discrete time periods. The assumptions about parameters are: $0 < c < 1$; $0 < k < 1$; and $v > 0$.

CHAPTER 3

1. How does the presence of a sales tax affect the *IS*, *LM*, and aggregate supply schedules? Explain the effects of a sales tax rate increase on the price level.

2. Under what conditions (if any) is the aggregate demand curve vertical? horizontal?

3. Archie and Veronica were overheard arguing after macro class:

   ARCHIE: Unemployment is caused by wages' being too high.

   VERONICA: Wage cuts lead to decreased consumption spending by workers and therefore to higher unemployment.

   Evaluate Archie and Veronica as macroeconomists.

4. State whether each of the following propositions is true or false, and explain your answer.

   a. Lowering unemployment requires decreasing the incomes of workers already employed.

   b. The *IS* curve is steeper when firms encounter a binding sales constraint.

c. The higher the payroll tax rate levied on firms, the flatter the aggregate supply curve.

d. An increase in the supply of labor (say, because of immigration) increases unemployment and lowers the price level in both Keynesian and Classical models.

e. With a rigid money wage and a Cobb/Douglas production function, $Y = N^\alpha K^{1-\alpha}$, the price elasticity of the aggregate supply curve is $1 - \alpha$.

f. The balanced-budget multiplier is positive in Keynesian models but negative in Classical models.

g. An income tax cut lowers real wages and increases the price level in both Keynesian and Classical models.

h. Movements upward and leftward along the aggregate demand schedule must involve lower interest rates.

i. The aggregate supply curve is horizontal if the production function is linear in the relevant range.

j. An increase in the money supply has a greater effect on the interest rate when nominal government expenditure is pegged than when real government expenditure is pegged.

CHAPTER 4

1. Neither the Quantity theory nor the Phillips curve, by itself, provides an adequate theory of inflation. Explain fully what you regard as an adequate theory of inflation. Make clear what role (if any) the Quantity theory and the Phillips curve play within your model.

2. Explain how the usual formula relating the nominal and real interest rates is an approximation. Show how the existence of taxes on nominal interest income affects the relationship between real and nominal interest rates.

3. State whether each of the following propositions is true or false, and explain your answer.

a. The steeper the short-run Phillips curve, the more likely it is that inflation will accelerate indefinitely.

b. Pegging the rate of growth of the money supply precludes accelerating inflation.

c. The steeper the short-run Phillips curve, the faster the economy reaches full equilibrium.

d. The long-run effect of an increase in autonomous expenditure on the nominal interest rate is independent of the interest elasticity of money demand.

4. Use the model with which we ended this chapter to investigate whether government expenditure should be used for contracyclical policy:

aggregate demand: $\qquad y = \phi g + \theta(m - p) + \psi \dot{p}$;

aggregate supply: $\qquad \dot{p} = \dot{\bar{p}} + a(\bar{p} - p)$;

policy reaction function: $\quad g = \bar{g} - \gamma(y - \bar{y})$.

Should the fiscal policy parameter, γ, be positive (as presumed by activists) or zero (as assumed by those favoring laissez-faire)? Explain your reasoning.

CHAPTER 5

1. Assuming that the income tax rate affects labor supply, rework the Sargent/Wallace analysis to show that systematic changes in the tax rate can affect the asymptotic variance of output.

2. Consider the following system:

$$Y = C + I + \bar{G};$$

$$C = cY^e;$$

$$I = vY + u.$$

$$c > 0 \qquad v > 0 \qquad c + v < 1 \qquad E(u) = 0 \qquad E(u^2) = \sigma_u^2.$$

Compare the implications of two hypotheses concerning income expectations: adaptive expectations, $Y^e = Y_{-1}$, and rational expectations, $Y^e = E_{-1}(Y)$. Explain whether the following statement is true or false: both the impact effect of government expenditure on output and the asymptotic variance of output are higher with adaptive expectations.

3. Poole, Friedman, and Sargent and Wallace have all contributed influential theoretical analyses of optimal monetary policy. Explain each of these contributions and compare the underlying assumptions of the three analyses.

4. State whether each of the following propositions is true or false, and explain your answer.

a. Changes in government spending have no effect on the budget deficit in the following economy:

$$Y = C + I + G;$$

$$C = 0.8E(Y - T);$$

$$T = 0.5Y;$$

$$I = 0.1E(Y).$$

E stands for rationally formed expectations.

b. A higher tax rate means more built-in stability for the following economy, whether income expectations are static—$(Y^d)^e = (1 - t)Y_{-1}$—or rationally formed—$(Y^d)^e = (1 - t)E(Y)$:

$$Y = C + A + u;$$

$$C = c(Y^d)^e.$$

$$E(u) = 0 \qquad E(u_i u_j) = \sigma_u^2 \quad \text{if} \quad i = j$$
$$= 0 \quad \text{if} \quad i \neq j.$$

A denotes autonomous expenditures.

c. The authorities should peg the price level rather than the money supply, to minimize the variance of output in the following model:

$$\text{supply:} \quad y = ay_{-1} + b(p - p^e) + u;$$

$$\text{demand:} \quad y = c(m - p) + v.$$

Here, y, m, p, and p^e are the logarithms of, respectively, output, the money supply, the price level, and the expected price level; a, b, and c are positive parameters; u and v are independent disturbances with zero means, constant variances, and no serial correlation. Agents form expectations rationally.

CHAPTER 6

1. Explain why some economists find the hypothesis of rational expectations appealing, and why others do not.

2. Explain and compare the ways the correspondence principle is interpreted by conventional macroeconomists, the recent analysts of perfect foresight models, and Post-Keynesians.

3. Under what conditions will an announced increase in the future money supply have effects only at the time of the announcement?

4. Consider the fixed-price version of Blanchard's model of the interaction between the real economy and the stock market. Suppose the monetary authority pegs the interest rate. In this case, how does output respond to an unanticipated increase in government spending? Can the expectation of a contractionary fiscal policy in the future cause a recession?

CHAPTER 7

1. Rework the Blinder/Solow analysis with bonds that mature at the end of one period (instead of consols). Are there any important differences in the analysis?

2. If bond yields were indexed, would this make bond-financed deficits more or less likely to involve stability?

3. Explain how the prediction that fiscal policy involves crowding-out depends on or is affected by each of the following:

   a. Adjustment costs for capital;

   b. Interest rate effects;

   c. Wealth effects;

   d. Wage and price changes;

   e. Rational expectations.

4. State whether each of the following propositions is true or false, and explain your answer.

   a. In a fixed-price model, bond financing necessarily involves instability if the central bank pegs the interest rate.

   b. In a fixed-price model, the full equilibrium effect on the interest rate of an increase in government expenditure must be higher than the impact-period effect, whether the spending is tax- or money-financed.

   c. In a fixed-price model, an open-market purchase of government bonds must be contractionary if budget deficits are bond-financed.

   d. The higher the marginal propensity to consume, the faster the speed of adjustment to full equilibrium under money-financed deficits.

   e. If the income tax system involves an exemption that is fixed in nominal terms, money-financed budget deficits must involve stability even if the natural rate of output is an exogenous constant.

CHAPTER 8

1. Consider a small, open economy in which all income (including interest income) is taxed. How will differences in the exchange-rate regime affect the impact of an income tax cut on the level of national output?

2. Add the government budget constraint written below to the flexible-exchange-rate version of the standard open-economy model. Examine the case of perfect capital mobility, taking the money supply as the residual policy variable. Compare the impact and long-run multipliers of government spending on national income, and consider whether the system is stable.

   $$G = tY + \dot{M}.$$

3. State whether each of the following propositions is true or false, and explain your answer.

a. Imports must increase following an increase in government spending in a small, open economy, whether the exchange rate is fixed or flexible.

b. The balanced-budget multiplier is one if the economy has perfect capital mobility and fixed exchange rates.

4. To our basic model of a small, open economy, add tariffs levied by foreign countries, so the relative price term in the domestic import function is $EP^m(1+t)/P^d$. Also, allow the domestic cost of living to depend on this tariff: $P = \alpha P^d + (1-\alpha)(1+t)EP^m$. Show that an increase in this foreign tariff rate causes a domestic recession, whether exchange rates are fixed or flexible.

CHAPTER 9

1. Does levying a domestic tariff on imports raise domestic employment in a small, open economy with intermediate imports? Explain how your answer depends on exchange-rate policy.

2. Explain fully the differences (both in structure and policy predictions) between the Mundell/Fleming model of an open economy and the portfolio equilibrium approach to the open economy.

3. Is crowding-out an issue for a small, open economy? Add government bonds to the fixed-price version of the portfolio balance model, and examine the efficacy of bond-financed deficits for a small, open economy.

4. Consider the following model of a small, open economy:

$$\text{IS:} \quad Y_t = -\gamma r_t + \delta(e_t + p^* - p_t) + u_t;$$

$$\text{LM:} \quad r_t = \alpha Y_t - \beta(m_t - p_t);$$

$$\text{covered interest arbitrage:} \quad r_t = r^* + E_t(e_{t+1}) - e_t;$$

$$\text{Phillips curve:} \quad p_t - p_{t-1} = \theta(Y_{t-1} - \bar{Y});$$

$$\text{monetary/exchange-rate policy:} \quad m_t - \bar{m} = \phi(e_t - \bar{e}).$$

All variables except r are logarithms. t is the time subscript; E is the expectations operator; the asterisk denotes a foreign variable; and u_t is a disturbance term with constant variance and no serial correlation. All private-sector parameters are positive. ϕ is the central bank parameter, which is zero under purely floating exchange rates and minus infinity under purely fixed exchange rates. Assuming the authority wants to minimize the asymptotic variance of output, should it follow a policy of "leaning against the wind" ($\phi < 0$) or a policy of "leaning with the wind" ($\phi > 0$)?

CHAPTER 10

1. Recent models of household behavior imply that temporary tax changes have little effect on consumption demand but may have a large effect on the quantity of goods supplied. Explain these models fully, and state whether you agree or disagree with this summary.

2. "The pursuit of a full-employment target which no one can measure or even define conceptually cannot be expected to contribute to the solution of the problem of reducing business cycle risk" (Lucas 1978, 357). Discuss the issues raised by this statement.

3. "The real (macroeconomic) issue is not the existence of a long-run static equilibrium with unemployment, but the possibility of protracted unemployment which the natural adjustments of a market economy remedy very slowly if at all" (Tobin 1975, 195–196). Discuss this view. How does it relate to the theories discussed in this chapter?

4. Derive the effects of tax rate policy and monetary policy on employment in a macro model that has unions and firms cooperating when setting wages and employment.

CHAPTER 11

1. Discuss whether more extensive use of indexing money wages would increase macroeconomic stability.

2. In the standard Keynesian model, the goods, money, and bond markets all clear while the labor market is in excess supply. In Weitzman's (1985) analysis of profit-sharing, the goods, money, and bond markets all clear while the labor market is in excess demand. Do either of these analyses violate Walras's law? Explain.

3. Explain what you regard to be the major current controversies in macroeconomic theory.

4. How do you assess the evidence concerning alternative theories of the business cycle?

REFERENCES

ADELMAN, I., and F.L. ADELMAN (1959), "The Dynamic Properties of the Klein-Goldberger Model," *Econometrica* 27, 596–625.

AKERLOF, G.A., and J. YELLEN (1985), "A Near Rational Model of the Business Cycle, with Wage and Price Inertia," *Quarterly Journal of Economics* 100, 823–838.

——— (1987), "Rational Models of Irrational Behavior," *The American Economic Review Proceedings* 77, 137–142.

ALTONJI, J.G. (1982), "The Intertemporal Substitution Model of Labour Market Fluctuations: An Empirical Analysis," *Review of Economic Studies* 49, 783–824.

ALTUG, S. (1985), "Gestation Lags and the Business Cycle: An Empirical Analysis," University of Minnesota, working paper.

ARGY, V., and J. SALOP (1983), "Prices and Output Effects of Monetary and Fiscal Expansion in a Two-Country World under Flexible Exchange Rates," *Oxford Economic Papers* 35, 228–246.

BAILEY, R.E., and W.M. SCARTH (1980), "Adjustment Costs and Aggregate Demand Theory," *Economica* 47, 423–431.

BARRO, R.J. (1974), "Are Government Bonds Net Wealth?" *Journal of Political Economy* 82, 1095–1117.

——— (1977), "Unanticipated Money Growth and Unemployment in the United States," *The American Economic Review* 67, 101–115.

BARRO, R.J., and H.I. GROSSMAN (1971), "A General Disequilibrium Model of Income and Employment," *The American Economic Review* 61, 82–93.

BAUMOL, W.J. (1961), "Pitfalls in Contracyclical Policies: Some Tools and Results," *Review of Economics and Statistics* 66, 21–26.

BLACKHOUSE, R.E. (1981), "Keynesian Unemployment and the One-Sector Neoclassical Growth Model," *Economic Journal* 91, 174–187.

BLANCHARD, O.J. (1981), "Output, the Stock Market, and Interest Rates," *The American Economic Review* 71, 132–143.

——— (1987), "Why Does Money Affect Output? A Survey," National Bureau of Economic Research, working paper no. 2285 [forthcoming (1987-88) in B. Friedman and F.H. Hahn, eds., *Handbook of Monetary Economics*, Amsterdam: North Holland].

BLANCHARD, O.J., R. DORNBUSCH, and R. LAYARD (1986), *Restoring Europe's Prosperity: Macroeconomic Papers from the Centre for European Policy Studies*, Cambridge, Mass.: The MIT Press.

BLANCHARD, O.J., and C.M. KAHN (1980), "The Solution of Linear Difference Models Under Rational Expectations," *Econometrica* 48, 1305–1311.

BLANCHARD, O.J., and N. KIYOTAKI (1986), "Monopolistic Competition and the Effects of Aggregate Demand," Massachusetts Institute of Technology, mimeo (forthcoming in *The American Economic Review*).

BLANCHARD, O.J., and L.H. SUMMERS (1986), "Hysteresis and the European Unemployment Problem," *NBER Macroeconomics Annual 1986* 1, 15–78.

——— (1987), "Hysteresis in Unemployment," *European Economic Review* 31, 288–295.

BLINDER, A.S. (1973), "Can Income Taxes Be Inflationary? An Expository Note," *National Tax Journal* 26, 295–301.

——— (1981), "Inventories and the Structure of Macro Models," *The American Economic Review Proceedings* 71, 11–16.

——— (1984), "Discussion," *The American Economic Review Proceedings* 74, 417–419.

——— (1986a), "Comment," *NBER Macroeconomics Annual 1986* 1, 335–343.

——— (1986b), "Keynes After Lucas," *Eastern Economic Journal* 12, 209–216.

——— (1986c), "A Skeptical Note on the New Econometrics," in M.H. Peston and R.E. Quandt, eds., *Prices, Competition and Equilibrium*, Oxford: Philip Allan Publishers.

——— (1987), "Keynes, Lucas, and Scientific Progress," *The American Economic Review Proceedings* 77, 130–135.

BLINDER, A.S., and R.M. SOLOW (1973), "Does Fiscal Policy Matter?" *Journal of Public Economics* 2, 319–337.

——— (1976), "Does Fiscal Policy Still Matter? A Reply," *Journal of Monetary Economics* 6, 501–510.

BOADWAY, R. (1980), "Corporate Taxation and Investment: A Synthesis of the Neoclassical Theory," *Canadian Journal of Economics* 13, 250–267.

BOOTHE, P., K. CLINTON, A. CÔTÉ, and D. LONGWORTH (1986), "International Asset Substitutability: A Summary of Research," in J. Sargent, ed., *Postwar Macroeconomic Development*, Toronto: University of Toronto Press.

BOYER, R.S. (1975), "Commodity Markets and Bond Markets in a Small, Fixed-Exchange Rate Economy," *Canadian Journal of Economics* 8, 1–23.

BRAINARD, W. (1967), "Uncertainty and the Effectiveness of Policy," *The American Economic Review* 57, 411–425.

BRANSON, W.H. (1972), "Macroeconomic Equilibrium with Portfolio Balance in Open Economies," Institute for International Economic Studies, Stockholm, seminar paper no. 22.

BRANSON, W.H., and J. ROTEMBERG (1980), "International Adjustment with Wage Rigidity," *European Economic Review* 13, 309–332.

BRECHLING, F. (1975), *Investment and Employment Decisions,* Manchester: Manchester University Press.

BUITER, W.H., and H.R. LORIE (1977), "Some Unfamiliar Properties of a Familiar Macroeconomic Model," *Economic Journal* 87, 743–754.

BUITER, W.H., and MILLER, M. (1981), "Monetary Policy and International Competitiveness," *Oxford Economic Papers* 33 (Supplement), 143–175.

——— (1982), "Real Exchange Rate Overshooting and the Output Cost of Bringing Down Inflation," *European Economic Review* 18, 85–123.

BUITER, W.H., and D.D. PURVIS (1983), "Oil, Disinflation, and Export Competitiveness: A Model of the 'Dutch Disease,' " in J.S. Bhandari and B.H. Putnam, eds., *Economic Interdependence and Flexible Exchange Rates,* Cambridge, Mass. and London, England: The MIT Press.

BURBIDGE, J.B. (1984), "Government Debt: Reply," *The American Economic Review* 74, 766–767.

CAGAN, P. (1956), "The Monetary Dynamics of Hyperinflation," in M. Friedman, ed., *Studies in the Quantity Theory of Money,* Chicago: University of Chicago Press.

CAMPBELL, J., and N.G. MANKIW (1986), "Are Output Fluctuations Transitory?" National Bureau of Economic Research working paper.

CHRIST, C.F. (1979), "On Fiscal and Monetary Policies and the Government Budget Constraint," *The American Economic Review* 69, 526–538.

CLOWER, R.W. (1965), "The Keynesian Counterrevolution: A Theoretical Appraisal," in F.H. Hahn and F.P.R. Brechling, eds., *The Theory of Interest Rates,* London: Macmillan.

DELONG, J.B., and L.H. SUMMERS (1986), "Is Increased Price Flexibility Stabilizing?" *The American Economic Review* 76, 1031–1044.

DENNISON, E.F. (1962), *The Sources of Economic Growth in the United States and the Alternatives Before Us,* New York: Committee for Economic Development.

DIAMOND, P.A. (1984), *A Search-Equilibrium Approach to the Micro Foundations of Macroeconomics,* Cambridge, Mass. and London, England: The MIT Press.

——— (1987), "Multiple Equilibria in Models of Credit," *The American Economic Review Proceedings* 77, 82–86.

DIXIT, A. (1980), "A Solution Technique for Rational Expectations Models with Applications to Exchange Rate and Interest Rate Determination," University of Warwick, mimeo.

DORNBUSCH, R. (1976), "Expectations and Exchange Rate Dynamics," *Journal of Political Economy* 84, 1161–1176.

FISCHER, S. (1980a), "Dynamic Inconsistency, Cooperation, and the Benevolent Dissembling Government," *Journal of Economic Dynamics and Control* 2, 93–107.

——— (1980b), "On Activist Monetary Policy with Rational Expectations," in S. Fischer, ed., *Rational Expectations and Economic Policy,* Chicago: University of Chicago Press for the National Bureau of Economic Research.

——— (1986), "1944, 1963 and 1985: Modiglianiesque Macro Models," National Bureau of Economic Research, working paper no. 1797.

FLAVIN, M.A. (1981), "The Adjustment of Consumption to Changing Expectations about Future Income," *Journal of Political Economy* 89, 974–1009.

FLEMING, J.M. (1962), "Domestic Financial Policies Under Fixed and Floating Exchange Rates," *International Monetary Fund Staff Papers* 9, 369–379.

FLEMMING, J.S. (1987), "Wage Flexibility and Employment Stability," *Oxford Economic Papers* 39, 161–174.

FRIEDMAN, M. (1948), "A Monetary and Fiscal Framework for Economic Stability," *The American Economic Review* 38, 245–264.

——— (1956), "The Quantity Theory of Money: A Restatement," in M. Friedman, ed., *Studies in the Quantity Theory of Money,* Chicago: University of Chicago Press.

——— (1957), *A Theory of the Consumption Function,* Princeton, N.J.: National Bureau of Economic Research and Princeton University Press.

——— (1959), *A Program for Monetary Stability,* New York: Fordham University Press.

——— (1968), "The Role of Monetary Policy," *The American Economic Review* 58, 1–17.

FRYDMAN, R., and E. PHELPS, (1984), *Individual Forecasting and Aggregate Outcomes: Rational Expectations Examined,* Cambridge, England: Cambridge University Press.

GEARY, P., and J. KENNAN (1982), "The Employment Real Wage Relationship: An International Study," *Journal of Political Economy* 90, 854–871.

GEWEKE, J. (1985), "Macroeconometric Modeling and the Theory of the Representative Agent," *The American Economic Review Proceedings* 75, 206–210.

GORDON, R.J. (1982), "Price Inertia and Policy Ineffectiveness in the United States, 1890–1980," *Journal of Political Economy* 90, 1087–1117.

GRAY, J.A. (1976), "Wage Indexation: A Macroeconomic Approach," *Journal of Monetary Economics* 2, 221–236.

——— (1984), "Dynamic Instability in Rational Expectations Models: An Attempt to Clarify," *International Economic Review* 25, 93–122.

GROSSMAN, H.I. (1983), "The Natural-Rate Hypothesis, the Rational-Expectations Hypothesis, and the Remarkable Survival of Non-Market-Clearing Assumptions," *Carnegie-Rochester Conference Series on Public Policy* 19, 225–245.

HAHN, F.H. and R.M. SOLOW (1986), "Is Wage Flexibility a Good Thing?" in W. Beckerman, ed., *Wage Rigidity and Unemployment*, Baltimore: The Johns Hopkins University Press.

HALL, R.E. (1978), "Stochastic Implications of the Life Cycle-Permanent Income Hypothesis: Theory and Evidence," *Journal of Political Economy* 86, 971–988.

——— (1980), "Labor Supply and Aggregate Fluctuations," *Carnegie-Rochester Conference Series on Public Policy* 12, 7–33.

——— (1986), "Comment," *NBER Macroeconomics Annual 1986* 1, 85–88.

HELLIWELL, J.F. (1986), "Supply-side Macro-economics," *Canadian Journal of Economics* 19, 597–625.

HENDRY, D.F. (1987), "Testing Feedback versus Feedforward Econometric Equations," Oxford University mimeo, August 1987 (forthcoming in the *Oxford Economic Papers*).

HOWITT, P. (1984), "Information and Coordination: A Review Article," *Economic Inquiry* 22, 429–446.

——— (1985), "Transaction Costs in the Theory of Unemployment," *The American Economic Review* 75, 88–100.

——— (1986a), "Conversations with Economists: A Review Essay," *Journal of Monetary Economics* 18, 103–118.

────── (1986b), "The Keynesian Recovery," *Canadian Journal of Economics* 19, 626–641.

────── (1986c), "Wage Flexibility and Employment," *Eastern Economic Journal* 12, 237–242.

JOHNSON, L. (1977), "Keynesian Dynamics and Growth," *Journal of Money, Credit and Banking* 9, 328–340.

KATZ, L.F. (1986), "Efficiency Wage Theories: A Partial Evaluation," *NBER Macroeconomics Annual 1986* 1, 235–275.

KEYNES, J.M. (1936), *The General Theory of Employment, Interest and Money*, London: Macmillan.

KLAMER, A. (1984), *The New Classical Macroeconomics*, Brighton, Sussex: Wheatsheaf Books.

KNIGHT, F.H. (1921), *Risk, Uncertainty and Profit*, London: London School of Economics.

KORMENDI, R.C. (1983), "Government Debt, Government Spending and Private Sector Behavior," *The American Economic Review* 73, 994–1009.

KOURI, P. (1976), "The Exchange Rate and the Balance of Payments in the Short Run and in the Long Run: A Monetary Approach," *Scandinavian Journal of Economics* 2, 280–304.

KYDLAND, F.E., and PRESCOTT, E.C. (1977), "Rules Rather than Discretion: The Inconsistency of Optimal Plans," *Journal of Political Economy* 85, 473–492.

────── (1982), "Time to Build and Aggregate Fluctuations," *Econometrica* 50, 1345–1370.

LAIDLER, D.E.W. (1968), "The Permanent Income Concept in a Macroeconomic Model," *Oxford Economic Papers* 20, 11–23.

────── (1986), "The New Classical Contribution to Macroeconomics," *Banca Nazionale del Lavoro Quarterly Review* 156, 27–55.

LILIEN, D.M. (1982), "Sectoral Shifts and Cyclical Unemployment," *Journal of Political Economy* 90, 777–793.

LUCAS, R.E., JR. (1972), "Expectations and the Neutrality of Money," *Journal of Economic Theory* 4, 103–124.

────── (1973), "Some International Evidence on Output–Inflation Tradeoffs," *The American Economic Review* 63, 326–334.

────── (1976), "Econometric Policy Evaluations: A Critique," in K. Brunner and A.H. Meltzer, eds., *The Phillips Curve and the Labor Market*, Amsterdam, New York, and Oxford: North Holland.

────── (1978), "Unemployment Policy," *The American Economic Review Proceedings* 68, 353–357.

────── (1980a), "Methods and Problems in Business Cycle Theory," *Journal of Money, Credit and Banking* 12, 696–715.

────── (1980b), "Two Illustrations of the Quantity Theory of Money," *The American Economic Review* 70, 1005–1014.

────── (1981), "Tobin and Monetarism: A Review Article," *Journal of Economic Literature* 19, 558–567.

────── (1985), "Models of Business Cycles," draft for Yrjo Jahnsson Lectures, Helsinki, Finland.

LUCAS, R.E., JR., and T.J. SARGENT (1979), "After Keynesian Macroeconomics," Federal Reserve Bank of Minneapolis *Quarterly Review* 3, 1–16.

McCALLUM, B.T. (1976), "Rational Expectations and the Estimation of Econometric Models: An Alternative Procedure," *International Economic Review* 17, 484–490.

———— (1978), "On Macroeconomic Instability from a Monetarist Policy Rule," *Economics Letters* 1, 121–124.

———— (1980), "Rational Expectations and Macroeconomic Stabilization Policy: An Overview," *Journal of Money, Credit and Banking* 12, 716–746.

———— (1982), "Macroeconomics After a Decade of Rational Expectations: Some Critical Issues," Federal Reserve Bank of Richmond *Economic Review* 68, 3–12.

———— (1983), "On Non-Uniqueness in Rational Expectations Models: An Attempt at Perspective," *Journal of Monetary Economics* 11, 139–168.

———— (1984), "Are Bond-Financed Deficits Inflationary? A Ricardian Analysis," *Journal of Political Economy* 92, 123–135.

———— (1986), "On 'Real' and 'Sticky-Price' Theories of the Business Cycle," *Journal of Money, Credit and Banking* 18, 397–414.

———— (1987), "The Development of Keynesian Macroeconomics," *The American Economic Review Proceedings* 77, 125–129.

McDONALD, I., and R.M. SOLOW (1981), "Wage Bargaining and Employment," *The American Economic Review* 71, 896–908.

———— (1985), "Wages and Employment in a Segmented Labour Market," *Quarterly Journal of Economics* 100, 1115–1141.

MAHMUD, S.F., A.L. ROBB, and W.M. SCARTH (1987), "On Estimating Dynamic Factor Demands," *Journal of Applied Econometrics* 2, 69–75.

MALINVAUD, E. (1977), *The Theory of Unemployment Reconsidered*, Oxford: Blackwell.

MANKIW, N.G. (1985), "Small Menu Costs and Large Business Cycles: A Macroeconomic Model of Monopoly," *Quarterly Journal of Economics* 100, 529–537.

———— (1986), "Issues in Keynesian Macroeconomics: A Review Essay," *Journal of Monetary Economics* 18, 217–223.

———— (1987), "Reflections on the New Keynesian Microfoundations," Harvard University, discussion paper no. 1318.

MANKIW, N.G., J. ROTEMBERG, and L.H. SUMMERS (1985), "Intertemporal Substitution in Macroeconomics," *Quarterly Journal of Economics* 100, 225–251.

METZLER, L.A. (1941), "The Nature and Stability of Inventory Cycles," *Review of Economics and Statistics* 23, 113–129.

MINFORD, P., and D. PEEL (1983), *Rational Expectations and the New Macroeconomcs*, Oxford: Martin Robertson.

MISHKIN, F.S. (1983), *A Rational Expectations Approach to Macroeconomics: Testing Policy Ineffectiveness and Efficient Market Models*, Chicago: University of Chicago Press.

MITCHELL, D.J.B. (1986), "Explanations of Wage Inflexibility: Institutions and Incentives," in W. Beckerman, ed., *Wage Rigidity and Unemployment*, Baltimore: The Johns Hopkins University Press.

MUNDELL, R.A. (1963), "Capital Mobility and Stabilization Policy under Fixed and Flexible Exchange Rates," *Canadian Journal of Economics and Political Science* 29, 475–485.

MUSSA, M. (1981), "Sticky Prices and Disequilibrium Adjustment in a Rational Model of the Inflationary Process," *The American Economic Review* 71, 1020–1027.

NEARY, J.P., and J.E. STIGLITZ (1983), "Toward a Reconstruction of Keynesian Economics: Expectations and Constrained Equilibria," *Quarterly Journal of Economics* 91 (supplement), 199–228.

NELSON, C., and C. PLOSSER (1982), "Trends and Random Walks in Macroeconomic Time Series: Some Evidence and Implications," *Journal of Monetary Economics* 10, 139–162.

PATINKIN, D. (1965), *Money, Interest, and Prices,* New York: Harper and Row.

PESARAN, M.H. (1982), "A Critique of the Proposed Tests of the Natural Rate–Rational Expectations Hypothesis," *Economic Journal* 92, 529–554.

PHELPS, E.S. (1982), "Cracks on the Demand Side: A Year of Crisis in Theoretical Macroeconomics," *The American Economic Review Proceedings* 72, 378–381.

POOLE, W. (1970), "Optimal Choice of Monetary Policy Instruments in a Simple Stochastic Macro Model," *Quarterly Journal of Economics* 85, 197–216.

POTERBA, J.M., J.J. ROTEMBERG, and L.H. SUMMERS (1986), "A Tax-Based Test for Nominal Rigidities," *The American Economic Review* 76, 659–675.

PRESCOTT, E.C. (1986), "Theory Ahead of Business Cycle Measurement," Federal Reserve Bank of Minneapolis *Quarterly Review* 10, 9–22.

PURVIS, D.D. (1985), "Public Sector Deficits, International Capital Movements, and the Domestic Economy: The Medium Term Is the Message," *Canadian Journal of Economics* 18, 723–742.

ROBINSON, J. (1970), "Capital Theory Up to Date," *Canadian Journal of Economics* 3, 309–317.

RODRIGUEZ, C.A. (1979), "Short and Long-Run Effects of Monetary and Fiscal Policies under Flexible Exchange Rates and Perfect Capital Mobility," *The American Economic Review* 69, 176–182.

ROGERSON, R.D. (1984), "Indivisible Labor, Lotteries and Equilibrium," Ph.D. dissertation, University of Minnesota, chapter 1.

ROWE, N. (1987), "An Extreme Keynesian Macro-economic Model with Formal Microeconomic Foundations," *Canadian Journal of Economics* 20, 306–320.

SACHS, J.D. (1980), "Wages, Flexible Exchange Rates and Macroeconomic Policy," *Quarterly Journal of Economics* 94, 731–747.

SALOP, S.C. (1979), "A Model of the Natural Unemployment Rate," *The American Economic Review* 69, 117–125.

SARGENT, T.J. (1973), "Rational Expectations, the Real Rate of Interest and the Natural Rate of Unemployment," *Brookings Papers on Economic Activity* 4, 429–472.

——— (1978), "Rational Expectations, Econometric Exogeneity, and Consumption," *Journal of Political Economy* 86, 673–700.

——— (1979), *Macroeconomic Theory,* New York: Academic Press.

——— (1982), "Beyond Demand and Supply Curves in Macroeconomics," *The American Economic Review Proceedings* 72, 382–389.

——— (1984), "Autoregressions, Expectations, and Advice," *The American Economic Review Proceedings* 74, 408–415.

——— (1986), *Rational Expectations and Inflation,* New York: Harper and Row.

——— (1987), *Dynamic Macroeconomic Theory,* Cambridge, Mass.: Harvard University Press.

SARGENT, T.J. and N. WALLACE (1975), " 'Rational' Expectations, the Optimal Monetary Instrument and the Optimal Money Supply Rule," *Journal of Political Economy* 83, 241–255.

——— (1976), "Rational Expectations and the Theory of Economic Policy," *Journal of Monetary Economics* 2, 169–183.

——— (1981), "Some Unpleasant Monetarist Arithmetic," Federal Reserve Bank of Minneapolis *Quarterly Review* 5, 1–17.

SCARTH, W.M. (1979), "Bond-Financed Fiscal Policy and the Problem of Instrument Instability," *Journal of Macroeconomics* 1, 107–117.

——— (1980), "Rational Expectations and the Instability of Bond-Financing," *Economics Letters* 6, 321–327.

——— (1984), "Adjustment Costs and Aggregate Supply Theory," *Canadian Journal of Economics* 17, 847–854.

——— (1985), "A Note on Non-Uniqueness in Rational Expectations Models," *Journal of Monetary Economics* 15, 247–254.

——— (1987a), "Can Economic Growth Make Monetarist Arithmetic Pleasant?" *Southern Economic Journal* 53, 1028–1036.

——— (1987b), "Profit-Sharing, Indexation and Macroeconomic Stability," McMaster University, mimeo.

SEATER, J.J. (1985), "Does Government Debt Matter? A Review," *Journal of Monetary Economics* 16, 121–132.

SHAH, A. (1984), "Crowding Out, Capital Accumulation, the Stock Market and Money-Financed Fiscal Policy," *Journal of Money, Credit and Banking* 16, 461–473.

SHAIKH, A. (1974), "Laws of Production and Laws of Algebra: The Humbug Production Function," *Review of Economics and Statistics* 56, 115–120.

SIMS, C.A. (1983), "Comparison of Interwar and Postwar Business Cycles: Monetarism Reconsidered," *The American Economic Review Proceedings* 73, 250–257.

SMYTH, D.J. (1974), "Built-in Flexibility of Taxation and Stability in a Simple Dynamic IS-LM Model," *Public Finance* 29, 111–113.

SOLOW, R.M. (1956), "A Contribution to the Theory of Economic Growth," *Quarterly Journal of Economics* 70, 65–94.

——— (1979), "Alternative Aproaches to Macroeconomics: A Partial View," *Canadian Journal of Economics* 12, 339–354.

——— (1986), "What Is a Nice Girl Like You Doing in a Place Like This? Macroeconomics After Fifty Years," *Eastern Economic Journal* 12, 191–198.

STIGLITZ, J.E. (1979), "Equilibrium in Product Markets with Imperfect Information," *The American Economic Review Proceedings* 69, 339–346.

—————— (1984), "Price Rigidities and Market Structure," *The American Economic Review Proceedings* 74, 350–355.

—————— (1986), "Theories of Wage Rigidity," in J.L. Butkiewicz, K.J. Koford, and J.B. Miller, eds., *Keynes' Economic Legacy: Contemporary Economic Theories,* New York: Praeger Publishers.

STONEMAN, P. (1979), "A Simple Diagrammatic Apparatus for the Investigation of a Macroeconomic Model of Temporary Equilibria," *Economica* 46, 61–66.

SUMMERS, L.H. (1986), "Some Skeptical Observations on Real Business Cycle Theory," Federal Reserve Bank of Minneapolis *Quarterly Review* 10, 23–27.

TAYLOR, J.B. (1977), "Conditions for Unique Solutions in Stochastic Macroeconomic Models with Rational Expectations," *Econometrica* 45, 1377–1385.

—————— (1979a), "Estimation and Control of a Macroeconomic Model with Rational Expectations," *Econometrica* 47, 1267–1286.

—————— (1979b), "Staggered Wage Setting in a Macro Model," *The American Economic Review* 69, 108–113.

—————— (1981), "Comments," *Brookings Papers on Economic Activity* 12, 434–438.

—————— (1986), "An Appeal for Rationality in the Policy Activism Debate," in R.W. Hafer, ed., *The Monetary Versus Fiscal Policy Debate,* Totowa, N.J.: Rowman & Allanheld.

TOBIN, J. (1969), "A General Equilibrium Approach to Monetary Theory," *Journal of Money, Credit and Banking* 1, 15–29.

—————— (1972), "Inflation and Unemployment," *The American Economic Review* 62, 1–18.

—————— (1975), "Keynesian Models of Recession and Depression," *The American Economic Review Proceedings* 65, 195–202.

—————— (1977), "How Dead Is Keynes?," *Economic Inquiry* 15, 459–468.

—————— (1980), "Stabilization Policy Ten Years After," *Brookings Papers on Economic Activity* 11, 19–72.

—————— (1986), "The Future of Keynesian Economics," *Eastern Economic Journal* 12, 347–356.

TUCKER, D. (1966), "Dynamic Income Adjustment to Money Supply Changes," *The American Economic Review* 56, 433–449.

TURNOVSKY, S.J. (1977), *Macroeconomic Analysis and Stabilization Policies,* London, New York, and Melbourne: Cambridge University Press.

—————— (1980), "The Choice of Monetary Instruments Under Alternative Forms of Price Expectations," *The Manchester School* 48, 39–62.

—————— (1983), "Exchange Market Intervention Policies in a Small Open Economy," in J.S. Bhandari and B.H. Putnam, eds., *Economic Interdependence and Flexible Exchange Rates,* Cambridge, Mass. and London, England: The MIT Press.

WEITZMAN, M.L. (1985), "The Simple Macroeconomics of Profit Sharing," *The American Economic Review* 75, 937–953.

—————— (1986), "Macroeconomic Implications of Profit Sharing," *NBER Macroeconomics Annual 1986* 1, 291–334.

WOGLOM, G. (1982), "Underemployment Equilibrium with Rational Expectations," *Quarterly Journal of Economics* 96, 89–107.

WOODFORD, M. (1987), "Three Questions about Sunspot Equilibria as an Explanation of Economic Fluctuations," *The American Economic Review Proceedings* 77, 93–98.

YARROW, G.K. (1977), "The Demand for Money Function and the Stability of Monetary Equilibrium," *Economic Journal* 87, 114–123.